VOYA Reader Two

Mary K. Chelton
and
Dorothy M. Broderick

The Scarecrow Press, Inc.
Lanham, Md., & London
1998

SCARECROW PRESS, INC.

Published in the United States of America
by Scarecrow Press, Inc.
4720 Boston Way
Lanham, Maryland 20706

Copyright © 1998 by Mary K. Chelton and Dorothy M. Broderick

All rights reserved. No part of this publication may be reproduced, stored in a retrieval system, or transmitted in any form or by any means, electronic, mechanical, photocopying, recording, or otherwise, without the prior permission of the publisher.

British Library Cataloguing in Publication Information Available

Library of Congress Cataloging-in-Publication Data

    VOYA reader two / [selected by] Mary K. Chelton and Dorothy M. Broderick.
      p. cm.
    Includes bibliographical references and index.
    ISBN 0-8108-3460-X (paper : alk. paper)
    1. Young adults' libraries—Activity programs—United States. 2. Young adults' libraries—Censorship—United States. I. Chelton, Mary K. II. Broderick, Dorothy M. III. Title: VOYA reader 2.
Z718.5.V69 1998
027.62'6—DC21   97-43610
                                                              CIP

∞™ The paper used in this publication meets the minimum requirements of American National Standard for Information Sciences—Permanence of Paper for Printed Library Materials, ANSI Z39.48–1984.
Manufactured in the United States of America.

Contents

Read Me! *Mary K. Chelton and Dorothy M. Broderick*   vii

CHALLENGES TO THE CENSORS

Annie on Trial: How It Feels to Be the Author of
   a Challenged Book
   Nancy Garden   3

Watch Out for "Don't Read This!" How a Library
   Youth Participation Group Was Silenced by Schools
   Yet Made Its Voice Heard
   Cathi Dunn MacRae   15

What Mean We, White Man?
   Roger Sutton   35

INTERGENERATIONAL PROGRAMS

Once Again, Alice in Wonderland
   Alan Bern   49

What We Did Together Over Their Summer Vacation:
   Reading Buddies in the Children's Room of the
   Oakland Public Main Library
   Alan Bern   57

Sidekicks: An Intergenerational Program
   Beth Karpas   65

Books Build Bridges: An Intergenerational Read-In
Martha Simpson and Barbara Blosveren 67

A POTPOURRI OF YA PROGRAMS

TAB: A Middle School/Public Library Success Story
Margaret Brown and Pat Muller 83

Bibliothecam Amissam Inveni! (I Found the Library)
Marilyn Brown and Anne Merkle 91

Books, Books, Books—Let Us Read: A Library Serving Sheltered and Incarcerated Youth
Pam Carlson 95

Best Books for Young Adults, Real Young Adult Opinions of the List, the Process, and the 1995 Selections
Lynn Cockett 101

Teenagers Work Well in the Berkeley Public Library
Kay Finney in collaboration with Kim McCombs 111

The Body in the Library: Who Dunnit?
Nancy Gorman 121

Relieving the Junior High Jitters
Kathryn L. Havris 123

YAs Need TLC. . . . Especially in the Summer
Lucretia Lipper 129

A Library Where Silence Is Banned
Cathi Dunn MacRae 135

Romancing the Young Teen
Mary Maggio 147

"Are You Afraid to Die?" 7th Graders Confront AIDS
Arthur S. Meyers 153

Contents

The Wall of Shame *Nancy Moore*	157
Sleuths in the Stacks *Merry Beth Oliveto and Sharon Vincent*	167
Programs with Boys and Girls Together *Frances Plesser*	171
The Empire Summer Puzzler *Carol Shama and Lindsay Ruth*	175
What a Summer We've Had *Joan Stainforth*	177
Locked in and Loving It *Janice T. Ungar*	181
Tapping Teen Talent in Queens: A Library-Based, LSCA-Funded Youth Development Success Story from New York *Barbara Osborne Williams*	187

FOCUS ON ADULTS

Books for the Beast: A Maryland How-We-Did-It-Good Self-Training Success Story! *Mary K. Chelton*	199
Teens in Transition: A Workshop on Teen Sexuality and AIDS for Youth-Serving Professionals *Mary Alice Deveny*	211
A Matter of Time: An Overview of Themes from the Carnegie Report *Jane Quinn*	219
Read My Genre: A Reader's Advisory Workshop *Judy Sasges*	233

For Young Adults Only—From Teen Volunteers to
   Young Adult Library Advisory Boards: North Regional/
   Broward Community College Library
   Leila J. Sprince   241

Cooperative Dialogue: Using an Instrument to Empower
   Kay E. Vandergrift   251

The Junior High School Comes to the Public Library
   Elizabeth Vollrath and Diane Kippenhan   261

About the Contributors   265

Read Me!

As computer users know all too well, when installing a new program the highlighted icon on the installation disk says Read Me! We borrow the phrase from the computer world to explain the structure of the book that follows. The "see" referrals are examples only and are not to be seen as excluding other articles within the volume that fall into the same category. Within each category, articles are arranged alphabetically by author. The date in brackets at the end of the article is when the original was published.

As with *The VOYA Reader* (Scarecrow, 1990), we make no claim to identify this as "the best of *VOYA*" because we are not capable of evaluating very different articles with very different emphases and say one is better than the other. The focus in this volume is primarily on programming library services for young adults. We have selected this focus because in monitoring youth oriented listservs we have encountered too many comments by youth librarians saying we should simply meet the information needs of the kids who walk through the door and then "leave them alone."

This view runs contrary to all the research available, particularly as detailed in the Carnegie Corporation's *A Matter of Time: Risk and Opportunity in the Nonschool Hours* (see Quinn, p. 212).

It is a very large mistake to misread the outer demeanor of adolescents as representing their inner needs. They may evoke the impression that they could care less about having adults in their lives, but in reality they are starved for positive interaction with adults. Most of all, they want to feel useful which is why intergenerational programming is met with such enthusiasm by the participating teenagers.

As the Carnegie Report documents, young people need places to go, things to do, and people who care about them. The library cannot magically meet the needs of all the young people in a school or community, but it can be one of the places to go providing things to do and service personnel who genuinely care about them. We are not talking about the all-too-cute caring provided by young adult librarians as "a pal," rather than as a bonafide adult role model.

There are as many ways to meet these needs as there are librarians. A program can be as elaborate as building a separate library (see "A Library Where Silence Is Banned" p. 132), providing adequate space and facilities in a new library (see Maggio, p. 144), writing a proposal for a grant that allows for elaborate programming (see Williams, p. 182), or a program costing nothing but staff time and imagination (see Gorman, p. 118).

The biggest challenge facing librarians is how to reach the truly disadvantaged youth in society. The Finney article (see p. 108) is a fine example of a library taking this challenge seriously as does the Williams article. As Quinn points out, the loss of youth recreation centers in Los Angeles coincides directly with the rise of gang activity. Young people need a sense of belonging and libraries can help meet that need if librarians take the challenge seriously.

While the present volume does not contain any articles on censorship related to the use of the Internet since the issue became headline news only recently, the entire question of censorship, whether of more traditional library materials or access to the Net is particularly pertinent in discussing services to the underprivileged among us. This is the segment of society least likely to be able to afford home computers or have access to extensive home libraries. When libraries bow to pressure, almost always exerted by the more affluent within a community, little attention is focused on how that decision impacts on those whose sole source of information is the school or public library. The young people most in need of the library are also the most penalized when censorship is rationalized by librarians as protection of the young.

There is a consistent adult denial about the interests and abilities of young people. As the TAB article (see p. 81) shows, there is great maturity in what middle school students identify as their favorite books. Since this is the age group librarians need to pay major attention to if they are not to lose them as they move into full adolescence, we ignore their abilities at our own risk.

With the decline in literature and service courses in what now pass for library schools, it is also essential that working librarians design in-service training courses to help each other learn through workshops what they need to know to do their jobs better (see Sasges and all articles in the final section). Of even more importance in many ways is the need for librarians to relate to other youth workers and parents within a community (see Deveny, p. 205). And it is particularly gratifying to find school and public librarians relating to each other and the Vollrath article (see p. 253) represents the ultimate in such potential cooperation.

Finally, it needs saying again and again that we make a serious mistake when we allow the adults of society to continue to think of adolescents as simply older children. They are not and have not been "older children" for some decades: they have their own literature, magazines, music, television shows, and even motion pictures. They are a dominant force in American society and their impact will grow as we see the largest group of teens arrive since the days of the baby boomers. Librarians cannot afford to ignore the group that will control the country very shortly. If altruism is not a good enough reason to serve the group then self-interest should be.

MARY K. CHELTON
DOROTHY M. BRODERICK

CHALLENGES TO THE CENSORS

Annie on Trial:
How It Feels to Be the Author of a Challenged Book
Nancy Garden

Setting the Scene

It was pouring rain and unseasonably cold in Kansas City when my partner, Sandra Scott, and I set off from our hotel. We were bound for the offices of Shook, Hardy & Bacon, the law firm handling the First Amendment suit involving my YA novel, *Annie on My Mind*. *Annie*, published in 1982 by Farrar, Straus & Giroux, is the story of two young women, high school seniors, who fall in love with each other.

Two years earlier, *Annie*, along with a book called *All American Boys* by Frank Mosca, had been donated to forty-two schools in and around Kansas City, in both Kansas and Missouri, by an organization called Project 21. (Project 21's purpose is to encourage schools to include accurate, positive materials about homosexuality in their libraries and curricula.) Not long after the donations, a fundamentalist minister and a small group of his supporters doused *Annie* with gasoline, dropped it into a metal bucket, and burned it in front of the Kansas City School District's office. As a result, there was a lot of media attention—and several school districts removed copies of the book they'd had on their shelves for years. One district put *Annie* on "restricted" shelves. Then, after protests, they returned it to general circulation, with the proviso that parents who don't want their children to read it must notify the school in writing. But in Olathe, Kansas, superintendent Dr. Ron Wimmer and the school board refused to restore the book, despite the fact that the librarians wanted to retain it. A number of students objected, and one, Amanda Greb, circulated a petition and passed out white ribbons for students to wear in protest. Finally, she and several other courageous students, led by Olathe East High School's student government president, Stevana

Case, filed suit against Wimmer and the school board for violating their First and Fourteenth Amendment rights. Stevie's father, Steve Case, who teaches in the district, and the other kids' parents joined the suit. Shook, Hardy & Bacon, backed by the American Civil Liberties Union, took the case on a *pro bono* basis, and the American Library Association, represented by Pat Scales, Ann Carlson Weeks, Dianne McAfee Hopkins, and others, lent its enormously helpful support. As attention focused increasingly on Olathe, the situation in the other districts where the book had been removed faded into the background.

Finally in fall of 1994, after many months of preparation, the Olathe suit went to trial.

Doing My Homework

As the author of the book, I wasn't a named plaintiff. In fact, I was probably the least important participant, but I did want to help, both for *Annie*'s sake and because I believe any challenge to any book endangers the First Amendment. Still, I entered this battle with equal measures of fear, rage, and eagerness—and sometimes a desire for it all to go away so I could work on my next book.

Early in August, when Sandy and I were in our cabin in Maine, John Bullock, one of the lawyers handling the case, called to ask me to testify. Reality, in the form of the fear and eagerness I mentioned above, struck hard.

John told me I'd probably be the first witness, and explained that I'd be asked about my purpose in writing *Annie*. He also said "educational suitability" would probably be a major issue, even though there's no legal definition of the term. Did I have or could I get statements from teachers and librarians who'd used the book? I said I thought I could, and set to work.

Then John shipped me about ten pounds of legal documents, including homophobic depositions from school board members and from two expert witnesses, a psychiatrist and a psychologist, whom the other side had hired. Like most gay people, I've been dealing with homophobia all my life, but as I read the experts' words, I felt so angry that I wasn't sure I'd be able to keep my temper if I was confronted with their bigotry in court. This was a First Amendment case, yes—but suppose homosexuality became the main issue? Suppose the other side tried to discredit the book by saying I'd written it to "recruit" straight kids? Suppose they tried to discredit me by "proving" homosexuality is a psychiatric disorder?

Luckily, though, both sides soon agreed not to use experts after all, and, for the moment, I relaxed. Even so, that decision was both good and bad. Now our side couldn't use the ALA experts who had helped prepare the case and/or given depositions about such matters as the Library Bill of Rights, school library policies, and the procedures by which the Young Adult Library Services Association (YALSA) chooses books for their Best Books for Young Adults lists. (*Annie* was a Best Book the year it was published, and has been on all subsequent "Best of the Best"-type lists.) Because those experts weren't going to be allowed to testify, the lawyers asked me to try to fill in some of the gaps. Linda Waddle, Deputy Executive Director of YALSA, briefed me thoroughly, and to my unending gratitude, made herself generally available as a knowledgeable and reassuring resource.

At around the same time, John sent me a list of gay YA titles the Olathe district had in its libraries; one of the other side's arguments, apparently, was going to be that since they already had gay books, they hadn't removed *Annie* because of its content. The legal assistant on our case, Debra Rinehart, was reading the books to see how they compared with *Annie*, but could I help?

I could; I've been keeping a list of gay YA books for years, and the Olathe books were on it. I'd read all except one, a book I've never been able to find. However, I felt I should refresh my memory, so, on a trip back to Massachusetts, where Sandy and I live in the winter, I managed to find library copies of most of the books I didn't own. Alice Stern, YA librarian at the Boston Public Library, kindly sent me one I hadn't been able to locate.

Soon I was spending a large portion of every day reading legal documents, rereading many of the books on Olathe's list, trying to memorize Best Books procedures, and, with the generous help of several friends and colleagues, contacting teachers and librarians who'd used *Annie*. I also tabulated and made abstracts of *Annie*'s reviews, fan mail, and "honors," plus articles and lists mentioning it. Michael Eisenberg of Farrar, Straus & Giroux, who along with *Annie*'s editor, Margaret

Ferguson, was tremendously supportive throughout, gathered sales figures for me to send to John. Finally, because the lawyers needed to know my background and qualifications, I dug out my old resume, updated it, and sent it off.

But although I still felt eager to testify, as the time to leave approached, butterflies swarmed in my stomach. Then the trial date was changed—and changed again. Sandy, bless her, dealt with the complexities of making and breaking plane reservations, and we worked out contingency plans for our dog, our cat, and my correspondence school students.

The more changes there were, the more apprehensive I felt. Every day, trying to maintain focus on the trial, I muttered Best Books' procedures to Pippin, our dog, as he and I took our usual early morning walk. Then I asked myself hostile questions, as if I were the other side's attorneys, and muttered the answers out loud, reminding myself that I must never lose my temper, be rude or sarcastic, or burst into tears, all of which I feared doing under cross examination. Soon I was waking up at night, again explaining to imaginary lawyers and to the judge (for there would be no jury) how Best Books are chosen, reciting my "qualifications" for writing a lesbian love story or any book at all, and asking myself the worst, most personal, and raunchiest questions I could imagine. Would the other side actually be allowed to do that? The experts were gone, but the school board members would still be testifying, and given the nature of some of their depositions, I felt I couldn't be sure.

On September 7, Sandy and I went back to Massachusetts and prepared to leave on the 9th for a September 11 trial date—but on September 11 we were back in Maine, waiting again. Soon there were other uncertainties as well. It now appeared that the trial might be held in two parts, with perhaps a week or more in between; we might not be able to stay—or return—for the second part. I might not be the first witness after all, which would mean I'd miss the beginning of the trial; only after I testified would I be allowed in the courtroom. Sandy, who's a retired attorney, assured me that this is normal, as are last-minute changes in trial dates, but I still found both unsettling.

More waking up at night. More rehearsing. More butterflies. More arrangements and rearrangements—and then on September 17, we were back in Massachusetts, packing once more.

We Arrive in Kansas City

And at last on that cold, rainy September day, we arrived at Shook, Hardy & Bacon.

We'd met John on an earlier trip to Kansas City, so greeting him was like greeting an old friend. And we'd both talked with legal assistant Debra Rinehart over the phone. She'd been our primary liaison for all the changes in dates and reservations; she seemed like an old friend, too. Gene Balloun, the older of the two partners handling the case, turned out to be one of the most compassionate and gentlemanly people I've ever met, and David Waxse, a big, friendly bear of a man, is so firmly committed to the First Amendment that when I started to ask if we would appeal if we lost, he answered "Yes" before I'd finished asking. Right away, they all made us feel confident and at home.

Still, when Gene was running me through my testimony and asked me to tell about my professional background, Sandy had to remind me to mention an editorial job I'd held for five years! She'd warned me that witnesses tend to get tired while they're being questioned, and that rehearsal certainly demonstrated how right she was. I was drained when it was over, and at 5:30 the next morning I was asking myself imaginary questions again. "It's a little like anticipating some awful medical procedure," I wrote in my journal right before we left for court, "except with that, you know your only responsibility is probably to bear it with as much dignity and poise as possible, and with this you know a lot depends on you—not only your own representation of your work, but the contribution—or mess—you can make of the whole issue."

The Trial Begins

The courthouse was huge, impressive, new—and nearly deserted. "Our" courtroom was on, as I remember, the fourth floor, where the halls were lined with plaques bearing photos and bios of past and present district court judges, most of them looking suitably solemn and wise. The hushed, austere atmosphere, with people in suits and dresses gathering in quiet but intense knots—some on "our" side, some on "theirs"—struck me as somewhat surrealistic and even a little silly. We all looked askance at one another, but pretended not to, the way people pretend not to look at people in wheelchairs; once in a while, though, we exchanged embarrassed, tentative smiles, as if some of us, at least, wanted to get to know each other, or at least were curious about who we all really were.

Sandy and I took a quick look at the courtroom, which was a lot smaller than I'd imagined, with only about six pew-like rows of benches for spectators. Then those of us on our side went into a small "witness room." It contained five or so fairly comfortable chairs, one window with drawn blinds, and a low table on which were a couple of catalogs, one offering Limoges china at outrageous prices. Jeff Blair, librarian at Olathe South High School, and I had a good laugh over that one!

For a while, people came and went. Steve Case brought that morning's Olathe paper, which had a front page article about Project 21's latest donation with a prominent sidebar about the trial. Steve kept me supplied with Olathe papers throughout the trial, and they, plus the constant presence of reporters, somehow made the whole thing seem more real, perhaps because neither the reporters nor the stories they wrote had the deferential attitude we all seemed to assume the moment we got off the elevator. The reporters were doing their real jobs; we, I felt, had become actors working on a script-in-progress.

Soon the lawyers arrived. Gene took me into a conference room and told me he was going to ask, "Ms. Garden, are you a lesbian?" and "How long have you and your partner been together?" if that was okay with me. It certainly was! I welcomed the opportunity to be up front about my sexual orientation, and to establish that Sandy and I, who've been together for twenty-six years, are a stable couple and unlike the Olathe school board members' idea of gay people.

And then word came that the trial was about to start. People rushed into the courtroom and the hall fell silent. Jeff and I, along with our side's star witness, Loretta Wood, the media specialist at Olathe East High School, were suddenly alone in the witness room.

The atmosphere was highly charged. Loretta wasn't called till 11:30, so we three had a long time to chat, joke, read, pace, speculate, and make trips to the water cooler and the restroom. Our nervousness was broken occasionally by people, most of them plaintiffs, stopping in to say hello, wish us luck, and give us general reports of what was going on in the courtroom. (Since we hadn't yet testified, no one could tell us specifics.) It was wonderful to see the kids and their parents, some of whom I hadn't met on earlier trips. I wish I'd been able to hear them testify!

When Loretta was finally called, Jeff and I withdrew into silence, I think both feeling, "Oh, God, now it's really happening!" As time passed that changed to a rather apprehensive, "What are they doing to her?" After about an hour there was a sudden flurry of activity in the hall, and Sandy, Loretta, and others burst in to tell us the judge, United States District Judge Thomas Van Bebber, had broken for lunch—after which Loretta would have to continue. Later, looking at the notes Sandy took for me (but couldn't show me till after I'd testified), I was amazed at the range of Loretta's testimony, from her own background and a description of library jobs, policies, and procedures, to specifics about the book and the complicated scenario surrounding its removal—even how the subject of homosexuality was presented in the Olathe schools. And I'd been worried about remembering the few facts I'd had to master!

At around 3:00 that afternoon, Loretta was finally through. But after a brief break the hall and witness room were again wrapped in silence and Jeff and I were left once more to ourselves, both of us tense and oddly sleepy. If I'm called, I prayed silently, please let me be awake!

But I wasn't called. Two of the plaintiffs, Amanda Greb and her mother, Cindy, testified, followed, finally, by Jeff—so late in the afternoon he was going to have to continue his testimony the next day. Jeff and the Grebs, everyone said, had done splendidly; the day had gone well for us. I was proud, pleased, and relieved, but I felt a bit like an injured athlete hearing second-hand about the progress of my team. "Tomorrow," the lawyers told me, "you'll definitely be called." And, they added, it now seemed there probably *would* be a week's break between the first and second parts of the trial.

My heart sank. That meant it was very unlikely Sandy and I would be able to hear the end of it.

"I wonder if I'll be as nervous today," I wrote in my journal the next morning, after muttering my testimony once more. "I do think I'm calmer, and more up for it today."

I did feel calmer when we walked into the courthouse, and by the time Jeff had testified and had come out beaming, saying it hadn't been too bad, I realized that the eagerness had returned and was beginning to counteract the fear. Even so, as the morning progressed and several of the plaintiffs testified, I did get a lot of exercise making nervousness-induced restroom trips!

Taking the Stand

Finally the moment arrived. I felt a little unreal as I walked to the stand, and at the same time, very alert. The other side's lawyers, especially the one who was obviously going to ask the questions if I was to be cross-examined, looked grim and stern; our group seemed more relaxed. I could see that our spectators and witnesses were sitting on the benches to my left as I sat in the witness box, and the other side's were to the right—like the bride and groom's sides at a wedding, Sam Pierron, one of the teenage plaintiffs, remarked later. Judge Van Bebber was to my left, above and behind me; I couldn't really see his face. But I could see Sandy's, and that, like our lawyers' calmness, made me feel better.

I'm afraid I don't remember much about my testimony, or the order in which I was asked questions. I remember being sworn in by a clerk who seemed friendly, and feeling surprised that I wasn't asked to swear on the Bible. I remember that the especially stern-looking lawyer from the other side objected as soon as I was sworn in, saying that he didn't see how the author's testimony was relevant. *Oh, no*, I thought, *please don't let them throw me out after I've come all this way!*

They didn't; the judge overruled the objection and Gene started questioning me. It's odd how those first stock questions—one's name and address, mostly—tend to settle one, and it's wonderful how a good lawyer like Gene will gradually ease one into the meat of one's testimony. I felt my voice wasn't strong enough at first, despite the microphone, and I bobbled words now and then as Gene took me through my background and experience. When I forgot to mention my work as an editor—all of it this time, not just one segment as before—Gene asked me about it specifically, without missing a beat, thereby prompting me and enabling me to get it in. The other side's lawyer objected, I'm pretty sure, to my being asked about my purpose in writing *Annie*—a pivotal part of my testimony—but the judge must have overruled him, for I was able to explain that I'd written it to tell a meaningful story, to fill a need for positive gay books that had existed when I was growing up and that still existed, and to show straight and gay kids alike that gay people aren't monsters and can live happy, healthy, productive lives. I think I got all that in, although I felt I had to rush to say it all before there was another objection. Gene asked, as planned, if I thought the book "glorified" homosexuality and I was able to answer that if glorifying something is making it better than it is, the book doesn't glorify homosexuality, because bad things as well as good ones happen to the gay characters. (A thin, simplistic answer, I think now, but one that did suit the situation.) I remember trying to gauge from Gene's expression if I was saying too much or too little. According to my journal, the other side objected a couple of times to my giving a "narrative answer," which I'm sure has a legal definition but which amused me, given the fact that as a writer, narrative is my business!

After some discussion, I was also allowed to testify as to how the "ideas" in *Annie* differed from those in the other gay YA titles in Olathe's school libraries; Jeff, I later learned, had been able to do that also. (The main difference is that *Annie*, which ends happily, is told from the point of view of a young lesbian.) Gene asked me, as planned, if I was a lesbian; I said yes, and was able to say that Sandy and I have been together for twenty-six years. The other side's lawyers showed no reaction—nor did Superintendent Ron Wimmer, who was sitting at the defense table the whole time.

And then came the moment I'd been dreading; Gene had no more questions and the other side was given the opportunity to cross-examine me. I tried to prepare myself for all those personal, homophobic questions I'd anticipated. But the other side declined—and suddenly, almost anticlimactically, it was over! As I joined Sandy and the others, I realized I was actually a little disappointed, although I was also so tremendously relieved I knew I must have been even more nervous than I'd thought.

The Defendants Testify

The next day, though, was in many ways the roughest, for that was the day three homophobic school board members testified. Even though I'd already read much of their testimony in their depositions, it still hurt to hear them say the book was "shallow," "unrealistic," "not educationally significant," and "not well written." It was especially upsetting that even after they admitted that there probably were gay kids in Olathe and that the gay kids were entitled to an education equal to that given straight kids, a couple of these school board members also admitted they hadn't thought about the effect the book's removal might have on gay kids, or considered the message its removal might send to them about their school district's official attitude toward them as human beings.

The school board president, who although unlicensed as a psychologist is a professor of psychology and counsels sexually confused kids, testified that homosexuality is a mental disorder, that homosexuals have adjustment problems and should refrain from "practicing," and so on. My heart raced while he spoke, and my head—what? "Buzzed" is the only word I can think of, I guess because my blood pressure must have risen. Later Sandy said she'd felt the same way, and told me that when she'd been in a position to hold a door for this man, she'd been tempted to say "I may be dysfunctional, but at least I'm polite." I kept thinking of Shylock's "Hath not a Jew eyes?" speech in *Merchant of Venice*, and I wanted to shout, "*Look* at me! I'm an ordinary person, with the same dreams and fears as you. I work; I love my partner; we own property together; we're active in our community; we have a dog and a cat; we've helped bring up two kids—we're really very conventional. We don't molest children; we aren't promiscuous; we aren't mentally ill or unstable." But of course I couldn't say that, any more than Sandy could make her wonderful remark. At one point, though, Gene asked this man if he'd read any of my other twenty-odd books (he hadn't), if he thought my life had been destroyed by homosexuality (he didn't know), and if he thought I'd been a creative person. He didn't know that either.

The school board president and one other board member who testified that day have connections to a right-wing religious college, and it was clear that they objected to the book at least partly on religious, Biblical, grounds. Another testified that the book wasn't "suitable or appropriate for high school students," that it "tended to promote and glorify," and was "not well written from the standpoint of overall purpose of content and what it was trying to promote (*sic*)." He said he felt that if the book remained on the shelves, "the public would view the board as advocating the homosexual life style."

All this was pretty grim, but the most astonishing statement came from the school board member who said she didn't think fiction had any place in a high school library!

As we'd feared, Sandy and I weren't able to return for the second part of the trial, during which Superintendent Ron Wimmer and one or two more school board members testified. We went back home, stayed in touch with John by telephone, and resumed our regular lives while waiting for Judge Van Bebber's decision.

The Decision

Late in the afternoon of November 29 the phone rang. Sandy answered it, and when she said "It's Gene!" I felt momentarily numb. But not for long. Judge Van Bebber, Gene said, had ruled that "the book was unconstitutionally removed from the shelves," and ordered that it be restored by January 2. My numbness gave way to relief, to joy—and to tremendous gratitude to the lawyers, librarians, and plaintiffs who had worked so hard and so long on *Annie*'s and the First Amendment's behalf. It felt awful being so far away; I wanted to jump on a plane and head back to Kansas so I could hug all those wonderful people!

The next call came on December 28, again late in the afternoon, only hours after I'd mailed this article—with a slightly different last paragraph—to Mary K. Chelton at *VOYA*. The Olathe school board, which had met on December 7 to discuss whether to appeal but hadn't released, or perhaps reached, any conclusion, were finally sending out the word: NO APPEAL! Judge Van Bebber's decision will stand, and the book has now been returned to school library shelves in Olathe.

Despite the ominous fact that the board's press release announcing their decision indicates that they will be revising their book selection process (which of course they have every right to do), I hope Van Bebber's decision will encourage all librarians who suddenly find themselves faced with a challenge. These are difficult times for librarians and teachers, writers and publishers, and we must stand firmly together in our resolve to protect the amendment that protects us and that allows people in this country free access to all ideas. *Annie* won, but there are other battles still to fight. [June 1996]

Watch Out for "Don't Read This!" How a Library Youth Participation Group Was Silenced by Schools Yet Made Its Voice Heard
Cathi Dunn MacRae

The general mayhem level is up several notches for dress rehearsal this brilliant May afternoon. For six months, sixteen teenagers have been crafting this play themselves, brainstorming, researching, scriptwriting, acting, coaching. Since April they have rehearsed it a dozen times, double cast, each playing three or more roles. Now eight players are sprawled around our public library meeting room with their ninth grade leaders, director Anna Salim and acting coach Nadia Haddad, adapting their staging for a middle school library tomorrow. Forsaking bitten fingernails, the cast forms a circle for their favorite exercise. "Tee tee tee TAH tee tah . . . whoop whoop whoop!" They chant in lusty call and response. Then they're on their tummies, relaxing to the croon of Nadia's voice. With a final ear-splitting whoop, they pop up like ten jacks-in-the-box. Now they're bonded and relaxed, flawlessly repeating their lines.

Tomorrow morning at the inhuman hour of seven, they'll be carpooling to the school for their first performance of many. I sit in the back of the room, my script abandoned, watching fifteen-year-old Anna hold the group in her capable hands. They don't seem to need me, their advisor, at all. I can go to my office for phone messages, in case any librarians in the Boulder middle and high schools on our "tour" have last-minute instructions. My stomach churns with something like stage fright.

I've been afraid to answer my phone since last week, when a middle school principal called out of the blue. Weeks before, she had asked for our script of *Don't Read This! A Dramatic Presentation by Teens for Teens to Raise Awareness of Censorship Issues.* Her school librarian then confirmed our appearance. But suddenly, the principal had objections to the script, which seemed to center around a single phrase, in a skit in which a father reads Michael Willhoite's *Daddy's Roommate* (Alyson,

1990) aloud to his children, without realizing until too late that it deals with gay parents. In this state, where voters denied gay rights in Amendment 2, I had been expecting some reaction to our treatment of gay issues. But I was taken aback when the objection, instead, was to "Saviors of Our Sinful Souls School," where the play's children had gotten Willhoite's book from their teacher. The author of that skit, Allison Barrett, fifteen, had been pleased with her rapier wit in naming the school. It got such a laugh in every rehearsal that we were wondering if the cast could say it straight-faced.

This principal thought the phrase was in poor taste, and would offend religious students viewing the play. I asked if she had read the rest of the script, in which viewpoints of Christians, Jews, Wiccans and atheists are represented in a balanced way. She replied that she did not see the script as balanced at all, since it encouraged students to read books "just because they are banned." When she related an incident in which parents bitterly complained to her for hosting a lesbian speaker in a program about diversity, I sensed that this principal's real agenda was to protect herself from similar complaints about our play. But I listened respectfully, trying to honor her point of view and come to some compromise without having to change the script. Anticipating possible complaints, our cast had voted to cancel any performance conditional on script changes.

In ensuing phone calls, this principal raised increasing objections. I realized I was getting nowhere when she echoed the sentiments of a parent character in our play, who objected to a YA novel about teen pregnancy being on a seventh grade reading list. "But the skit shows two parents with opposing views discussing that book," I pointed out, "leaving the issue open-ended and suggesting a talk with the teacher." But since this principal herself doubted that *Send No Blessings* by Phyllis Reynolds Naylor (Atheneum, 1990) was appropriate for seventh graders (she had not read it), the mere discussion of the issue on-stage for her students seemed suspect. At last, I arranged to bring cast representatives to testify before her parent-teacher curriculum committee that would decide whether to allow our performance.

Just three days before dress rehearsal, four cast members had so articulately defended their play before that committee, that they converted its parents and teachers to enthusiastic support. The committee was convinced of the importance of raising these issues for their seventh graders, but they were also convinced that classes attending the play must have curriculum backup so those issues would not appear in a vacuum. There wasn't time to prepare such support in just two weeks before our scheduled appearance. Could we delay our presentation until fall, or maybe send a video instead?

Our play's intrepid defenders exchanged glances. We had advertised for bookings six weeks earlier, with a letter to both principals and school librarians explaining the play's controversial nature, and offering further information before dates were confirmed. I had recommended the very discussion time and classroom support, already planned with this school's librarian, that was now being broached to us as a new idea. The two other middle schools which requested scripts decided to limit attendance to students with parental permission. Now this school was reneging due to its own poor planning. For our budgetless production, I had searched in vain for a volunteer to videotape the play. We could never remount our complex show months later, so we gracefully accepted this school's cancellation.

The principal who initiated the complaint had not attended; we never met face to face. But within a day or two, a second middle school canceled, pleading the same lack of time to prepare curriculum support. While I was wondering why they hadn't been planning such support for the month since they scheduled us, a third middle school canceled our "too raw" production.

I was mystified until a librarian from another middle school, my good friend Nancy Moore (See *The Wall of Shame*, p. 157), reported that her principal had just attended a district administration meeting, where copies of the *Don't Read This!"* script were circulated. Of course I guessed the source of that hefty photocopying job, though I had not realized I was offering the script for general distribution. The mystery of our sudden cancellations was solved. Nancy assured me that we would still perform at her school. She had already battled her principal, with righteous First Amendment determination, convincing him to use permission slips rather than cancel, and was planning long discussion periods around the performance.

But even Nancy had trouble with "Saviors of our Sinful Souls School." She knew its author Allison well, and could just hear the phrase rolling off her acerbic tongue. Nancy and I wrangled long over that line. She saw the phrase as offensive to Christians (though Allison had Moslems in mind when she wrote it). I saw its value as comic relief during an excruciatingly serious play, exquisitely timed to keep the young audience with their peer performers. It was merely irreverent, hardly strong stuff when compared to Beavis and Butthead-type humor beloved by teenagers. Boulder was plagued with an advanced case of political correctness, to which these kids were thumbing their noses. Besides, our script addressed freedom of religion issues very fairly. But Nancy reminded me that humor at anyone's expense is a cruel thing, convincing me that if the phrase possibly offended only a few, it could undermine our entire cause. I agreed to discuss it privately with Allison, who had great respect for Nancy, leaving the decision to change it, or not, up to her—a heavy burden.

The week before dress rehearsal strung tight with tension as Allison and I agonize over that line. Were we knuckling under to censorship ourselves if we changed it? Allison finally asked the cast: "Is anyone here offended by Saviors of Our Sinful Souls?"

Everyone was shocked when Lisa and Erik, our two devout Christians, admitted that it made them uncomfortable, feeling like a put-down of their faith. Since everyone always laughed so much, they confessed, it was easier to join in than reveal how they felt. Peer pressure in action. The room was utterly silent as the group pondered this shocking revelation.

I filled the silence with a reminder that our Library Director, Marcelee Gralapp, when informed of the flap about the line and the school cancellations, refused to dictate to the cast what they should do. "It's the kids' decision," she declared. "Let them know the Library is behind them, whatever they choose to do."

Expressing amazement that a powerful and unknown adult placed such confidence in them, YAAB rose to the occasion. Now that the truth was out, Allison insisted on changing the line which bothered her friends. Everyone agreed, with great relief. But what new name would not identify the school with any particular faith? Andy, who hardly ever said a word beyond his lines, suggested shyly, "How about Institute for the Advancement of Juvenile Moral Development?"

Instantly, the cast was in chaos. Their mirth surpassed any giggles the original line ever earned. Everyone said it together ten times, fast.

That was a few days ago. Now it's dress rehearsal, and I'm leaving the kids on their own while I run to my office to check messages. More accurately, I'm creeping to my cubbyhole, laden with dread. "Please, no more cancellations," I beg the universe—*all* gods, I add, anxious not to offend. Voice Mail instructs me to call the librarian at the school where we perform tomorrow. "Just final arrangements," I reassure myself while punching the number.

"I'm sorry to give you such late notice," says the librarian, after four o'clock. "We're going to have to cancel your play tomorrow. Our principal says that censorship is a non-issue in our school, and it doesn't make sense to get our students worked up about something which doesn't concern them. I must say I agree with him."

I am speechless. Can this be a librarian who misses the point about Freedom to Read? I find my voice. "Did *you* read the script?" I ask.

"Yes, but we haven't had any challenges to books here," she answers. "I am very careful to let students know if a book they're checking out is on an appropriate level. Your play would just raise issues our seventh graders wouldn't understand."

I may have mumbled that some of the play's authors are seventh graders, but I am out of steam. Why had this school booked our play in the first place? Its title alone should have told them we were addressing an issue they didn't think was an issue. I hang up quickly.

I am more enraged by rudeness than by anything else. Less than twenty-four hours before a performance booked weeks ago, this school offhandedly cancels elaborate plans involving volunteer parent drivers, the cast's excuses from their own classes, and our debut. How can I face my wired cast with the news that suddenly there's no play tomorrow?

It takes a very long time for any of us to be grateful for this experience, but it is the best thing that could have happened to these sixteen creative but naive youths who thought they had something to tell their peers about censorship.

When they wrote *Don't Read This!* they had no idea what censorship really meant. They had felt righteous indignation when reading about it in books, newspapers, or the Banned Books list issued by the American Library Association. Incidents in their own schools upset them. Ingrid Ulbrich and James Reling, two founding members of their group, the

Young Adult Advisory Board (YAAB) had participated in a 1991 Banned Books Week program at the Tattered Cover Bookstore in Denver. Ingrid and James became so inflamed about America's censorship epidemic that they had been fanning those flames ever since within YAAB. The group longed to inform as many of their peers as possible that their Freedom to Read was being threatened. They knew that other teenagers would also see it as adults keeping youth ignorant of "what is happening in the world we are inheriting," as YAAB would eventually write in their script. Already youth was ignorant the issue even existed.

This particular YAAB group had strong dramatic and writing talent, so a play written and performed by themselves was an obvious way to reach their peers with this message. They would combine skits dramatizing reasons books are banned, with their own booktalks of favorite banned books, inspiring their audience to read the wonderful books often withheld from them. (YAAB knew booktalks worked because they had been hooked by mine.)

In September 1993, YAAB began planning their presentation in earnest. They pored over ALA's Banned Books kit and sampled titles from its list, read Joan DelFattore's *What Johnny Shouldn't Read* (Yale University Press, 1992), collected clippings about local book challenges. In November they attended a booktalk training workshop with national expert Joni Bodart. They transformed her tips into booktalks so excellent they rivaled Bodart's own. After testing their talks on each other, YAAB formed scriptwriting committees to focus on three major areas in book censorship: historical/political issues, sexuality, and religion. Each committee explored its issue and wrote skits to illustrate it.

As editor, I meshed thirteen booktalks with the skits into a dramatic whole, adding a "Listbearer" to cite complaints against each title from the Banned Books list, and a "Questioner" to prod the audience to form its own opinions. The audience would also participate by adding to YAAB's paper chain, each link bearing a title of one banned book read by a student. By collecting links during performances, and all summer during Book Quest, our YA summer reading game, YAAB hoped to build a chain long enough to encircle our whole library during September's Banned Books Week. Then "everyone can see how book censorship imprisons us," their script proclaimed. YAAB also offered an award to the "Banned Books Champion of Boulder," the teen who made the most

Challenges to the Censors

chain links of banned books she or he had read.

By late March 1994 the script was complete, and twenty-nine parts were double-cast among sixteen players. Performances were scheduled for May and June in nine schools, our main public library and a branch, and Boulder Bookstore, an independent bookseller which sponsors many young adult library events.

In response to initial criticisms from the two schools which asked for the script, I included this "important note" in the confirmation letter sent to all scheduled schools in April:

> Due to the potentially controversial nature of this production, which mentions racism, religion, teen pregnancy, the gay population, and even political correctness—all issues for which books have been challenged in America recently—two Boulder middle schools have decided to require parental permission to attend our presentation.
>
> The Boulder Public Library administration and myself stand behind this program, which we believe eloquently expresses essential First Amendment freedoms, communicated youth to youth. We admire its balanced representation of all sides of sensitive censorship issues. Sometimes the performers use humor and irony to relieve the seriousness of the content, but we assure you they show respect for diverse opinions, since the very exercise of planning the production has taught them that is what the First Amendment means.
>
> We at the Library are committed to allowing these young writers and actors free expression, and the opportunity to share their awareness of Constitutional rights with their peers. In supporting their own Right to Read, they literally demonstrate each young person's right to know, to formulate his or her own opinions based on what really happens in the world.
>
> We understand that middle schools are concerned about parents' possible reactions to controversial issues presented in school, especially to the youngest students. We trust schools to know and judge their own communities. The student producers of *Don't Read This!* range from seventh grade up (average age 14), and are passionately dedicated to getting their message across to their peers. We thank you for doing all you can to allow your students access to that crucial message. We are sure that everyone who sees the play will be moved and challenged to think.

With the wisdom of hindsight, I realize that this plea for student access to their peers in the exercise of free expression may have triggered the very opposite. As a librarian, I forget how radical these precepts sound to those who don't face the First Amendment every day in their work. My defense of free expression for youth may have waved the red flag in front of the bulls who believe that mere kids aren't equipped to handle that. My statement also may have stimulated the schools' already lurking fear of parents' intrusion. Though our presentation was balanced with the diverse opinions that the First Amendment protects, it was criticized for not showing both sides. How could censorship have two sides if our Constitution protects everyone's side? My statement could not counteract such muddled thinking.

It was only when four of the nine schools which booked us canceled performances, when one school postponed their all-school assembly to reconsider and then opened it to only two drama classes, when another school allowed YAAB's appearance only if they refrained from asking students to join their paper chain "political protest," when most "captive audiences" were restricted by parental permission slips, that the young authors of an anti-censorship play knew what censorship really meant.

Ingrid, YAAB's senior guiding light and ideological "mother" of their project, and Anna, its freshman director, eloquently expressed YAAB's reactions in their article for the newsletter of Boulder County Safeguard Law Related Education Program (Fall 1994):

> As two teenagers, we have been viewed as young, immature, and ignorant. Because of this, adults often dismiss what we say.... Adults often feel the need to take charge of our lives and control what enters our minds.

> [When our production] was canceled, ... YAAB was enraged. And amused. YAAB had been silenced, yet the play about censorship had been banned. The irony never escaped us, and we began to wonder about the integrity of the First Amendment.

> Religion, speech, press, assembly, and petition are all forums for spreading ideas. That was exactly what we wanted to do ....We chose our audience to be our peers, because we saw how censorship affected every one of us, and them. But how could we capture a group of teens and make them listen? School!

Challenges to the Censors

We, the young, immature, and ignorant YAABites, thought that schools were established for education, learning, and enlightenment. These were the values we wanted to promote regarding censorship, but the schools didn't understand. They saw our program of banned books as making a political statement, or forcing others to believe that book banning is evil. YAAB struggled to understand the points of view of these four schools, and failed.

I'm facing ten eager young actors, glowing with anticipation at the end of a successful dress rehearsal. I am also failing to understand these four schools, or how I can squelch all this enthusiasm by axing YAAB's debut performance.

"I have some upsetting news," I begin, barely controlling the quiver in my voice which betrays my private session in the ladies' room, with Kleenex™. "We won't be performing tomorrow." I parrot the reasons the school librarian gave me, and let the cast have their own reactions. Disbelief. Outrage. Tears. The timing of this fourth cancellation makes it hit harder than all the others. They are just kids, powerless. And I am powerless to stop that big adult thumb from squishing them. Devastated, YAAB glumly packs up to go home.

"I guarantee this will hit the news," I pep talk. "We're still performing in five schools, and those audiences are going to be wondering what's so controversial that students in four other schools aren't allowed to see it."

Could I keep this promise? So far, our local paper *The Daily Camera* has ignored our press releases. I describe our cancellations to the library's publicist, Colleen Miller. "I think it's time for little reminder calls to the press," says Colleen with a gleam in her eye.

YAAB Hits the News

Two days later, on Saturday, May 7, the article *Drama Draws "Censors"* appears in Boulder's *Daily Camera*, placing YAAB's opinions that their play was banned alongside the four school officials' assertions that "the issue is more complex than that" due to timing, "the captive audience," and censorship as a "non-issue." The details behind the complaints were eclipsed, but the reporter displayed both sides for the public to examine. ALA's *Newsletter on Intellectual Freedom* reprinted the article in its July 1994 issue.

On our new opening date of May 10, postponed so often it seemed a mirage, YAAB was quietly manic when they performed at Casey Middle School. Afterward they asked their audience, "Did anything in our production offend you?" Nearly collapsing with relief when the answer was no, the cast stood taller with every stimulating question they fielded from this first audience they had been allowed to reach.

Twenty miles away through winding Boulder Canyon, YAAB triumphed again in the small mountain town of Nederland. With a paper chain made by the entire junior high student body which attended the play, librarian Ann Cornfield "chained" her school library, delivering a huge box of links to us when school was out for the summer. Nederland Junior-Senior High School was the only school whose students joined the chain as a group.

On May 19, Nederland's *Mountain-Ear* newspaper described their hosting of YAAB's "literate, peaceful objection to the banning of books" as "unlike some other schools in the Boulder Valley School District." Principal Ed Ellis justified YAAB's appearance to "expose students to issues they must face in today's world . . . . We didn't just invite YAAB here because they are controversial. We had a whole unit preparing them for the play. Because we are more isolated than urban schools, we have to bring more things to them."

During that first tour week, YAAB felt the heat turn up in gratifying contrast to the chill of cancellations beforehand. Reporter Mary George from the *Denver Post* tried to bring a photographer to get live shots on a school stage. All three scheduled schools declined to host the *Post*. So the cast bunched together outside our main library, waving their Banned Books placards and "chaining" themselves solemnly for the lens. George's May 16 story *Schools Spurn Student Play on Censorship* hit the AP wire. This time, YAAB's view that "they are the target of their play's topic" was set against some principals' dissenting voices, and others' support. George unearthed further elucidation of our eleventh hour cancellation, quoting the principal as needing "to draw the line when it comes to furthering people's causes with my students." He did not explain how our Constitution constituted a cause. That same day, three YAAB members went live on the air for Peter Boyle's call-in talk radio show on KTLK in Denver. Calls ranged from a man who wanted them to admit that they supported "sodomizing" by presenting books with homosexual themes (Boyle hung up on him), to Boulder's American Civil Liberties Union chapter offering legal support.

The students rushed from the radio station back to Boulder in time to perform at Boulder High School, especially nerve-wracking as the school most players attended. As soon as I returned home from a seemingly endless day, KNUS radio called for a phone interview with their talk show host Tom Jensen. Journalists, I was learning, seem supportive because they champion free speech, but their own agendas sometimes emerge. It was a struggle to stop Jensen from corralling me into insulting the school administration.

Advocating for Youth and the First Amendment

Every time I ran this gauntlet with or for "my kids," my own commitment to the First Amendment blazed stronger, a flare lighting the treacherous path I trod. As YAAB posed for their *Denver Post* photos, a passerby watched with interest. She later confessed to being a librarian who had lost her job over a Banned Books Week display in a local library she could not name, since she was currently in litigation. Though my library director was firmly behind me, I was thankful for this chance spectator's warning. Somehow, I had to champion YAAB while watching my own step.

In my career-long commitment to youth participation, I had found it impossible to avoid identifying with those for whom I advocated. I had led these kids into this stew where we were now simmering together— or more accurately, had encouraged and guided them when they picked this pot to jump in. Like *Saturday Night Live*'s mimic of President Clinton, "I feel your pain" became my anthem. Few adults experience being inside teenage skin again, and most of us are thankful for that. As YAAB's faithful supporter, I walked in their moccasins on hot coals, acutely reliving the sense of powerlessness youth feels in an adult-controlled world. I couldn't help experiencing it as they did; it *was* an ageist issue. Adults were denying youth their voice, their opportunity to address their peers about issues essential to development as "free" Americans.

This "silencing," as Ingrid and Anna called it, became the heart of the issue for us. It felt as if someone had placed big pieces of tape over *our* mouths. While gagged, YAAB could not reach half the students they had targeted (a residual casualty was the promotion of our summer reading game which was part of the play). For some reason, it was okay to remove the tape to address the other half. While gagged, I had to avoid antagonizing school officials with whom I must continue to work, and convey that my threatening "sales pitch" was only to allow youth to exercise the voice guaranteed by the Constitution. What a relief it is to remove that gag among *VOYA* readers!

When YAAB did its first public performance on May 14 at our Meadows Library branch, the spare all-adult audience proved our conviction; what red-blooded American teenager would turn up at a library, of all places, on a gorgeous spring Saturday afternoon, to hear about an issue unknown as an issue? No one mentions to typical teenagers that the Freedom to Read is a cornerstone of their rights as American citizens that may be lost if they don't defend it. Also, being teenagers, they don't read the papers to discover that the battle is raging in their own town. The absence of teenagers in YAAB's first public audience underlined the fact that schools were where we had to be to reach them, the same schools which barred us.

But every adult who attended had read the papers. Among their "warm fuzzies" offered during post-play discussion was permission to call the schools' actions censorship. When YAAB asked their usual question, "Was anyone here offended by this production?" Deanna and Matt Young responded eloquently, later repeating in a letter to the editor of the *Daily Camera*:

> The librarian who advises the group was careful to use the word "canceled" rather than "censored." We think, however, that "censored" is precisely the right word, because of the manner of the cancellations: on short notice, after the play had been booked and a date set, and after a principals' meeting at which photocopies of the script were circulated.
>
> Some of the principals were reportedly afraid that someone would be offended by the play. We fail to see how anyone not interested in censoring books would be offended, and we want to congratulate those principals who stood by their commitment to show the play.

We want the other principals, however, to know that their fears were justified. We were offended—by their timorous censorship of a thoughtful and evenhanded production whose message they ought to study more carefully and their students need to hear.

Another letter to the editor reacted to the librarian's claim that censorship was a "non-issue" at her school. "Anyone capable of such a mindless statement has no place in any school. . . . Lack of 'concern' about a subject on the part of students cannot possibly excuse inaction by a school."

A few days later, the *Daily Camera* printed kudos from another reader: "The cast members . . . hope to spread the word about the injustice of one person or group attempting to limit what another can read. Let's support Boulder teens . . . who are making a positive contribution to our community."

We never saw any negative criticism from *Daily Camera* readers, but a telephone threat on my library voice mail was unsettling. A man who identified himself as a right-wing Christian and also a Jew promised to be in our play's audience. If he witnessed anything which offended him in our production, he guaranteed he would stop our performance immediately. During the minute he spoke on my message, he became increasingly agitated, nearly inarticulate by the time he hung up. He left no number to call back, and failed to mention which performance he planned to attend. After conferring with our library director, I made an official report to the police, requesting that officers attend our remaining two public showings in case of a disturbance.

Our last two school performances went without a hitch. The language arts teacher hosting us at Fairview High School also taught in one of the middle schools which had canceled us. After seeing the play, she announced to her class and our cast that she was ashamed of her colleagues at the other school. Part of her class's assignment was to read a banned book; one of her students commented that he *was* offended by some opinions quoted in our play, but figured that was the point, to cause enough discomfort to make our audience think.

Nancy Moore's Base Line Middle School was our last. After the play, she organized small group breakouts with teachers facilitating each discussion. One parent had approached Nancy beforehand, saying she was disturbed by our encouragement of young people to flout authority. So Nancy invited her to attend. Not only was this mother full of praise when she actually saw the play, but she was impressed by the thoughtful comments from the seventh grade audience. Score one for a parent discovering that young people can think for themselves!

Dan the Video Man Saves the Day

Before our final public appearances, to be held after school closed for the summer, I conferred with Carla Selby, the local ACLU chapter head who heard us on the radio. Since we didn't want to sue the schools (gulp!), Carla wondered what ACLU could do to help spread our message, beyond their Board resolution commending YAAB's project. My light bulb blinked. Would she have any contacts to help us make a video?

Less than twenty-four hours later, Carla sent Dan Culberson to our doorstep. A freelance videographer, he offered to make the video of our dreams. He would tape YAAB's live performances, including discussion sessions, then take YAAB into the studio. The finished product would air on public access cable television during Banned Books Week; then we could use the video for any educational purpose. All this came free; he would volunteer his time, and TCI Cable Television would provide the studio.

Leaping from the depths, we now walked on air. Dan kept turning up reliably with his videocam, promising YAAB they could assist him later in the studio on camera and sound. Suddenly we realized we would need music for a soundtrack, and I began to suspect that video is a very different animal from a play. YAAB discussed songs to enhance their message, from John Lennon's *Imagine* to Enya. Hassling with recording companies for permission to use recorded music was a headache. Yoko gave a flat no—or her representative gave the standard answer from Lennon's estate. Months later, we received permission to use Peter, Paul & Mary's 1965 recording of Bob Dylan's *The Times They Are A-Changin'*. YAAB especially loved its line telling mothers and fathers not to criticize what they can't understand. (Moccasin time again—I was their age when I too felt unbearably moved by that line!)

Challenges to the Censors

We still needed instrumental music to fill some gaps. At our cast party, I discovered that our own YAABite Ashley Burns was an accomplished pianist and composer. Another light bulb: more youth participation! A volunteer from our local public radio station, KGNU, recorded Ashley playing her *Elfin Dance*, *Breeze*, and *The Untold Dream* for our video soundtrack. Now we're learning how to copyright original music.

Ever More Fascinating Bookings

The presence of uniformed police at our main library performance on June 11 did not mar the excitement of the day, a simultaneous kickoff for our Book Quest summer reading game, designed for statewide use by some of the same kids. Our agitated protester either never turned up, or slunk off when he saw the police. Once again, the audience was reluctant to end the post-play discussion, especially with Denver ABC-TV affiliate Channel 9's camera whirring. Their resulting thirty-second news clip about us was easy to miss if you blinked, but still gratifying.

All this publicity brought an additional booking. On June 14 the cast went to an airport hotel to perform for Women in Communications, a professional group which annually sponsored a First Amendment fund-raiser. A free dinner and generous compliments from adults who got the point were an unbeatable combination.

On a high, YAAB swung into their last and most anticipated performance four days later. They all enjoy shopping at Boulder Bookstore, a superb independent bookseller on Boulder's renowned Pearl Street Mall. Now they got to perform there, in one of Boulder's most historic buildings, below stained glass windows in its glorious ballroom, in the very spot where many had attended signings by authors such as Douglas Adams. The bookstore's publicity staff Lisa Gesner and Tami Wachtel were committed to our entire project. The play was only the first step, for they would participate in our grand finale during Banned Books Week.

After relaxing into summer, YAAB revved up again for an unexpected encore performance on July 24, at Columbine Unitarian Universalist Church in Littleton, south of Denver. It proved to be their most sparkling moment as these folks, known for humanitarian ideals, embraced YAAB during their packed church service. Such wholehearted support from these people of all ages buoyed our performers into their most passionate rendition. Afterwards, YAAB received their first standing ovation (it was not to be their last), and the congregation lingered long to fill out hundreds of chain links.

Three days later YAAB was in the television studio for a seven-hour taping session. Though their live staging was bare bones, now they used makeup and dressed differently for each of their multiple parts. For the first time, Romeo wore a cape, and Juliet traded a tee shirt for a gown. Francesca Lia Block's *Weetzie Bat* (HarperCollins, 1989) booktalker wore California palm tree sunglasses and dangly earrings, and Margaret Atwood's handmaid wore her white veil and red robe. To economize, taping was completed in only two sessions, but YAAB's performance had grown so polished, few retakes were needed. Dan would edit in time to premiere the video during Banned Books Week, when it would run simultaneously on Boulder Public Access Cable Channel 54/62, in the main Boulder Public Library, and in Boulder Bookstore.

The Chain Parade

YAAB had vowed to "chain the library," which stretched across nearly two city blocks and spanned Boulder Creek. They mapped a route around the outside of this sprawling building: to cross the creek would require weaving back indoors. Would it work? Would we have enough links to reach the chain all the way around?

Infected by YAAB's enthusiasm, the Boulder Bookstore staff decided to make a chain too, offering their customers a free "I Read Banned Books" button for contributing links. Another light bulb zinged: how about connecting the library's chain to the bookstore's?

So the Chain Parade was born. On Saturday, October 1, the last day of Banned Books Week, YAAB and as many volunteers as they could hustle would encircle the library, and then carry the chain three blocks to the bookstore, where the two chains would join to surround the store. Then they would march up and down Pearl Street Mall.

Complex negotiations commence with the police about parade permits and traffic obstruction. I truly do not know if this can be done, because I have no idea how long the chain will be, or how many volunteers will turn up. But I promise the police to be good, book several staff members to marshal our parade, and get very nervous.

The *Daily Camera*'s youth columnist Clay Evans gives us a big boost to kick off the week. In his September 24 column, after declaiming the "creepy irony" of banning books like *Fahrenheit 451*, Evans demonstrates that he is one of the few adults to get the point: "Usually the people most affected by book bans—the kids—are completely left out of the debate." He quotes YAAB's Dylan Burns, thirteen: "We don't need protecting. . . . Do they want us to be sheep when we grow up? Because that's what's going to happen if [book banning] is allowed." Summarizing YAAB's experience with their play, Evans gets it again. "Amid all the bluster and bombast of know-it-all adults wagging fingers, . . . something is being forgotten: kids are smart and they are their own best censors." He concludes with a plea for the public to join YAAB's chain: "I encourage anybody who in interested in the First Amendment to stop by and support these efforts this week. These kids are in the trenches, fighting battles that preserve everyone's freedom."

During each day of Banned Books Week, YAAB swarms the library preparing the chain. They staff a table by the circulation desk, urging the public to make links by referring to copies of ALA's Banned Books list. The video plays repeatedly as they direct patrons to nearby displays of banned books. Another YAAB team is holed up in a library storeroom stapling links together, the chain expanding like a creeping mass of algae. Periodically they check link collection boxes all over the library, which are never empty. The public is responding! Patrons get hooked on the Banned Books list, poring over it to exclaim over the senselessness of complaints against their favorite classics. Old ladies discuss a lifetime of reading with these nice young people; teens and children plop down on the floor to fill out *Where's Waldo?* and Dr. Seuss links. YAAB handles all queries with aplomb; by now they are more articulate than I am. The competition for Banned Books Champion of Boulder, the teen who makes the most links, heats up among over three hundred teen contributors. A twenty-dollar gift certificate from Cover to Cover Books is at stake. Meanwhile, Boulder Bookstore runs the video continuously and loops their growing chain through their window display of banned books.

I watch for Saturday weather predictions. Colorado enjoys over three hundred days of sunshine annually. We have indoor rain plans, but rain would stop our march to the bookstore.

When October 1st dawns, the *Denver Post* gives our Chain Parade a plug. We're feeling confident. Our monster chain oozes all over the storeroom. It takes four YAABites an hour to feed it downstairs over the railing to lurk behind the auditorium, awaiting its debut. A Banned Books Read-in by local lawmakers is our prelude; we hope to draft the audience as chainbearers. Three YAAB booktalkers perform, then library staffer Ghada Elturk speaks movingly about her family's horrific experience of government censorship in Lebanon. Her three teenage daughters gave over 150 links to our chain.

At last I announce the Banned Books Champion: YAAB's own Ashley Burns, music composer and reader of 295 banned books in her fifteen years. Both runners-up Nadia Haddad and Felina Tanner also broke 200 books. (I only read 197 in my tripled years.)

The moment has arrived. YAAB parade leaders Linda Reling and Aron Kelly drag one end of the chain across the stage, their team towing behind them. About twenty chainbearer draftees line up at the auditorium exit. The chain unwinds from its massive pile. One glance out the window explains our sparse turnout (beyond the CU Buffaloes game). For the first time in weeks, it's raining. But this light drizzle can't stop us.

We've hardly crossed the vestibule before our paper chain becomes a dead weight. It's snagging on everything. We push gamely onward, snaking around the first corner of the building. We stop and start, as YAAB messengers run back and forth helping to keep the chain moving. The chain breaks once, then again, then constantly. We're stuck, and the parade has hardly begun.

The skies open. Within seconds everyone is soaked. As we race back inside, sopping chainbearers abandon their disintegrating links.

Inside, we regroup in the art gallery lobby. We are starting the rain plan, which I have instantly reduced to dragging the chain across our indoor bridge to the door at the opposite end of the library. An unbelievable mound of chain still crouches behind the auditorium. Some volunteers have disappeared; we beg folks to stay. It's hailing golf balls outside.

An hour later we are still dragging. Once YAAB reaches the entrance two blocks away, they insist on bringing the chain back to the starting point, since the whole pile has not yet unwound. Less than ten volunteers remain. Patrons are not joining in anymore, but simply stare at us crazed chainbearers yelling and yanking. The paper creature trips on every barrier to its writhing route. YAAB chain-fixers race back and forth, brandishing staplers.

This is hardly the glory we imagined. All YAAB has left, besides miles of chain, is determination. Our few hardy volunteers, from little kids to a gleefully sporting elderly man, hang in there as saints in our eyes. When the gallery appears at trail's end, everyone yanks with renewed vigor.

At last the entire chain is heaped once more in a glorious pile, mangled and tattered from its journey, surrounded by proud chainbearers. We've done it!

Six thousand links extended for one-third of a mile. The world record paper chain might be over 36 miles long, made in 1993 by university students in Ireland, but we're still pretty proud. With so few helpers, we could never have dragged it to the bookstore even in sunshine; their additional thousand links would have approached half a mile. While the bookstore staff is disappointed, I am relieved that we are not entangled among zillions of ripped links in traffic, pleading with the cops not to arrest us!

Intellectual Freedom Champions

YAAB has done what they set out to do, but they are not finished yet. On November 6, they appear as special guests at the Colorado Library Association's conference at Keystone ski resort. There they proudly accept CLA's 1994 Intellectual Freedom Award, alongside a second award recipient, Theresa Marsh, an Evergreen librarian who withstood attempts to remove forty books from her elementary school library in an incident mentioned in our play. YAAB's nominator Virginia Boucher cites them for "presenting and defending *Don't Read This!* . . . initiated *by* teens and *for* teens, giving them a chance to hear, discuss, and *do* something to support the freedom to read." As eight YAAB members stand on the banquet platform to receive their Colorado red sandstone award, hundreds of librarians rise in a standing ovation.

Youth participation doesn't get any better than this. For all of us, it's a ten-hankie award.

Where does YAAB go from this lofty pinnacle? They're pretty cocky after being recognized in Keystone, even before their award was presented, as "the kids from the video." They have appeared in national and local media, and in reports by the ACLU and People for the American Way. Allison has been interviewed by one of her favorite authors, Nancy Garden, and Ingrid received a letter from Theodore Taylor, author of her booktalk title *The Cay* (Avon, 1970). Already bursting with new ideas, YAAB struggles to fill the hole left by their beloved Ingrid when she went to MIT in the fall of 1994. Whatever YAAB does in the future, they will persevere, with the vision and confidence they have acquired.

But *Don't Read This!* carried even more valuable lessons. What began as an exercise of and about free expression among youth, transformed its sixteen young creators, through the very suppression which they questioned, into lifelong defenders of the First Amendment. They know, on the deepest personal level, what censorship means. Being "silenced" taught them more about our precious freedoms than most Americans ever learn.

If some technical problems with the video's sound can be overcome, YAAB hopes to find national distribution for *Don't Read This!* [*Editors' note*: While national distribution did not prove possible, the entire text of the script is available in the appendix of *Youth Participation in School and Public Libraries: It Works* (ALA/YALSA, 1995.)]

Cast and Creators of *Don't Read This!*

Allison Barrett, Ashley Burns, Dylan Burns, Pixy Dougherty, Malinda Dunckley, Nora Gully, Nadia Haddad, Erik Hansen, Anne Pizzi, Linda Reling, Anna Salim, Olivia Simantob, Lisa Sweeney, Felina Tanner, Ingrid Ulbrich, Andy Wallace. [June 1995]

What Mean We, White Man?
Roger Sutton

The Lone Ranger and Tonto are riding cross the range, and they spot a stagecoach being held up by outlaws. "Tonto!" says the Lone Ranger. 'We have to stop the outlaws!" "OK, Keemosabe," says Tonto, and they stop the outlaws. Then they're riding along again, and they see cattle rustlers trying to steal some cattle. "Tonto!" says the Lone Ranger. "We have to stop the cattle rustlers." "OK, Keemosabe," says Tonto, and they stop the cattle rustlers. So after this, Tonto and the Lone Ranger make camp and settle in for the night. But in the morning, when they awake, they're surrounded by Indians. "Tonto!" says the Lone Ranger. "We have to stop the Indians!" Says Tonto, "What mean *we*, white man?"

I've always loved that joke: it has that wonderful kind of punch line at which people don't know if they're allowed to laugh.

"What mean we?" is a question now being asked of and by the day-to-day culture as well as in the academy—a question often expressed in terms of "political correctness," and, depending upon who's asking, the question is phrased with indignation, irony, or honest bewilderment.

For librarians serving children and youth, it is not a new question. We—by which I mean librarians—have recognized the need for a culturally comprehensive literature for young people for at least the past thirty-five years. Before then, there were books about minority children, of course, but by and large they were books by white writers, implicitly for white children. The worthy goal of many of these books was to foster empathy for young people who looked or talked "different." But how do young people who *are* different, that is, minority, or foreign-born, or disabled, see themselves in books designed for those who think them different? (Young people all think themselves different, anyway, and I'm not sure that's a separate discussion.) I have an old anthology of "teenage" short stories called *Stories to Live By*, published in 1960. There is one story in it called "Incident on a Train," in which Annette, a light-skinned black girl, mistakenly is seated in a "whites only" train car. In a prefatory note, the reader is asked, "How do you feel about integration?" "Who do you think is meant by 'you'"? The answer is implicit in Annette's speech delivered upon moving to the Negro car after a bigoted white woman tattles to the conductor: "I am a Negro, but as a good representative of my race I should abide by the rules. They may be changed someday, but until they are, I shall obey them."[1] "We" don't have to worry about her causing trouble, now do we?

The Council on Interracial Books for Children has been significant in calling for good books *for* minority children, as well as about them. The Council has run a contest to find new minority writers and calls attention to the good books that are being published. More controversially, it has called for the elimination of stereotyping and the cessation of negative images of minorities in children's books. Among the books the council has criticized are Ezra Jack Keats's *The Snowy Day* (for its pictorial depiction of a large black woman, the protagonist's mother) and Margot Zemach's *Jake and Honeybunch Go to Heaven* (for, among other problems, the pictorial depictions of blacks in heaven eating ribs and listening to jazz).[2] In a Council editorial, Sanford Berman called for amending the ALA's Library Bill of Rights and its Policy on Access for Minors:

> Intellectual freedom advocates need to consider if indeed, a juvenile work that distorts the experience of a given ethnic or racial group, questions the humanity of young, older or disabled persons, or posits the superiority of men over women so violates Fourteenth Amendment strictures against denial of equal protection and due process that it just doesn't belong on the open shelves of a children's library collection.[3]

First of all, librarians should not be doing the Supreme Court's job of interpreting the Constitution (and Berman's interpretation has found little judicial favor). Second, it seems peculiar to address the violation of constitutional protection of one group by limiting another group's right to read. Berman's proposal would limit children's First Amendment rights while doing nothing for the oppressed groups with which he is concerned.

Both *The Snowy Day* and *Jake and Honeybunch Go to Heaven* are by white author/illustrators, and it has been suggested that the CIBC has a policy of going after white writers who tackle minority subjects. My own unscientific perusal of back issues of the *CIBC Bulletin* does not entirely bear this out, (with, for example, reviewer Doris Seale handling Paul Goble with entirely good humor) but there does seem to be a tendency in the reviews to say that white writers don't often get it right.

Is it fair to say that only members of a minority culture can accurately convey the experience of that culture? Many liberals and conservatives alike would have us flip the question, asking if minorities can accurately reflect the dominant culture. The questions, however, aren't equal: minorities absorb far more of the dominant white culture than the other way around. They have to. Still, the first question is a good one. Here is an answer by Ann Cameron, a white writer who has written about minority children, most notably in *The Stories That Julian Tells* (Pantheon, 1981):

> It seems to me that people who advise "write what you know" drastically underestimate the human capacity for imagining what lies beyond our immediate knowledge and for understanding what is new to us. Equally they overestimate the extent to which we know ourselves. A culture like a person, has blind spots—traits for which their very familiarity the culture cannot see. Often the writer who is an outsider—an African writing about the United States, an American writing about China—sees in a way that enriches him as an observer, the culture he observes, and the culture he comes from.[4]

I think Ann Cameron is correct. If we cannot reach beyond the bounds of race, ethnicity, sex, sexual orientation, and class, literature is useless, leaving writers few options beyond Joni Mitchell-style confessional lyrics: This is what happened to *me* and this is how I feel about it. If literature—language—is meant to communicate, there's a presupposition that we have something to say to each other, and hear from each other. It is a way to jump out of our own skins. South African writer Nadine Gordimer said in a *Booklist* interview with Hazel Rochman that

> as for writers writing about this or that or the other, it's extraordinary that people should question this. How does a writer write from the point of view of a child? Or from the point of view of an old person when you are 17 years old? How does a writer change sex? If you say that living as we do in a society where we are rubbing up against each other—even under

apartheid—every day in many different circumstances, if given those conditions, you cannot ever have a black character, then you could only write about yourself. It's denying what writing is. How could the famous soliloquy of Molly Bloom have been written by James Joyce? Has any woman ever written anything as incredibly intimate? I mean, how did Joyce know how a woman feels before she's going to get her period? How does he know? I can't tell you. There's an intuition. There's an empathy with other people's lives that writers have—not sympathy, but empathy.[5]

Also, if we cannot, in writing, imagine another person's experience, we cannot do so in reading, another way to jump from our skins. Why bother at all?

As an example from the children's book field, I would like to tell you a story YA novelist Ron Koertge told at a conference I attended last year. Ron Koertge wrote *The Arizona Kid*, a book I think of as the first YA novel with a sense of humor about gay people. A sense of humor is a good thing to have; it helps a lot in the job of taking the world seriously. Spending the summer with his gay Uncle Wes in Tucson, Billy is learning about life and horses, and hopefully pursuing his First Time with a girl he meets named Cara Mae. One night, Billy and Cara Mae are out for dinner when they run into Wes who, Billy notices, is wearing jeans. "Tight jeans. Very tight jeans."

"Are those your pants?" I hissed.

"Of course they're my pants. Why?"

"They're so tight."

"They're supposed to be tight."

I toyed with a broken tortilla chip. "When are you going to be home tonight?"

"Gosh, whenever you say, Dad. But can I have ten dollars for a condom after the movie?"[6]

Here's a book that dares to say, yes, gay men *do* wear tight jeans, and yes that would make even a nice teenager nervous, and it's no big deal; that scene is funny and real, and touching in the way it demonstrates that Uncle Wes and Billy love each other. Anyway, Koertge got a letter from a man who said something like, "loved your book, great to see a gay writer do such a positive book for teens," etc. Ron wrote back, and said, "I'm not gay, but thank you very much for your compliments to my book." So then the man writes back *again*, and asks Ron what business he thought he had writing about the gay community? The book hadn't changed a bit.

As librarians, we are more concerned with evaluating books, rather than writing them, so I would like to explore the question of cultural authenticity from the point of view of reviewing and selecting books for children and young adults. The people who review books at *The Bulletin of the Center for Children's Books* are all white, and, excepting myself, female. This is in opposition to the *CIBC Bulletin*, where there is a policy that each book reviewed will be reviewed by a member of the group with which the book is concerned, that is, a book about an Asian-American child should be reviewed by an Asian-American.[7] (Not by a child or young adult, however, and that's a cultural gap we all have to be aware of.)

I like to think that I review the book in front of me, not the author behind it. But like any reviewer, I have preferences and prejudices, topics I know a lot about and more topics about which I know very little. When I review a book about astronomy or salamanders, for example, I take a lot on faith, assuming that the author or illustrator knows what he or she is talking about. I'm confident commenting on effective presentation, clear language and conveyance of ideas, and the presence or absence of an index, but unless I have knowledge of a topic, I have to assume the basic information is correct. Sometimes the book itself can tip you off to its mistakes: fuzzy thinking, self-contradictions, poor copyediting, or sweeping generalizations are clues that all is not right, and that a look in other books or a call to the reference desk is in order. Hazel Rochman tells me that she worries about the converse of this know-nothing dilemma, and asks whether her detailed knowledge of South Africa (where she grew up) and subsequently more authoritative reviews of books about that country, only points up her inadequacies in reviewing books about countries with which she is less familiar. "What am I missing?" she wonders.

Most reviews, however, call upon reviewers' strengths as well as limitations (and knowing the difference is half the battle). When I reviewed Fred and Patricia McKissack's biography of black contralto Marian Anderson (Enslow, 1991), for example, I obviously had no ethnic heritage from which to speak with any cultural authority (a sticky term, and I don't know if I believe in it), but I am an Anderson fan and an opera buff and found factual errors and omissions in the book. So how does my review stack up against one by a reviewer who may be black, but does not care for opera? And again, how does my review of that mythical salamander book compare with one by a biology teacher?

People are a lot more slippery than salamanders, and fiction as slippery as people. A reliable encyclopedia can prove or disprove a salamander characteristic, but how do we evaluate "authenticity" in fiction? How do we distinguish between a stereotype and a portrayal we just don't like? In her article "Equality and Ambiguity in Library Service to Children," Donnarae MacCann states that "stereotyping cannot be ignored by book selectors,"[8] but she fails to tell us what a stereotype is or how to detect it. Is it like pornography, we know it when we see it?

One problem in defining stereotyping as it is used in this context is that we are seeking to evaluate books as to their moral effectiveness: stereotypes are wrong, harmful, leading impressionable child readers to a misunderstanding of a fellow human being. Both the CIBC and Donnarae MacCann make an argument for exempting young people from policies of unimpeded access. McCann writes,

"Generally speaking, a credible public policy toward Zemach's Jake story is achieved if copies of the book are accessible to those studying graphic art, or to those analyzing specimens of American racism."[9] In other words, not the young children for whom the book is intended. And I find it rather chilling the idea of a librarian interrogating any patron as to his or her qualifications for reading a book.

To evaluate a piece of literature in terms of its moral or its political correctness is certainly within the wide province of criticism. But to use it as a standard of book selection is, I think, a mistake. You can't point at people the same way you can at salamanders and say: this is true about (fill in the blank) people. This is demeaning of (fill in the blank) people. To do so is to indulge in stereotyping, and the only disagreement is over exactly what the stereotype is to be.

Another problem in defining stereotyping is that, by its nature, its presence depends upon considerations found in other books, outside the book in hand. The reason people get upset about Zemach's spareribs in heaven, for example, is that they have had to eat those spareribs so many times before. Is that Zemach's responsibility? And what credence does the "but black people [like many people] *do* eat spareribs" argument hold? Or, as I recall the publisher of *Jake and Honeybunch* saying on the radio, "What's wrong with eating spareribs?"

Nothing's wrong with eating spareribs, but spareribs alone do not provide a balanced diet. Please understand that I speak metaphorically: will Zemach's book be the only one in the library that depicts black people eating? If it is, then the problem is with the library, not the book. This is where I think the CIBC and MacCann err. Both seem to view the book selection process as one of exclusion, keeping out materials that do not meet (as yet undefined) standards of nonstereotyping. It would, I think, be better to demand an inclusive approach to collection development, an approach that views the collection as a whole, not one that takes it one-book-at-a-time.

I did find a set of "Guidelines for Choosing Books on African-American Themes," written by Beryle Banfield in the *CIBC Bulletin*. While much she says is sensible, "Recognize that good books on African American themes are crucial to the healthy development of *all* children," for example, too much else is unabashed mythification, approving only those books that hold to an uplifting, didactic line.

> Does the book illuminate critical aspects of the Black experience? Does it, for example, depict positive and warm family relationships; Black responses to various forms of oppression; the development of customs, traditions and institutions; supportive relationship among various members of the Black community; the role of Black women?[10]

Complicated and difficult family relationships are usually far more interesting and enlightening than stories of happy families: Virginia Hamilton's *Sweet Whispers, Brother Rush* is proof of that, as is Richard Wright's *Native Son* or Richard Rodriguez's *Hunger of Memory*. To use literature as a manual for role-modeling ("Will the material and its presentation contribute to the development of a positive self-concept by the child of African descent?")[11] is stifling to both writer and reader.

In fact, I worry that despite all our raised consciousness, we haven't eradicated our stereotypes, we've only changed them. Aunt Jemima may be among the missing, but what about the many books about wise, helpful, and God-fearing black people who exist but to help out their troubled white neighbors? What about the spate of nostalgic picture books that rosy-up the past at the expense of any real plot? This is a trend

I have seen in picture books about black families, but such gorgeously illustrated sentimentality is by no means limited to those books: kinder, gentler, and boring describes too many pictures books today.

Instead, what about Karen Williams's *Galimoto* (Morrow, 1990), about a young Malawi boy who spends the day collecting scrap wire to make a toy car? I mention this book specifically because it was denounced by Opal Moore in *Wilson Library Bulletin* as the "celebration of a Western material icon."[12] That strikes me as a singularly humorless response, and sentimental in the way it seems to deny Africa technology. How would a Malawian feel about that boy's pastime? It depends, I suppose, on which Malawian you talk to. And the boy himself? He seems to be having a fine time, oblivious to grownup wrangling.

For a more political story, what about Reviva Schermbrucker and Niki Daly's *Charlie's House* (Viking, 1991)? Charlie lives in a black South African township, and spends a day building a dollhouse of mud, filled with all the out-of-reach things Charlie would love to have: his own room, a TV, an indoor bathroom, and electricity. The pictures of the trash he uses to construct his dreams are heartbreaking, but his imagination and persistence are exhilarating.

What about *Amazing Grace*, by Mary Hoffman and Caroline Birch (Dial, 1991)? Grace is a young black girl who loves to pretend she's Joan of Arc, Anansi the Spider, Hiawatha and Mowgli. But she discovers she can't be Peter Pan in the school play because, as schoolmate Natalie tells her, she's black. Grace *is* amazing, and she gets the part.

Incidentally, *Booklist* included *Amazing Grace* on a recommended list about "African-Americans."[13] That may be current usage, but not for Grace: the book is a British import. What do we call her? Does it matter? In any case, each of these books shows a black child overcoming adversity that is actual or implied, but that adversity has been particularized, and so has the child.

Native Americans in children's books no longer go woo-woo-woo and wear warpaint, but the new stereotype is just as wearing: having a special relationship with Mother Earth, they stand as an ecological exemplary to us all, and they talk like slow, quiet, gods.

Instead, what about Kirkpatrick Hill's *Toughboy and Sister* (McElderry, 1990), about a contemporary Alaskan Athabascan brother and sister who face the death of their father from an alcoholic binge?

This book isn't about a stereotypic drunken Indian: it shows us a very real problem in the Native American community and elsewhere, and about two brave kids who survive it.

And grandmas of all races no longer make cookies—they make quilts, and then they die. But in Takaaki Nomura's *Grandpa's Town* (Kane/Miller, 1991), a Japanese boy learns that his recently widowed grandfather is *not* lonely, does *not* want to come live with the boy and his mother, and instead takes his grandson to visit the community's men's bath, where Grandpa has lots of friends.

In a story (autobiographical, one senses) set in modern Japan, Allen Say pulls a switch on the stereotype of American immigrants longing for "the old country," parents clinging to "the old ways." *Tree of Cranes* (Houghton, 1991) is about a Japanese mother longing for her homeland, but what she misses is a California Christmas, having moved to Japan in her youth. It is a lovely mystery to her son when she decorates a Japanese pine with paper cranes. It was, says the now grown narrator, "my first Christmas."[14]

Stereotypes, whether insulting or ennobling, are clichés. Like many clichés, they may have at one time possessed some truth, but that truth is now erased by overuse and underwork: resorts taken by people who don't want to think. And they often aren't true. I remember my childhood shock when I put together the paradox of "many hands make light work" and "too many cooks spoil the soup."

I feel I'm on firmer ground when I discuss stereotyping as a literary failure, rather than a social one. In assessing a book's literary quality I am certainly making a value judgment, just as are the people who have called *Jake and Honeybunch* racist. So when I say firmer ground I don't mean higher ground. I can't tell you, because I don't know, if a given novel is culturally authentic. I don't know who can tell you that. I can tell you if I've read the same story, seen the same characters, anticipated the same plot twists five times already this year. Stereotypes are flat and uncomplicated and unsurprising, failures of the imagination that stop a story cold. There can be pleasure in reading what you've read before— and *Sweet Valley High* is a double example of that—but it is static, the simulation of an experience felt before, lacking the stimulation of discovery.

But what do we do with the stereotypes that are downright inaccurate and hateful? Some people have criticized *Gone with the Wind* for what is perceived as its racist portrait of happy slaves. There is a good argument there, but it is by no means clear-cut. We cannot say with any certainty, for example, that Mammy *would not have been like that*. But what about some of Margaret Mitchell's more offhand remarks, such as the one about Scarlett throwing up when she gets the "niggery smell" of the slave cabins?[15] That comes just before the God-as-My-Witness scene, and is forgotten in the drama. What do we do with that? First, we know it as a lie and we hope it makes us angry. Do we remove *Gone with the Wind* from the library? No. We can't keep *Gone with the Wind* a secret. Do we keep it away from young people? No. There are too many good things about the book.

I would like to think that there is no reason to share a book with young people which contains such a lie and such an insult. I'm worried, though, about giving that power to anyone else: the promise of censorship turns each of us into a self-righteous despot. If I forbid that, what happens when somebody wants to forbid me? And the personal pronoun is on purpose, because it is hard not to take personally. Imagine you're a gay person, like me, and read this:

> Some homosexuals may object to our speaking of "queer gays." They may call it a put-down, an expression of scorn and contempt. So let's agree that we—the author of this book and its readers—aren't being scornful or contemptuous when we use this term; we're only being descriptive. The behavior and, often, the looks of the kinds of gays we're talking about are very odd, very unlike what we usually expect of other people, that's what we mean by calling them queer gays."[16]

What mean we, indeed, Mary! That quote is from Morton Hunt's *Gay: What Teenagers Should Know About Homosexuality and the AIDS Crisis*, published for young people in 1987. Think about that paragraph, and insert your own ethnicity, religious affiliation, whatever, every time you hear *queer gays*. While you're at it, add a pejorative swing. And think about how it feels to be insulted by an author who doesn't even recognize that you're in the audience.

When your own button is pushed, things look different. When I first read Hunt's paragraph I said, who does he think he *is*. How dare *he* tell *me* about what it is like for me? But if I tell Hunt he can't be allowed to be hateful about me, I run the risk of not being allowed to be hateful about Morton Hunt, which is something I very much like to be. And I can do lots of things: I can write a book of my own. I can read another book. In a library, I can surround Morton Hunt with friends, such as *When Someone You Know Is Gay*, by Daniel and Susan Cohen (Evans, 1989), a married couple who realize that the "Someone You Know" may be you. I can surround Morton Hunt with friendly enemies (Larry Kramer comes to mind here); that is, those who know me and still give me a hard time. The "we of me" that Carson McCullers's' Frankie longed for in *Member of the Wedding* has to include all of the above: it's the only way we discover who we really are.

Notes

1. Mabel Cleland Widdemer, Incident on a Train, collected in *Stories to Live By*, ed. by Marjorie Vetter. Platt & Munk, 1960, p. 234-241.

2. Beryle Banfield and Geraldine L. Wilson, The Black Experience through White Eyes—The Same Old Story Once Again, *Interracial Books for Children Bulletin*, v. 14, no. 5, 1983, p. 9.

3. Sanford Berman, *Interracial Books for Children Bulletin*, v. 14, no. 6, 1983. p. 3.

4. Ann Cameron, Write What You Care About, *School Library Journal*, June, 1989, p. 50.

5. Hazel Rochman, Booklist Interview: Nadine Gordimer, *Booklist*, September 15, 1990, p. 100.

6. Ron Koertge, *The Arizona Kid*, Joy Street, Little, Brown, 1988, p. 157.

7. *The Interracial Books for Children Bulletin's* headnote for its "Bookshelf" column reads: "all books that relate to minority themes are evaluated by members of the minority group depicted."

8. Donnarae MacCann, Equality and Ambiguity in Library Service for Children, in *Social Responsibility in Librarianship: Essays in Equality*, MacCann, ed., McFarland, 1989, p. xxx.

9. MacCann, p. 89.

10. Beryle Banfield, Guidelines for Choosing Books on African American Themes, *Interracial Books for Children Bulletin*, v. 16, no. 7, 1985, p. 10.

11. Banfield, p. 10.

12. Donnarae MacCann and Olga Richards, Picture Books about Blacks: an Interview with Opal Moore, *Wilson Library Bulletin*, June, 1991, p. 28.

13. Ilene Cooper. The African American Experience in Children's Books, *Booklist*, February 1, 1992, p. 1036.

14. Allen Say, *Tree of Cranes*, Houghton Mifflin. 1991, p. 32.

15. Margaret Mitchell, *Gone with the Wind*, Macmillan, 1936, p. 427.

16. Morton Hunt, *Gay: What Teenagers Should Know About Homosexuality and the AIDS Crisis*. Farrar Straus & Giroux. 1987, p. 167. [August 1992]

INTERGENERATIONAL PROGRAMS

Once Again, Alice in Wonderland
Alan Bern

In pinafore and with her hair tied back with a ribbon, looking as if she had just stepped out of a John Tenniel illustration, Alice bit into a home-baked chocolate chip cookie and announced that she felt as if she were growing taller; then she slipped around the southwest corner of the Berkeley Public Library's North Branch and out of sight. A milling crowd of four dozen preschoolers and kindergartners hardly noticed: from a balcony one flight up, the Queen of Hearts had just called out for a game of croquet to be played with pink beach balls and pink plastic flamingos as mallets, and players were gathering. Suddenly out from behind a tree emerged another Alice, much taller, on stilts in fact, in a long flamingo-pink gown and wearing a blond wig! The crowd of children froze and looked up at him, gazing with appreciation.

In filling in for North Branch Young Adult Librarian Debbie Carton while she was on family leave, I inherited the ongoing Teen Playreaders Group. For the preceding few years a slowly-changing group of eight to twelve teens had been devoted to meeting weekly in order to read aloud plays as diverse as Aristophanes's *The Frogs* and Alfred Uhry's *Driving Miss Daisy*. Previously Debbie Carton had directed informal productions such as the one using *The Berkeley Anthology*, an Edgar Lee Masters-like series of monologues of deceased Berkeleyans, written in part by the Playreaders and performed by them for a family audience, each reader popping up from behind a chair-as-gravestone. Before beginning my tenure at Berkeley Public North Branch, I had read an article[1] which described teens acting out picture books for a family audience, including young children. After several weeks of meeting with Teen Playreaders I suggested this idea to the group, which included several of my new recruits. The idea met with a kind of neutral interest and a little puzzlement. I suggested adapting one of my favorite picture books, Chris Van Allsburg's *The Stranger*, which I believe is suitable material for audiences of nearly all ages. This suggestion received very little reaction. I continued to raise the issue for several weeks until one of the Playreaders suggested, during one of our brainstorming, that we think of trying our minds at *Alice in Wonderland*: he had participated in a production of it at a summer camp, which he described in some detail. Immediately interest jumped up a few notches.

Soon, however, we had embarked on the production of a major motion picture, including scenes of virtual reality as yet unimagined by humans or androids. I had no formal training or experience in drama, let alone in film. How to contain some wonderful and wild ideas enough to do a production? I held to the idea that little kids were our best audience, and we went happily along, brainstorming when we were not reading new plays.

North Branch is a small, often extremely busy branch, almost too small for its circulation. When faced with my idea of the Playreaders performing for small children, my supervisor Francisca Schneider, a former children's librarian, suggested I look outside.

"Ah," I thought, "perfect for noise, action, and small children." This is when I began to think of a production in terms of the space(s) outdoors and, almost automatically, in terms of action and props. There was very little budget for the program, and this, combined with my lack of experience in directing, led me to the notion of doing a few scenes from *Alice*. I visualized these scenes as physical *stations* outside on the lawn. With the input of the Playreaders and of other Young Adult Librarians in the system, I came up with a half dozen feasible scenes.

We opened the show with a juggling teen, who captured the kids' attention, both with his juggling and his bantering with the audience. Approximately fifty children, ages three to five, attended with their parents; I had advertised the production for four- to seven-year-olds, but the adults, in their wisdom, brought the younger children. Perfect for our show! The juggling ended; sitting silently behind him had been Alice in her white dress at the foot of her sister. A teen playreader narrator read from the opening of *Alice in Wonderland*:

> Alice was beginning to get very tired of sitting by her sister on the bank, and of having nothing to do: once or twice she had peeped into the book her sister was reading, but it had no pictures or conversations in it, "and what is the use of a book," thought Alice, "without pictures or conversation?"

Alice's Sister then began reading flatly out of a dully-written textbook, but did not proceed long enough to put anyone to sleep. Meanwhile out from my van, which I had parked close by, emerged the White Rabbit, running, halting, long ears flapping, looking at her watch, exclaiming that she was late, and then taking off with Alice close behind.

Alice in Wonderland seems to have nearly universal appeal, and one of the most intriguing and well-remembered movements is the beginning where Alice follows the rabbit down the hole. Of course, I had not dug a deep hole, but the idea of putting some open-ended barrels through some bushes had seemed a nice analogy. Finding the barrels had not been easy, but I had finally solicited a donation of some fiber barrels once used to hold garlic powder: fiber barrels containing foodstuffs can be washed and aired out to dry; other costlier barrels might have contained solvents of petroleum products and could not have been properly cleaned or the ends easily and safely cut away. Since Alice and the White Rabbit were leading the young children through the barrels, the relationship of active audience participation in the performance was immediately established. I had punched small holes in the barrels and tied them loosely to strong branches of the bushes. Teen Playreaders and I had glued decorations on the outsides and, especially, the insides of the barrels: colored sheets and odd cut-outs from magazines, all non-staining and non-sticking materials to view as one went through the barrels. When people went through them, the barrels rocked gently without rolling or breaking the ropes.

The White Rabbit and Alice led; excited children followed. Many went through quite quickly, but some took their time, testing the barrels for steadiness and safety. Participating parents and my wife ("Alice" by name) and I were there to help the more careful kids through. On the other side of the bushes was a whole new world, a new scene indeed: there sat the caterpillar blowing bubbles. The narrator read:

> The Caterpillar and Alice looked at each other for some time in silence: at last the Caterpillar took the hookah out of its mouth, and addressed her in a languid, sleepy voice.
>
> The Caterpillar spoke as slowly as he could to Alice,
>
> "Who are you?"

In wonderfully elongated tones. Alice, hands on hips, listened with some patience.

Suddenly, behind Alice, was that White Rabbit again, checking the time and exclaiming, "I'm late! I'm late!" The kids turned around and there stood the Dodo Bird all ready for the Caucus Race. Alice and the White Rabbit began to chase around and around the Dodo Bird with the kids following close behind. What a race! Several times, and carefully, they switched directions until the Dodo Bird yelled,

"The race is over!"
The White Rabbit asked,
"But who has won?"
After thinking for a moment, the Dodo said,
Everybody has won, and all must have prizes."
Again the white Rabbit,
"But who is to give the prizes?"
And the Dodo responded,
"Why, she, of course" . . . pointing to Alice with one finger.

Alice gave out bags of popcorn tied with ribbon as prizes to each child. Children munched, shared with their parents, and chatted for an instant.

When the White Rabbit appeared again, late as always, the children were ready to move; next they found Alice at "A Mad Tea-party," where the Mad Hatter, the March Hare, and the Mouse conversed nonsensically as Carroll had them. Upon seeing Alice, all huddled in one corner of the table, they cried out,

"No room! No room!"

Although there was plenty of room. The March Hare offered Alice some wine, though there was none, as she noticed and he immediately admitted. After a short game of musical chairs among these characters dressed in hats, coats, and masks, somehow room was made for Alice though at first there had seemed to be none. Once again food (chocolate chip cookies and lemonade) was offered to the children. The children stood in lines and were served by the Mad Tea-Partyers, pleased to be so close to them.

Parents saved the uneaten and undrunk portions from the Mad Tea-Party as again the children followed the White Rabbit to the next station, Painting the Roses Red, *The Queen's Croquet-Ground.*

> "Would you tell me," said Alice, a little timidly, "why you are painting those roses?"

The children were offered watercolor markers by two overseeing teens, the Guards, to help color white paper roses mounted on heavy cardboard; they explained to Alice and the children that the roses should have been colored; I had not expected this activity to be as popular as it was. Groups of children colored while others waited their turns; coloring went in layers over and over on the same paper roses, and many of the children did not want to finish. Suddenly from a porch overlooking the lawn, came a loud, royal proclamation: the Queen, in proper crown and with her scepter upraised shouted, "Can you play croquet?" to Alice who answered in the affirmative. There followed a croquet game played chaotically by a number of the teen playreaders all at once with pink flamingos purchased at a garden supply store and large pink balls and spiny rubber dog toys (the porcupines) from a toy store. The Queen, calling for a trial, threatened to behead all the players, especially Alice.

After the game had gone on for a few minutes, Alice, munching on a chocolate chip cookie, announced that she felt odd; immediately following her announcement, on the other side of the game, the White Rabbit again proclaimed how late it was. The crowd turned toward the shouting Rabbit, and, as they did, around a corner and out from behind a tree came a much taller Alice, dressed in a pink dress and walking on tall stilts! He walked and wobbled and argued with the Queen, who, of course, wanted to pronounce the sentence "Off with her head" even before the verdict.

The production wound down with the throwing of thousands of playing cards (donated by a local gambling hall), which floated over all of us and which the children happily picked (a.k.a. *cleaned*) up, per an improvised suggestion of the Dormouse, and kept in packs. In the last scene, under the tree behind which the stilted Alice had emerged, sat the original Alice at her sister's knee. The children circled the seated ones and then dispersed.

All props, including lemonade, paper cups, raw materials for the cookies, markers, and flamingos cost under $70; Playreaders made their own costumes, which varied wildly in complexity. Branch staff donated masks, belts, yarn, and hats. Playreaders made all signs and paper props. A Playreader and I designed and photocopied the flyer, which I distributed to local schools and minimally to other branches: this was, after all, a local affair, and we did not want it to be too large. I let the regular patrons and neighbors in close proximity know of the event with flyers posted and handed out in order to head off complaints of loud noise and lack of parking. I kept and distributed an updated phone tree of Playreaders; this came in very handy when two of the Playreaders could not make the production. Fortunately the format was loose enough to absorb the loss of performers and go on with the show.

Under the leadership of the Director of Library Services, Regina Minudri, and Senior Librarian Francisca Goldsmith, Young Adult Services have done very well at the Berkeley Public Library. They have truly supported and facilitated imaginative programming for teens such as the Playreaders group, an All Staff Day on Young Adult Services, and a mural painting project now under way. Their support coupled with the enthusiastic backing of the Supervising Librarian at North Branch, Francisca Schneider, and the additional implicit, and often helpful, endorsement of other branch staff made my programming job easier. Needless to say the children loved the food, the participation, the prizes. The children loved watching the teens perform, just as the teens loved performing for them. The scenes themselves were very simple: I had photocopied small portions of *Alice in Wonderland* for the Playreaders to study, but little actual memorization was necessary. Because participation was paramount, children could miss a bit of a scene if they lagged behind and still catch up to all the fun.

Alice in Wonderland probably explains the issues as well as I can: as Alice grows and shrinks, Carroll is telling us, among other things about aging and growing up. Are we not all our previous ages in one as we grow? Do our memories of childhood not live on with us as he suggests they do at the end of *Alice in Wonderland*? I am reminded of a touching scene in the wonderful film *Mrs. Miniver* (based on the novel of the same title by Jan Struther and the 1942 Academy Award winner for Best Picture), in which Mrs. Miniver and her husband recite parts of *Alice in*

Wonderland to each other for comfort in their bomb shelter as the Germans bomb their home overhead. Perhaps I am sentimentalizing these patterns, but I think not; I am a believer in the "right to regress" as well as the "tendency to look up to." After the production I watched Teen Playreaders continue to play with the barrels, rolling in them vigorously and then rolling them more carefully as they put the younger children in them. I watch the children in awe of the Alice-on-stilts. I take off my Panama hat (which I wore during the production to make my place in the joyous atmosphere) to all participants; and I suggest that more such productions take place, to aid the generations in joining and communicating. Perhaps the Playreaders should go on the road next to a nursing home . . .

Notes

1. Carol Albano and Susan Holden, "Practically Speaking: Stories on Stage," *School Library Journal,* Feb. 1990: 40.

All direct quotations taken from: Lewis Carroll, *Alice's Adventures in Wonderland* (Woodbury, NY: Bobley Publishing, ©1979). [December 1994]

What We Did Together Over Their Summer Vacation: Reading Buddies in the Children's Room of the Oakland Public Main Library

Alan Bern

How It All Began

In early 1994 the Coordinator of Children's Services at Oakland Public Library, Julie Odofin, was approached by a local learning disabilities and reading specialist, Nancy McKee-Jolda, who had observed young adults working successfully with kids in several of our branches during the previous summer—these young adults worked in many of our branches that summer and were, in fact, employed in the Clinton Administration's 1993 Summer of Service program. From her professional experience and from her family life, Ms. McKee-Jolda knew the value of reading in enhancing all aspects of kids' lives, both in and out of school. She saw that improving reading skills helps children pursue and achieve goals and have a strong sense of accomplishment in doing so. She also wished to promote a stronger sense of community among youth in our East Bay Area. Further, she had an intuition that teens, especially younger teens, could work effectively with younger kids to help improve the kids' reading skills. Our Coordinator of Children's Services, Ms. Odofin, who also has experience as a Young Adult Librarian, has a keen eye for potential programs. She suggested to staff in the Children's Room that we all meet together with Ms. McKee-Jolda. Together Ms. Odofin and Ms. McKee-Jolda presented the idea to us in the Children's room. They wanted the Children's Room to sponsor an informal reading program of teens tutoring younger kids. Ms. McKee-Jolda had in mind teens from her daughter's middle school in an ethnically diverse, but mostly middle class, neighborhood. We liked the idea, but hesitated because of our already overflowing work load. Ms. McKee-Jolda assured us that she would be present to supervise the teens. We were also worried about what exactly the teens would do. We could not sponsor the program if they were actually going to teach the kids to read; we ourselves did not feel competent to do that, and we discussed with Ms. McKee-Jolda the thin line between teaching and helping. We knew that Ms. McKee-Jolda had skills in that arena, but she could by no means work with all the kids. We also knew that the teens could not do reader's advisory although we were not against them talking to the kids about their interests. Ms. McKee-Jolda assured us that the teens would be reading to the kids, reading along with the kids, or listening to the kids read; in other words, the teens would help the kids (and us) create an atmosphere more conducive to reading and enjoying reading. As for reader's advisory, Ms. McKee-Jolda was overjoyed to refer those issues to us, the librarians.

We in the Children's Room were used to working with teen volunteers. For years teens had helped with an enormous range of activities, from stamping and taping (reinforcing) books to moving furniture for programs to handing out reading club prizes. We prized our good relations with teens; they had helped us operate a busy Children's Room. Furthermore, we knew that we supplied a friendly atmosphere for these teen volunteers. In some cases this was the part of the library in which the teens were most comfortable. As we all know, the transition to adulthood is uneven at best and fraught with regressions. But, in any case, this program was different. It combined teens and kids in ways that we felt might give some new things to each group.

A Grand Summer for All

Our gamble paid off! We worked out a rotating schedule with our Adult Reading Specialist Volunteer so that all the teens she had recruited, including her own daughter, could have chances to come in and work with the kids and still have their own summer holidays. We solicited teachers of local daycare centers, which run through the summer, and found classes that could come in to take advantage of the teen Reading Buddies program, a name suggested during one of our preliminary meetings by my supervisor, the Senior Librarian in the Children's Room, Pat Lichter.

Intergenerational Programs

Some of the kids in the daycare classes, ages five to seven, were children of recent immigrants and were learning two languages at once. Reading Buddies asked individual kids what kinds of stories or activities they enjoyed. With our help they then located books which the kids might enjoy. The Buddies helped the kids with their English by reading to the kids, and the kids, when they could, would read with the Buddies, or to the Buddies, independently. The Buddies also kept notes regarding kids' interests, books read, future books to read, skills, and new words discovered by the kids. Ms. McKee-Jolda gave reading suggestions to the Buddies, which included: (1) make certain that the kid with whom you are reading can see the page, and (2) track the words with your finger as you read them. These daycare classes also participated in our Summer Reading Program, and the Buddies helped us by keeping track of what the daycare class members, as well as other participants in the Summer Reading Program, had read and what prizes they had earned.

The teen buddies were themselves quite creative. In early meetings with Ms. McKee-Jolda, we had discussed other possible activities that the teens and kids might enjoy doing in the library: puppet shows had been mentioned, as well as magic shows and even writing and drawing. Several Buddies were interested in puppet shows. We offered them some puppet scripts, several of which we had retrieved from an Internet listserv, and helped the Buddies work on their ideas. The magic shows came off more informally, but were equally as popular. In both cases library materials were the centers of the activities. Drawing was sometimes used by Buddies to help kids respond to what they had read. Some kids wrote postcards to family and friends with the help of the Buddies, often writing about what they had been reading. As Ms. McKee-Jolda pointed out in her final report, the Buddies' work covered the three major elements of reading and literacy: oral (talking about interests and books), reading, and writing.

The remarkable Ms. McKee-Jolda, indeed, was instrumental in making the program what it was; the program would have been a far different one without her. Ms. McKee-Jolda brought many years of specialized experience as a reading and learning specialist to the project, but I believe that the project would also be valuable if a library staff member or an adult volunteer had only (1) experience working with kids and teens, and (2) a strong commitment to serving both groups. For it was the relationships of the Buddies and kids which struck us all as the central focus. They all loved working (and playing) together. Ms. McKee-Jolda performed a program evaluation using forms she had drawn up for the Buddies to fill out. To quote her final report:

> The Piedmont Middle School Buddies felt they made a worthwhile contribution to the young readers. Many spoke about learning to know individuals from among a type of people they didn't often encounter. There was a clear theme in the comments of pride and accomplishment based on dealing with new situations in a responsible way, meeting challenges, and working for a good purpose. Here are a few of their comments: "We gave the children a feeling that reading is fun and worthwhile." "I learned that many children, especially children of immigrants, struggle with reading because their parents can't read English. We have to help these parents and children." "I re-established how much I like working with younger kids." "I learned how to help young people read a little better."" I learned that keeping kids occupied is hard work."

What valuable lessons to learn and experiences to have. They are as lucky to have been in the program as the kids they worked with.

We also obtained feedback from the daycare teachers and kids' parents. The teachers reported that their students' interest in reading had increased. Kids asked to do more reading when they were in the classroom. The teachers and parents also believed that their students' reading skills had actually improved; after only two weeks in the program, some kids asked for more advanced books to read. We have no hard evidence that reading skills improved in such a short time period, but to increase the enjoyment of reading as an activity is perhaps our primary goal, especially for this age group.

The summer ended on a wonderful upbeat note in the Children's Room. We threw a party for all participants in the Summer Reading Game. Nearly 300 showed up, including many classes, some of whom had participated in Reading Buddies. Also present were many of the volunteers who had worked in the Children's Room throughout the summer, including many of the teen Reading Buddies. The teens helped us with the party, which included serving refreshments and handing out prizes for the Summer Reading Game; many of the teens also won prizes, and all our volunteers were presented with individualized Certificates of Appreciation (designed on, and printed from, a microcomputer program), handed out in ceremonial fashion.

We in the Children's Room evaluated the program (quite positively), and then in concert with Ms. McKee-Jolda we came up with ideas for a future program, in other words to continue in 1995.

Ms. McKee-Jolda suggested that this next time we begin with an interest survey for all participating kids. Kids connect best with teens over particular books based on particular interests. She recommended asking for the following: 3 things I usually do after school or on the weekend, 3 things I really like to do or would like to try, any hobbies or collections I have, places I have visited.

Ms. McKee-Jolda also suggested using a bulletin board to keep track of Reading Buddies activities and continuing the more structured activities such as puppet shows, magic shows, adding perhaps more topical activities based on materials in the library, not limited to books. Ms. McKee-Jolda hopes for more gender mixing in future programs, but not until kids (and teens) are ready for it. Kids are less shy with a buddy, and if they want to continue with the same buddy all summer, that should be facilitated.

Once More with Feeling

In the second year of the Reading Buddies program (summer 1995), much was the same, but there were also some important differences from the first year of the program (summer 1994). Ms. McKee-Jolda continued as the volunteer coordinator, and she put together a fine group of volunteer buddies. In addition we at the Children's Room expanded our publicity of the program and were able to draw in some volunteer buddies from our local neighborhood and from other parts of Oakland as well. Several of these buddies were older than the younger teens Ms. McKee-Jolda had recruited. As in 1994, we contacted a teacher at a local daycare center: the kids in 1995's class were a little older and had more advanced reading skills than in 1994's class. We also advertised the program more widely for younger kids, and we were able to draw in more neighborhood kids and kids from throughout the city: this addition and the addition of new buddies improved the program by increasing the numbers of participants and by diversifying participation throughout the population.

We hope to continue to solicit new buddies throughout this next year for the 1996 program and have orientation materials available in the spring for potential buddies not initially connected to Ms. McKee-Jolda's recruiting. During our wrap-up evaluation of the 1995 program, Lisa Fung, the Children's Room's library assistant, suggested that Ms. McKee-Jolda offer a midway orientation for buddies who join the program after the program has begun. We all felt that this would be of great help to the program and a way to help new buddies feel included. We also envision a flyer with an announcement on one side and a short, but specific description of the program on the opposite side so that the buddies, the younger kids, and the parents of kids and buddies, as well as library staff, will have a clearer, more detailed picture of the program, its activities and goals. This flyer can be used for school and neighborhood outreach in the spring and for publicity at events such as a local Summer Activity Fair taking place also in the spring. More publicity is also needed in order to make it clear that Reading Buddies is a fun, enrichment program, not a tutoring or teaching program: many parents, especially, request the latter for their kids, but we at Oakland Public Library continue to feel that these types of programs should be offered by school districts.

Ms. McKee-Jolda implemented a looser scheduling structure for her group of buddies in 1995, and she did not find this to be as efficient. With her stricter scheduling in 1994, she had found that the buddies had been able to make a greater commitment to the program and to the kids, and, in fact, had gotten more out of the program themselves. Many of the buddies thrive on more activities and more responsibilities. Young teens are both earnest and capable as we have been reminded by our experience with Reading Buddies and as Leah Blakely, Project Director, Southeast Case Management Unit, Lutheran Social Services, has shown in the Inner City of Chicago where she has helped young teens become literacy tutors to their elders; but they do need structure, which may include timelines, lists of duties, and other specific details. Volunteers such as Ms. McKee-Jolda are perfectly situated to create and follow up on these details.

Unavoidably several regular summer library programs were planned at the same time as Reading Buddies in 1995: we were concerned that these programs, which included a comics drawing and writing workshop and a small animals viewing and petting program, would conflict with

Reading Buddies. Just the reverse: because of how well these programs worked during Reading Buddies, we planned other programs to coincide with the time period. For some kids and buddies these programs were incentives to participate in Reading Buddies. The library as cultural center has begun to take on a new, more concrete meaning in the Children's Room. Although buddies did put on a successful magic show in 1995, some of the "performances" of puppet and magic shows put on by buddies in 1994 were replaced by one-to-one work and smaller group activities. Many of these activities are directly or indirectly connected with reading and writing. These include chess, cards, origami, comics, and work on our new 486 computer which has CD-ROM educational programs and kids' word processing programs—our use of Kid's Catalog to do a summer reading hunt will have to wait until next summer since the software is not yet installed. Activities such as these often imply books or other materials or include other activities; e.g., we have a large supply of origami books for kids to use with origami materials, and learning about comic book creation and production led one group of kids and buddies to produce, on an ongoing basis, comics and posters of their own. Chess has become so popular that a chess club is now ongoing and has become its own independent activity. And yet through all this diversification, there were always kids who preferred to find books (on their own or with buddies) and then work on reading and writing with their buddies; this was even true during the popular comics and small animal programs.

The Future

We will continue Reading Buddies and allow it to change and diversify in directions that are feasible and fit into the image of the library as cultural center. Ms. McKee-Jolda remarked near the end of the 1995 program that language enhancement and enrichment (which improve reading and writing skills) can occur through a variety of means, and Reading Buddies offers kids a number of options to enhance and enrich their skills while having fun. [February 1996]

Sidekicks: An Intergenerational Program
Beth Karpas

For the third year in a row, Clermont County Public Library, a nine-branch system in southwestern Ohio, and Clermont Senior Services, Inc. have combined forces to produce an intergenerational summer program for young adults and senior citizens. This program is *Sidekicks: Kids and Seniors Together.*

Begun in 1992 at one of the library's more rural branches with fourteen students, the program has expanded to four branches and over forty young adults. Each summer, new participants attend a three-week training course at their local library branch. Clermont Senior Services provides the technical background for these sessions. The course covers issues such as aging awareness, sensory changes, and grief. After training, Sidekicks meet with a librarian to plan service activities for local seniors. These have included: nursing home visits, a traveling pets group, and unbirthday presents for Meals on Wheels recipients.

For the past two years, Sidekicks has received a grant to fund an interbranch activity at the county senior center. The 1993 Kids Again Carnival was sponsored by two branches. This mini-fair included games and old-fashioned photo facades. The 1994 Kids Again Ice Cream Social was sponsored by four branches. Activities included kick the can, ice cream, dancing, and a cake walk. The young adults staffed the activities and socialized with the seniors. Some Sidekicks and seniors even exchanged names and phone numbers.

While the initial Sidekicks program continues each summer, the individual branch groups are evolving as well. One is planning to form a library advisory council. Another is considering a summer social for local, home based seniors. Even during the school year, young adults continue to talk about the program. Best of all, the Sidekicks have taken what they learned from training sessions and begun to apply it to their own community. After the last summer meeting at our branch, two boys went to a nearby senior's home and spent the afternoon helping her with her garden. When asked why, the Sidekicks replied, "We just didn't want it [Sidekicks] to end." [April 1995]

Books Build Bridges: An Intergenerational Read-In

Martha Simpson and Barbara Blosveren

Overview

People of all ages come to the library to choose books for their reading enjoyment. Although adults, teens, and children may frequent a library, rarely do these different groups have an opportunity to interact. Members of the Stratford Library Association's Young Adult and Children's Departments set out to bridge this gap among the age groups by organizing a one day intergenerational reading program. The plan called for pairing local senior citizens with young adults, who would then read picture books to children from the first, second, and third grades. Books Build Bridges was held in April, 1995, and was a huge success.

Other libraries have initiated programs that involved two generations of readers. This article recounts SLA's experience in planning and implementing a reading day in which three generations of patrons shared their love for books.

Planning the Event

In December 1994, Young Adult librarian Debra Billings [now Debra Adams] submitted her proposal to the library administration and Children's Department. She envisioned Books Build Bridges as a one day program to be held during the Stratford public schools' spring vacation, which also happened to coincide with National Library Week. YA and senior volunteers would be required to attend a one-hour training session on Tuesday, April 18, 1995, and the program would take place on Thursday, April 20. Minimal funding was requested in order to provide refreshments on both days for the participants, and for the printing of publicity materials.

Program Objectives

1. To allow young adults and seniors an opportunity to work together, thus overcoming the age barrier that sometimes exists between these two groups.
2. To demonstrate to children the importance of books by arranging an enjoyable reading experience with young adults and seniors.
3. To provide young adults and seniors with the positive volunteer experience of contributing their services and time to the library and the youngsters of the community, and to serve as good reading role models for the children.
4. To give young adults and children a worthwhile, yet fun, activity in which they could participate during their April vacation from school.

In January, 1995, the proposal was enthusiastically accepted by the administration. At that point, Children's Department librarian Martha Simpson joined Debby and YA Department Head Barbara Blosveren in planning the program. They reserved the library's community room, the Lovell Room, for April 18 and 20. The first step was to set up publicity for the event. Debby met with Tom Holehan, Department Head of Programming and Public Relations at Stratford Library, to discuss publicity ideas. In the ensuing weeks, Tom produced flyers promoting Books Build Bridges and mailed publicity releases to all the local newspapers. He also invited members of the press to attend the orientation sessions and reading programs.

Barbara and Debby then set to work recruiting young adult and senior readers for the program.

Recruiting Volunteer Readers

Stratford Library Association is fortunate to be located next to the Baldwin Center, which is the town's community center for senior citizens. In December, Debby met with Marie Guman, Outreach

Intergenerational Programs 69

Coordinator at the Baldwin Center, to discuss plans for the intergenerational program. Mrs. Guman was extremely enthusiastic and placed a notice in the Baldwin Center newsletter requesting volunteers. She also posted a sign-up sheet at the Center. As the seniors registered, Mrs. Guman gave Debby their names and phone numbers. Seniors also called the Young Adult Department to volunteer after reading the Baldwin Center newsletter, seeing flyers at the library, and reading articles in the local newspapers.

In February, Barbara and Debby attended the library noon book review series to publicize the intergenerational program. Since many of the patrons who attend this program are seniors, and they are all interested in reading, this was another good source for locating volunteers. The librarians explained that seniors could, at that time, sign up to learn more about the program without actually committing to it. This no-pressure attitude encouraged more people to register.

Attracting young adult readers was the next task. The Stratford Library has an active teen volunteer program throughout the year. The Young Adult Department also sponsors the Youth Review Board, a group of 7th-10th grade students who read, review, and recommend young adult books. Flyers publicizing Books Build Bridges were distributed at Youth Review Board meetings and given to young adult volunteers encouraging them to participate in the program.

Another source for YA readers was provided by the Community Service Advisory Committee of the Stratford Youth and Family Advisory Board, on which Barbara serves. The Committee's purpose is to promote teen volunteerism among agencies in the community, including the schools, library, Baldwin Center, health agencies, and others. In February, Community Connections Week was held at the middle schools in Stratford. Barbara addressed teens on the opportunites for volunteering at the library, and specifically discussed Books Build Bridges. Many teens signed up for the program at that time.

With the master list of possible senior and young adult volunteers in hand, the Young Adult librarians made phone calls to schedule people for an orientation session and to confirm that they would be available on the day of the program.

Signing up Children

In March, after securing the young adult and senior readers, first, second, and third grade children were invited to register for the program. Initially, Debby and Barbara had planned to offer three story sessions on April 20, at 11 a.m., 2 p.m., and 3 p.m. Flyers announcing the program were displayed in the Children's and Young Adult Departments, and at the Information and Circulation Desks. Interested patrons were directed to sign up for one of the time slots at the Children's Department. Debby drafted a letter publicizing the program and sent it to the Stratford elementary schools along with flyers. Children's Department librarians also encouraged the parents of preschoolers who attended storyhours to sign up their first through third graders for the special program.

While the morning session was filling up nicely, fewer children were signing up for the two afternoon sessions. In order to ensure a good size group, it was decided to eliminate the 3 p.m. slot, and just run the program at 11 a.m. and 2 p.m.

Putting It All Together

Everything kicked into high gear during the first week in April. The Young Adult staff telephoned the volunteer readers to remind them of their commitment and to sign them up for either the 11 a.m. or 2 p.m. training session to be held on April 18. Debby and Martha discussed the information to be covered on that day and produced a schedule for the one-hour orientation meetings. Tom contacted the local newspapers and cleared his own schedule so that he would be available to take photographs that day. The Children's Department librarians selected approximately 100 picture books that would appeal to six-to-ten-year-olds to bring to the training sessions. The variety of books included humor, folklore, multicultural stories, fairy tales, old favorites, and new releases. All librarians continued to encourage children to sign up for the 11 a.m. or 2 p.m. story times. Barbara bought refreshments for both the orientation and programming sessions. Martha devised an evaluation sheet for participants to complete at the conclusion of the Thursday program. The entire library was abuzz with anticipation for this first-time-ever intergenerational event.

Training

The training sessions were held in the Lovell Room on Tuesday, April 18. A small stage had been set up at the front of the room, and there were chairs for about thirty people, with a table of refreshments at one side. A cart holding the picture books stood near the stage.

For both the morning and afternoon sessions, Debby, Martha, and Barbara greeted the YAs and seniors and asked them to sign an attendance sheet as they entered the room. When all the volunteers were seated, Barbara welcomed everyone, introduced Debby and Martha, and explained the program. She then introduced Tom, who would be taking photographs of the event, and explained that the media had been invited to come on Thursday. She also invited teens to join the Youth Review Board and to sign up to help out as a YA volunteer for the summer.

Debby told the volunteers what to expect on the day of the Books Build Bridges program:
1. Chairs would be arranged in small circular groups. Ideally, one YA and one senior would be in each group, reading to one to three children, depending on how many attended.
2. Upon entering, volunteers and children would sign in, make themselves name tags, and find a place to sit.
3. Barbara and Debby would give introductory speeches.
4. Martha would do a warm-up activity with the group.
5. YA and senior volunteers would read to children.
6. When they had finished reading, participants could have some refreshments.
7. Everyone would be asked to fill out an evaluation form and offer their comments about the program.

Debby then turned the orientation session over to Martha.

Martha's job was to give the volunteers a crash course on storytelling. She stepped onto the stage and began by explaining that SLA Children's librarians always start their preschool storyhours with a fingerplay. Since the group on Thursday would be comprised of older children, young adults, and seniors, she would be doing a more complicated activity than she does with the preschoolers. Martha asked everyone to stand up, stretch, and make sure they had enough room to move their arms. She then led them through "My Hat It Has Three Corners" (see text below).

My Hat, It Has Three Corners

My hat, it has three corners
Three corners has my hat.
And had it not three corners
It would not be my hat.

Gestures

Most words have an accompanying gesture. Following are the words and the movements that go with them: MY (point to yourself), HAT (put hands on head), IT (point straight out), HAS (no gesture), THREE (hold up 3 fingers), CORNERS (left hand touches right elbow), AND (no gestures), HAD (no gesture), NOT (Shake head), WOULD (no gesture), BE (no gesture).

Instructions:

1. Sing or speak the words of the song once through without gestures.
2. Explain that most words have a gesture, which you will be teaching them.
3. Go over one line at a time, teaching the accompanying gestures. Have the group repeat each line after you until they know the entire song.
4. Now comes the tricky part! Tell the group that they will sing the song and do the movements again, but instead of speaking the first word (my), they will only do the gesture.
5. Repeat this process for all the words that have an accompanying movement, dropping one additional spoken word each time you repeat the song, until the only spoken words left are the ones without gestures.
6. Try to do each round of the song faster. Everyone's hands will be flying, trying to keep up. Don't worry about making mistakes—that's part of the fun!

By the end of this activity, the ice was broken, people were laughing, and everyone felt relaxed.

After the warm-up, Martha pulled up a chair to face the volunteers and went over some storytelling basics.

Intergenerational Programs

Tips for Volunteer Readers

1. Choose a book that suits your personality, one that you feel comfortable reading. If you are good at making up funny voices, you may want to select a book with a lot of dialogue. You may also want to take a few books to try out at home, and decide which you would like to read on the day of the program.
2. Practice reading aloud several times before the program, so that you become very familiar with the book.
3. During the program, read loud enough so that your listeners can hear you, but not so loud that you distract people in other groups. Read clearly, at a steady pace, and with expression. Remember to show the pictures to your audience as you read.
4. Most of all, relax and have fun! Children love to have someone read to them, and they will appreciate the time you spend with them.

She then demonstrated this by telling one of her favorite read-aloud stories, *Harry and the Terrible Whatzit* by Dick Gackenbach. After the story, she answered questions from the group.

Then it was time for the highlight of the meeting—choosing a book to read! Martha reminded the volunteers to register for either the 11 a.m. or 2 p.m. slot on Thursday, while Debby and Barbara laid out the books on the edge of the stage for better visibility.

The YAs and seniors enthusiastically pored over the picture books and made their selections. Because of the wide variety of titles, everyone was able to find something to their liking. Some preferred the classic stories, fairy tales, and legends with which they had grown up, but just as many were drawn to the recently published titles and multicultural stories. A few people took two or three books to try out at home and decide which one they would like to read on Thursday.

From the number of preregistered volunteers, Debby and Martha had decided to schedule nine or ten groups for each of the program sessions. In order to maintain a somewhat even balance between the number of young adults and seniors for each time, volunteers were sometimes asked to switch their slot, if possible. There was no attempt to assign specific pairings on Tuesday.

Orientation took about an hour, as planned, with a total of twenty YAs and sixteen seniors in attendance. There were some additional seniors who said they had storytelling experience and would like to participate in the program, but were not able to come in for the training. They were phoned and scheduled for one of the time slots. Debby, Barbara, and Martha were very satisfied with the way these sessions had gone, and looked forward to Thursday's programs.

Program Day

In preparation for the day's event, nine groups of five chairs were arranged in the Lovell Room. A table of refreshments stood at one side. Another table held pencils, markers, name tags, attendance sheets (one for children, another for readers), evaluation sheets, and sign-up sheets for the Youth Review Board and YA summer volunteers. A cart with additional picture books was also available.

Barbara, Debby, and Martha met the seniors, young adults, children and their parents as they entered the room. Participants were told to make themselves a name tag and sign an attendance sheet. The librarians helped the readers and children find seats, making sure that each group had a YA and a senior. (As it turned out, nine YAs and eleven seniors attended the morning session, so two lucky groups had three readers.) Parents helped their children settle in and people in the groups introduced themselves to one another.

Tom and members of the local press were on hand to take photographs and interview participants during the morning session. The event officially began when Edythe Landes, the Director of the library, welcomed everyone to Stratford Library Association's first intergenerational reading program. Mrs. Landes spoke about the importance of storytelling, promoting literacy, and using the library to fill recreational as well as informational needs. She congratulated the participants for taking advantage of this valuable opportunity for three generations to share their love for books, and promised that Books Build Bridges would become an annual event if this pilot project proved successful. She then turned the program over to Barbara.

Barbara first told the parents of the first to third grade children that they were not required to stay for the hour-long program. Most of the parents left at that point, relieved to have some time for themselves. A few opted to stay and listen to the stories with their children. Barbara again welcomed the patrons on behalf of the Young Adult and Children's Departments, introduced Tom and told the group that he and members of the press would be observing and taking photographs. She reminded YAs that they could sign up for the Youth Review Board and to volunteer in the library if they chose to do so. Next, Debby held up the evaluation sheets and asked each participant to complete one before they left. Martha conducted the warm-up exercise, "My Hat It Has Three Corners" for the group. Then she turned the program over to the seniors, YAs, and children.

The readers worked out among themselves who would go first, and they enthusiastically dove into their tasks. The children, two or three per group, responded by listening, laughing, pointing to the pictures, commenting on the stories, and generally enjoying themselves. Tom and the reporters moved through the room, snapping photos and taking notes. Debby, Martha, and Barbara walked from group to group, observing but not interfering. From the looks on the faces of the participants, and the happy noise of people sharing books, the event appeared to be a great success.

As each group finished their stories, they enjoyed their refreshments and completed the evaluation form. Children received help from their parents or a volunteer reader. Many people spoke to the librarians about how much fun they had and expressed an interest in repeating the experience. The morning program lasted slightly over an hour, due to the press speaking to the participants after they finished reading.

The afternoon program had the same number of readers (eleven YAs and nine seniors) but only eleven children, so each group contained only one or two youngsters. Although the groups were smaller than in the morning, the children relished the special attention they received. In fact, after listening to their two stories, many of the children grabbed a third book from the cart and insisted that a YA or senior read that, too! As it turned out, it was just as well that the 3 p.m. program was canceled, since the 2 p.m. session ran overtime!

Evaluations

By all accounts, Books Build Bridges was a spectacular success. Several teens signed up to participate on the Youth Review Board and to volunteer for other library programs. Seniors also expressed an interest in becoming involved in more library activities. Many of the children went upstairs to the Children's Department after the program to check out additional books to read. Photographs and articles about the program were published in the town's newspapers and in *Connecticut Libraries*, published by the Connecticut Library Association. The library administration gave its stamp of approval by announcing that Books Build Bridges would become an annual event at Stratford Library Association.

Most of all, the three generations of participants appreciated the experience. Every one of them marked on their evaluation form (see Evaluation Form) that they enjoyed participating in the program and would like to do it again. Following are some of the responses to question #5 "What did you like best about the program?" Some children said, "I liked the books," "Having someone read to me," "Cookies," "The lady," "The whole thing," "Being read to by adults, there were good stories." A few parents added: "Interaction of volunteers and children," "The enjoyment the children had."

The seniors commented: "Everything," "Interaction with the teenager and the little ones," "Children were very eager to hear the stories," "Well-organized, cheerful group," "The young man who read with me was just great," "Children were very interested. . . .There were many children in this space, but there were no problems," "The child we read to was great," "The children's interest," "Looking at the new (to me) books and the actual reading."

The young adults wrote: "That senior citizens participated with Young Adults, and the children enjoyed it very much," "Being able to share literature with others," "That they were older children so they could understand," "It gives adults, young adults, and children a chance to be together and have fun with all generations," "Reading and discussing the stories," "Youngsters, teens, and seniors worked together," "Getting to meet new people and pleasing the children with books," "Small groups of kids," "The stories," "We got to get kids excited while reading and make them happy."

When Debby Billings first proposed Books Build Bridges, everyone thought it was a good idea, but people were concerned about the logistics. The element of juggling the schedules of three disparate groups was tricky, but careful planning, the commitment of the librarians involved, the cooperation between the YA and Children's Departments, the support of the entire library staff, and the enthusiasm of the participants made the program a rewarding experience for all.

Programming Tips

Set aside a wide variety of picture books, at least twice as many as you think you'll need. Choose books that are in top condition, appeal to the targeted age group, have eye-grabbing illustrations, and that are fun to read. Keep in mind the ethnic and cultural background of your community and include something for all interests.

Success Stories

While the entire program went well, there were a few small but significant success stories which Martha, Debby, and Barbara observed. One instance involved two boys who came to the library every day after school. Although they were not disruptive, they were always restless—wandering through the stacks, moving from the YA Department downstairs to the Children's Room upstairs and then back again, taking magazines and not reading them, etc. Clearly, these boys didn't know what to do with themselves. When they found out about Books Build Bridges, they were eager to participate. The experience turned out to be just the type of involvement the boys needed. They chose and read their books with great enthusiasm, and really related with the youngsters. Both boys later volunteered to work in the library to fulfill a community service requirement for their conformation class, and also participated in other Young Adult activities.

A grandmother with plenty of experience reading to children connected with an insecure boy in another success story. A teenage girl had volunteered to read at both the morning and afternoon sessions.

However, she also had to babysit her three younger cousins. During the morning program, she read to them—reluctantly, because she had been babysitting for her cousins all week and she would have preferred reading to someone else. But in the afternoon, she absolutely refused to read to them again. Two of the children settled into another group, but one boy was just as stubborn. Luckily, one woman came to the rescue. She had brought a large canvas bag with her. In it were her own well-read copies of Dr. Seuss books and a large plush Cat in the Hat. She placed the Cat on the boy's lap, sat down next to him, and began to read. The boy was enraptured, and his cousin gratefully found a seat in another group. The interaction between the boy and the senior who read to him was one of the highlights of the entire day.

Evaluation Form

Thank you for participating in Stratford Library Association's first intergenerational reading program! Please take a few minutes to give us your opinions about this program.

1. Who are you? (check one)
_____ Senior citizen / adult
_____ Young adult
_____ First grade student
_____ Second grade student
_____ Third grade student

2. Where did you hear about the program?
_____ Children's Department flyer or program
_____ Young Adult Department flyer or program
_____ Senior or Adult program
_____ Flyer at Circulation (where you check out books)
_____ At school
_____ In the newspaper (which one?)
_____ Other (please explain)

3. Did you enjoy participating in the program?
_____ Yes _____ No

4. What days and times would be best for you to participate in this program again?

_____ Saturdays _____ In the summer _____ School vacations
_____ Mornings _____ Afternoons _____ evenings
_____ Other (please explain)
5. What did you like best about the program?
6. What would you want to change about the program?
7. Would you like to participate in this program next year:
_____ Yes _____ No
8. Other comments: [February 1996]

A POTPOURRI OF YA PROGRAMS

TAB: A Middle School/Public Library Success Story

Margaret Brown and Pat Muller

What does it stand for? Teen Advisory Board, those indispensable, indefatigable, incredible kids who are willing to read books for the Arlington (VA) Public Library and review them. Or, Talking About Books, the thing our TAB students do best. Or, Teens Are Beneficial, to the well-being of our Young Adult collection and programs, to the library in general, and to the state of mind of each librarian fortunate enough to work with them.

In the fall of 1990, our Young Adult Division began a pilot TAB program at Thomas Jefferson Middle School in Arlington. Martha Walke, an English teacher there, had expressed a willingness to work with us in setting up an after-school reading and reviewing group with books supplied by the public library. All students in grades six through eight were eligible, and we met every other week after school to talk about publishers' advances and newly accessioned books in the Young Adult collection. We printed a 4x6 yellow TAB review card, based on one used in Baltimore County, and devised a checkout system.

That year TAB was a big success. We had about twenty-five regular participants, many of whom attended a YA Best Books discussion in Baltimore and held their own among young adult librarians in defending their favorite titles. We sweetened the task of reading with bookmarks from a local TCBY which promised a free frozen yogurt after the tenth title—and we provided the transportation for the payoff one day after school. For their efforts, a pizza party and buttons that proclaimed the bearer "Star Reader." At the end of the year the TAB students designed their own bookmark which listed their favorite reads of the year.

The following year we expanded TAB into all four middle schools, with a public library staff person and a school teacher or librarian as coadvisors at each location. One group elected to meet in the mornings during the school day and restrict the numbers to ten from each grade. One school alternated meeting for a brown-bag lunch in an empty classroom and meeting after school. Each group took on its own personality and each had its favorite authors. One group became a science fiction/Orson Scott Card fan club. We arranged some special programs for our TAB students, such as an Australian storyteller one year, and authors Suzanne Staples and Walter Dean Myers another. Each winter we have also had a joint TAB meeting of all the schools to talk about Best Books nominations. One TAB group does its own recruiting by visiting fifth graders at the local feeder elementary schools and talking about books, and TAB events, such as our make-your-own-sundae parties. (Food is an essential ingredient here, second only to books.) Not only have more sixth graders appeared in the fall to join TAB at this particular school, but another pleasant and unexpected result has been the springing up of an elementary TAB group, based on the middle-school model and named by its fifth-grade participants, Books R Us.

We now have well over one hundred students reading and reviewing books for us. Because alumni from the middle school TABs asked to continue in ninth grade, last year we initiated a separate countywide high school meeting, held once a month from 6:30-7:30 p.m., with pizza, at the Central Library. Many of our original students continue, and this year the group consists of both freshmen and sophomores. Because TAB proved such a great way to get to know Arlington students and their reading habits, this year a bilingual YA librarian is piloting a HILT (High Intensity Language Training) TAB group for students learning English.

There have been some problems associated with the breadth of our TAB program. Finding enough new young adult books to give to the students is one. We decided to write to publishers, explain our program, and ask to be put on their lists for advance copies. It worked, and now we maintain a collection of about 50–60 review titles, and are receiving more all the time. But even those books proved not enough, so we negotiated with the library to let us buy four sets of McNaughton rental books, all titles included on the Best Books list. Using these books, we were able to assure that students had access to the new books, and that they were prepared for the regional Best Books discussion.

But the benefits, of course, are endless. The library staff has a much better understanding of what kids are reading and want to read. When we go to middle schools to give booktalks in the spring, we are armed with the top choices from all the TAB groups, and even incorporate some of their favorites into our own summer reading list. We mark TAB favorites in the library with a metallic gold seal for easy finding and maintain a display year-round. When we give a young adult program at the library, we have ready-made mailing lists of potentially interested students. We know what's going on in the schools and can speak to some kids by name when we visit. We take students with us whenever we can to area book discussion programs, last year in October to the Books for the Beast in Baltimore County and in January to Washington, DC, for the regional Best Books discussion. When the library has needed volunteers, for example at the grand opening of our new Central building two years ago, or for children's programs in the summer, we have recruited easily from among our TAB friends. In fact, our next project is to start a summer volunteer program, beginning with a corps of TAB students.

Those in TAB who have reached the age of fourteen are eligible to apply for paid employment with the library as pages, and we have hired four so far. Our own YA page has been a TAB member for four years now and reads and reviews easily five to six books a month for us, many more in the summer. He is our resident expert on new YA books.

TAB members have testified at County Board budget hearings on behalf of the library, and they contribute articles to *Buzzword*, the monthly TAB newsletter. Last spring we held an open house for teens and their parents, and have asked TAB students to speak about "Books I'd Like My Parents to Read."

What more could we possibly squeeze from this concept called TAB? Well, Martha Walke, now librarian at Thomas Jefferson Middle School, has an idea. In this age when computers threaten to replace books as the medium of the moment, why not harness the technology to spread the word about books? Specifically, why not use the Global Schoolhouse, a computer network linking students nationally and internationally, to Talk About Books worldwide? Wouldn't it be wonderful if a TAB group suddenly popped up in Arkansas, or in England?

We attended a Washington, DC, Children's Book Guild program in December 1993 about the future of young adult literature, and the mood of the group was gloomy. "Teens don't read," was the prevailing opinion. "Love for the written word is disappearing." We in Arlington don't pretend to have all the answers to that one, but we do feel that the success of our TAB groups sends a message that is clear: Teens Are reading Books! It's up to us as librarians to make it easy and enjoyable for them to keep on reading.

Williamsburg Middle School 1994 Teen Advisory Board Favorites

Alcott. *Little Women.* Classic story of the four March sisters, growing up poor, but with humor and affection, in 19th century New England.

Card. *Xenocide.* Exciting sequel to *Ender's Game* and *Speaker for the Dead,* in which the planet of Lusitania is ordered destroyed to save humankind from a deadly virus.

Card. *Prentice Alvin.* Epic tale in which Alvin the Maker must battle the forces of evil in a magical alternate America.

Dickinson. *A Bone from a Dry Sea.* Parallel stories of Vinny, an archeologist's daughter who finds the bone of a prehistoric female, and Li, who lives the life Vinny is searching to uncover.

Drucker. *Kindertransport.* Olga must leave her parents at the age of five and journey to England on a train with other Jewish children fleeing Hitler's Germany.

Duncan. *Who Killed My Daughter?* A true story which details how Lois Duncan consulted psychics and uncovered clues missed by the police to find out why her teenage daughter was murdered.

Furlong. *Wise Child.* Abandoned by her parents, nine-year-old Wise Child learns the ways of herbs and magic from the witch woman, Juniper. Also by Furlong: *Juniper.*

Jordan. *Juniper Game.* Juniper's telepathic powers transport her back to the Middle Ages to witness a young woman being accused of witchcraft.

Jordan. *Winter of Fire.* Elsha at 16 has a vision and discovers that she has the power to save her people, the Quelled, from a life of brutal enslavement in a world of ice.

L'Amour. *Comstock Lode* and *The Lonesome Gods.* Two classic tales of the West by a master storyteller.

Lowry. *The Giver.* Jonas is chosen to become the receiver of memories

by his society and discovers the terrible truth about how they live.
Paulsen. *Nightjohn*. Sarny's life as a slave is brutal and becomes dangerous as well, when a new field hand with horrible scars teaches her to read.
Reiss. *The Upstairs Room*. A Dutch Jewish girl describes the years spent in hiding in the bedroom of a farmer during World War II.
Wrede. *Calling on Dragons*. Queen Cimorene of the Enchanted Forest asks for help from the King of Dragons when the Society of Wizards starts making mischief once again.

Kenmore Middle School 1994 Teen Advisory Board Favorites

Alcock. *Singer to the Sea God*. When he and his companions flee their island home after the king's court is turned to stone, Phaidon begins to believe in the gods and monsters that his uncle has always scorned.
Anderson. *Bus People*. The lives of the passengers on Bertram's "fruitcake bus" are shaped by the experiences and problems each has faced because of different disabilities.
Drucker. *Kindertransport*. Olga must leave her parents at the age of five and journey to England on a train with other Jewish children fleeing Hitler's Germany.
Pfeffer. *The Ring of Truth*. Since the death of her parents, 16-year-old Sloan has lived a privileged, protected life with her grandmother, the matriarch of a prominent political family, until the drunken advances of an elected official lead to a public scandal.
Ruby. *Miriam's Well*. When Miriam develops bone cancer, she finds herself the focus of a battle between the medical and legal establishments and the small Christian sect to which she and her family belong.
Sleator. *Oddballs: Stories*. A collection of stories based on experiences from the author's youth and peopled with an unusual assortment of family and friends.
Temple. *Grab Hands and Run*. After his father disappears, 12-year-old Felipe, his mother and younger sister set out on a dangerous journey, trying to make their way from their home in El Salvador to Canada.
Temple. *Taste of Salt: A Story of Modern Haiti*. In the hospital after being

beaten by Macoutes, 17-year-old Djo tells the story of his impoverished life to a young woman who, like him, has been working with the social reformer Father Aristide to fight the repression in Haiti.

Voigt. *The Wings of a Falcon.* Fourteen-year-old Oriel and his friend Griff flee the slavery of Damall's Island and seek a new life on the mainland, where they face raiding Wolfers, rival armies and other dangers.

Swanson Middle School 1994 Teen Advisory Board Favorites.

Avi. *The Man Who Was Poe.* When 11-year-old Edmund's Rhode Island family disappears in 1848, Edgar Allan Poe agrees to investigate.

Cooney. *The Face on the Milk Carton.* Teenager Janie Johnson realizes the "missing child" pictured on the milk carton is herself, but finds it hard to believe her parents are kidnappers.

Cooper. *The Sleep of Stone.* When the man she loves brings his betrothed to his great house, Ghysia, the Shapechanger, exacts a terrible revenge.

Dickinson. *Eva.* Thirteen-year-old Eva awakes from a coma following a traffic accident to discover that the operation she needed to save her life has changed her into another kind of being.

Drucker. *Kindertransport.* The author describes the perils of life in Germany under Hitler and the evacuation of many Jewish children to England during World War II.

Duncan. *Don't Look Behind You.* Seventeen-year-old April and her family are forced to go into hiding when her father, a witness in a federal court case, begins to receive death threats.

Duncan. *Locked in Time.* Nore Robbins reluctantly visits her stepmother's Louisiana plantation and finds her new family odd and surrounded by evil and mystery.

Griffin. *Switching Well.* Two 12-year-old girls in Texas, Ada in 1891 and Amber in 1991, switch places through a magic well and try desperately to return to their own times.

Hahn. *Stepping on the Cracks.* During World War II, 11-year-old Margaret decides to help the school bully hide his brother, an army deserter.

Hillerman. *Dance Hall of the Dead.* Detective Joe Leaphorn is called to investigate when two seventh graders, a Navajo and a Zuni boy, disappear.

Keyes. *Flowers for Algernon.* Charlie, a gentle, retarded man, participates in an experiment which turns him into a genius—but only temporarily.

Rinaldi. *Wolf by the Ears.* Harriet Hemings, rumored to be the daughter of Thomas Jefferson, must make a painful choice: to stay in the comfort of Monticello or to seek freedom from slavery.

Thomas Jefferson Middle School 1994 Teen Advisory Board Favorites

Alcock. *Singer to the Sea God.* When he and his companions flee their island home after the king's court is turned to stone, Phaidon begins to believe in the gods and monsters that his uncle has always scorned.

Arrick. *What You Don't Know Can Kill You.* Ellen is recently graduated from high school and her life and future seem perfect until a blood test proves she is HIV positive, and a nightmare begins for her and her family.

Avi. *True Confessions of Charlotte Doyle.* As the lone female on a transatlantic voyage in 1832, Charlotte learns that the Captain is murderous and the crew rebellious.

Lowry. *The Giver.* Given his lifetime assignment at the ceremony of twelve, Jonas becomes the receiver of memories shared by only one other and discovers the terrible truth about the society in which he lives.

Nasu. *Children of the Paper Crane.* The true story of Sadako Sasaki and her struggle to survive after the bombing of Hiroshima.

Norman. *Albion's Dream: A Novel of Terror.* Edward's involvement with a mysterious adventure game leads to a confrontation with his boarding school's tyrannical headmaster and evil doctor.

Rodda. *Finders Keepers.* While playing a computer game, Patrick is transported to a parallel world and invited to participate in a game show in which he must find three lost items to win several fabulous prizes.

Service. *Being of Two Minds*. Connie's ability to share "mental visits" with the prince of Thulgaria proves useful when he is mysteriously kidnapped. [December 1994]

Bibliothecam Amissam Inveni!
(I Found the Library)

Marilyn Brown and Anne Merkle

How do we top a successful Young Adult Reading Club? In the summer of 1993 we introduced a reading club for teens entering sixth grade and older. We had what we considered an excellent beginning with 125 teens participating in this club. We wanted to build upon this enthusiasm and felt that in 1994 we needed something flashy, something different, a reading club that would keep this group and others coming to the library all summer.

After hours of brainstorming we selected a reading club based on David Macaulay's book, *Motel of Mysteries*. This is a book set far into the future. The plot is the discovery of a motel by archaeologists. They have no idea what it is they have discovered, but believe that it is significant. The archaeologists name and describe their discoveries based on their understanding of ancient cultures.

Our idea, like Macaulay's book, was to provide a story of discovery based on artifacts found at an imaginary archaeological dig and an unearthed building. We used facets of local history to humorously describe the setting. Throughout the ruins artifacts were discovered, and the identity of a building became known as the artifacts were identified. Our library was the dig site, of course.

An enjoyable part of this program was producing the artifacts. After some discussion, we decided on black-and-white film because we felt colored photographs would give away too many details. We loaded the camera with the first roll of film and began searching out unusual shots of everyday library paraphernalia. By the end of the picture-taking session we had used three rolls of film. We took pictures of items around the library: for example, a cord to a computer, handles on the card catalog, or the blade of a fan. Hours spent wandering throughout the library creating and taking interesting shots proved to be worthwhile. It was a challenge to select the forty-two pictures and mat them with unusually shaped construction paper mats to make identification more difficult. Each artifact was placed in a plastic folder and numbered one through forty-two. Twenty-eight were put in one notebook marked ARTIFACTS and the other fourteen made up a second notebook titled MORE ARTIFACTS? Teens needed to complete the first notebook to qualify for the Grand Prize Drawing. The second notebook was a challenge for the prolific readers who would need more to do throughout the summer.

The Summer Reading Club at the library began June 14, 1994. We sent fliers advertising the program to the area junior and senior high schools. As members signed up they received the Archaeological Dig story, the rules, and a log sheet to keep track of their reading. For every 100 pages read, an artifact tag was earned. At this point, they looked through the first Artifacts notebook and chose a picture to identify. Members wrote what they thought the photograph depicted on their identification tag, along with the number of the artifact they had chosen to identify. They then gave the tag to a library staff member who placed it on a binder ring. There was one ring per number. This was done so teens could read how others identified the same artifact. We informed the members that there was no "right" answer. As a result, some of the identifications were very creative.

To complete the first notebook of twenty-eight pictures, a member needed to read 2,800 pages or twelve to fifteen books. Not all of the 234 members completed the first notebook, but all had a good time trying. Twenty-five teens were eligible for the drawing and fifteen completed both notebooks. Those that finished really enjoyed the challenge.

What would we change? Looking back at the program, we decided we were too ambitious. Our advice to ourselves would be to use fewer pictures in the main notebook. Some parents and teens felt that the requirement of 2,800 pages was too difficult. Using the total number of pages as the goal did give the impression that a lot of reading was needed to reach the goal. Another year we will look into a different method of earning artifacts.

The Archaeological Dig Reading Club was easy to administer. Teens were signed up and were given the story and the log. When they returned to the library with their log, we totaled the number of pages read and gave them the artifact tags. They looked through the notebook and identified their artifacts. We collected the tags and displayed them. There was little to file or keep at the library. The notebooks, tags, and prize drawing box took space on only one shelf.

The program provided a different and challenging summer reading club that had readers wandering throughout the library looking at it from a totally different perspective. [April 1995]

Books, Books, Books—Let Us Read: A Library Serving Sheltered and Incarcerated Youth
Pam Carlson

First days with young adults—do you remember yours? I do. I am the librarian at Orangewood Children's Home in Orange County, California. The County's largest emergency shelter for children, the Home provides protective custody for those who have been removed from their homes due to abuse, neglect, or abandonment. At any one time, we have approximately 200 children in residence, approximately fifty of them teens.

The adolescent girls were scheduled to visit the library first. As a veteran of one library school class aimed at young adults, as a former teenager, and as a reader of young adult books, I was ready. I had both current and old favorite titles on display, along with a selection of magazines. And since I enjoy crafts, I had a project all prepared. When the girls arrived at the door, I heard one ask her counselor why they were here. Her reply? "It's library time, there are books to read, and best of all, it's only an hour, so no matter what we do, surely you can survive that short a time!" With such enthusiasm, how could I miss?

As the girls came in, I explained the procedure for checking out books and requesting titles we did not have on hand. I gave some short booktalks and told them that after they had selected books to borrow, they could work on the craft project and listen to the radio for the remainder of the session. By the end of the hour, most were looking forward to coming back. One girl thanked me as she left, saying with some surprise, "That was fun—I thought you were going to make us *read* the whole time."

The library program at Orangewood, "Library STARS," was begun by the Orange County Public Library in late 1989 as an LSCA grant-funded program. Although Orangewood serves approximately 2,700 children each year, ranging in age from two days to seventeen years, our original goal was to establish library service for the target ages of five to twelve by providing weekly programs and purchasing books for the cottages the children live in. Orangewood is not a stereotypical shelter with a cold, institutional atmosphere. The children live in Spanish style cottages with tile roofs, attend an on-site school staffed by excellent, committed teachers, and participate in a variety of activities planned by the staff or offered by volunteers. There is a pool, a gym, an outside basketball court, a large playing field, and a playground. For the past four years, there have even been proms for the teens complete with donated prom dresses and tuxes, catered dinners, and live entertainment.

We did not originally plan to work with the teens or with the school, concerned that we would be busy enough working with our target group. After all, "Library STARS" was only funded for a year, at the end of which the full-time on-site Librarian's position was scheduled to be eliminated. While the Adult and Children's Specialists of Orange County Public Library were committed to continuing programs for the five to twelve year olds, they were not prepared to work with other groups. And we did not want to start any activities that might have to be abandoned.

However, things happen. Toward the end of the first year, we were asked by enthusiastic staff working with the Adolescent Girls to select materials for their cottage library. We bought books on how to get jobs, on college entrance requirements, the SAT and GED, on teen pregnancy and motherhood, cookbooks and a variety of paperback novels. They housed the books in a glass-door bookcase and established their own checkout system. Later, after attending a workshop on family literacy, we decided to adapt the Grandparents and Books read-aloud program for use at Orangewood. Our Superb Storytellers group consists of four students (fifth grade and up) who read to our preschoolers and elementary age students. Several teens have participated, giving up time with their friends to be a part of the weekly bedtime story hour for our six to eight year olds.

August 1990 meant the end of grant funding. But OCPL Administration was convinced of the program's importance and agreed to continue Library STARS as an ongoing service, staffed by a full-time librarian. Since then, a former classroom has been converted into a library with furniture from one of our refurbished branches and shelving donated by a local company. OCPL provides a materials and a supply budget to purchase new titles for the collection, and we receive many donations as well. We have books in English, Spanish and Vietnamese, on all reading levels. No one is judged for the length or type of book he or she chooses to read. For our teen patrons, we stock a good selection of magazines and paperbacks. The latter are popular with both kids and staff because of their low price and ease of transport. Also—and this is particularly important in the case of our Juvenile Hall program—paperbacks have less potential use as weapons for those few who might be inclined to use a book as such.

Expanding to Juvenile Hall

In 1992, I began library service to the security risk students residing in Juvenile Hall. On the first day, I filled a bookcart with paperbacks, took some "show and tell" items—seashells and a shark's jaw—and books on shells and the ocean over to the Hall, just a short walk from Orangewood. The first class consisted of approximately fifteen boys. They listened politely, asked questions about the things I had brought, and checked out books. One tall, skinny guy in the back had his legs draped over the desk in front of him during the whole presentation and gave only token attention to what was going on. He made no move to come to the cart when the others came to look at books. I asked him if he wanted to check anything out, thinking that he could not care less about reading. His reply began a friendship: "I have about twelve books in my room right now and I don't have time to read them so I don't want to add any more. But if you have a copy of *The Once and Future King*, I'd like to finish reading it. My roommate tore out the last chapter." I happened to have a copy in the library so I took it over that afternoon. I saw him every week after that, until he went to the California Youth Authority to serve out his sentence. He always had some suggestion for an addition to our collection.

What They Read

What are our most requested books? Poetry, especially *love* poetry, drawing, mysteries, romance, Stephen King, Dean Koontz, Joan Lowery Nixon, Lois Duncan, Sidney Sheldon, V.C. Andrews, Louis L'Amour, the *Chronicles of Narnia*, *Choose Your Own Adventure*, comics such as

Garfield, Calvin and Hobbes, and the *Far Side,* college entrance requirements, pregnancy (with plenty of illustrations), and more poetry. The other day I received my first request for one of Rush Limbaugh's books. Popular magazines include *Transworld Skateboarding, Surfer, Glamour, Mad, Sassy,* and *Low Rider.*

Although we have an on-line catalog in the library, the collection here is separate from that of the rest of the county library system. With the addition of a new circulation system this spring, our books will be visible in the catalog, but not available for outside patron holds. This is to save me, the only staff member, from becoming completely overloaded. Our patrons will, however, be able to request materials from other branches. Since our service population is transitory, we do not issue individual library cards. Instead we use the old-fashioned method for checking out books—signing book cards. This is helpful not only for knowing where the books are but for showing kids what they have checked out as well.

Like other kids, our patrons use the library to find information for homework assignments and to satisfy personal interests. The Orangewood Home school here has just revamped its high school curriculum. Now students will be coming to the library with advanced literature and writing classes as a component of their English as a Second Language studies, and to learn life skills. The teachers plan the course content and use the library as a resource as they do in other high school libraries. I will also have student aides: some clerical and some to assist with our toddler story time. The goal for all of us is to get the kids to see the library as a good place to be, a place to get information and to get materials to read for fun. They are encouraged to use the public library upon release from Orangewood.

Besides visiting the library with their teachers, the kids make weekly library visits with their cottage staff. Considered a privilege, these times are less formal than when they come during school hours. We often make crafts, sew, bake (after all, it's important to know how to read recipes), or play board games. Everyone is encouraged to check out at least one book to read later. To help insure the return of library books, each cottage has a library box in which finished books are placed until the next visit to the library.

In addition to school and cottage activities, there are occasional special library events, such as author appearances and reading programs. One activity particularly popular with our teens was our murder mystery dinner. After eating, they used their detective skills a la *Clue* to solve the "murder" of the Orangewood Children's Home director. Photos were taken of the "victim" both alive and dead—strangled by his own tie (what a good sport); of suspects—counseling staff and teachers; and of murder locations—the pool, Anaheim Stadium, and Disneyland. A list of possible weapons was also given out. The first five to solve the mystery received trophies.

Funding for programs and summer reading incentives is provided by donations from a variety of sources, principally our children's support auxiliary, La Casa. With their help, we have taken field trips to some of the OCPL branches, and an annual train trip to San Juan Capistrano. La Casa also provides funds to purchase paperback books to give away to each new child admitted to the Home. Coupons donated by businesses have allowed us to encourage reading trips to local fast-food restaurants and miniature golf courses.

One unique program planned especially for the Juvenile Hall students was our "Slice of Life" luncheon, designed to help the participants understand that events in life do not always turn out as we hope. Participants ordered meal items from a menu consisting of a listing of authors and titles. No one knew what he or she was getting—until their selections were served. They might be lucky—"Stephen King" could equal bread; *Sounder* meat—or not so lucky—those ordering "Louis L'Amour" and "Garfield" got a spoon and ketchup! Since the kitchen staff prepared the food, all I brought were the menus. At the end of the luncheon, we played an adaptation of the *Price Is Right* TV game show to give away some books and magazines. The kids bid and the one who came closest to "the actual retail price" won that item. For at least one boy, this was the first book he had ever owned.

Problems? We have lost some paperbacks and magazines to personal collections. Kids sometimes take their library books with them when they are released from Orangewood or Juvenile Hall. At other times, books are left behind in the cottage, where they are picked up to be read by someone else. Some kids have even tried to disguise favorite titles as their own by tearing out identifying labels and removing spine labels. Sometimes this works, but if I'm in a cottage, I can usually spot "my" books and take them back for repair. My rule of thumb is that the day after I list an item as lost, it will be returned by one of the kids or a staff member. We have had very little plaguing (gang writing) in the books, with most of what has been written in pencil and therefore erasable. Overall, the books are treated with respect—probably this is due to the feelings the kids have for their beloved librarian. Also, I remind them of our small budget. If they damage or keep a book or magazine, we can't afford to replace it.

There are some new goals we would like to accomplish this year. I want to involve more of our Hispanic teens in reading to Spanish speaking preschoolers. We also want to increase the opportunities the kids have to display their reading and dramatic skills by using reader's theater, either during the regular Orangewood talent shows or on specially-planned occasions. The teachers at Juvenile Hall want to work especially with teen fathers. We are working with them to provide information on how to read to children, where to find children's books, what is appropriate, and so on. We may also set up a story time during visiting hours at the Hall for children who come to visit their fathers or brothers.

The Orangewood "Branch" of the Orange County Public Library is succeeding in getting the teens at the Home and Juvenile Hall excited about reading. In the words of the kids themselves, "Thank you sooo much for the books! We are enjoying them sooo much!" This past Christmas I received several gifts from classes at the Hall. Some were hand-made cards carrying messages such as, "Without you, I wouldn't gain the knowledge that I need to absorb to become someone special," and "Thanks for bringing all the books for us to read. They helped my time go by much faster. . . ." One of my favorites was an original carol sung aloud by the students who wrote it. It echoes my feelings about the library service Library STARS provides to sheltered and incarcerated teens:

> Books, books, books, let us read;
> Books, books, books, they will teach;
> Every request that she grants us
> Helps us read without a fuss;
> A Merry Christmas wish we bring to you; Hope you'll bring more books that are new. [August 1994]

Best Books for Young Adults, Real Young Adult Opinions of the List, the Process, and the 1995 Selections

Lynn Cockett

The Young Adult Library Services Association (YALSA) provides a flyer called "How Did This Book Make the List," a description of the Best Books for Young Adults (BBYA) list, and the criteria for selecting the titles that are included each year. The committee receives a set of guidelines and uses it to make all of their decisions.

From 1993 to 1995, young adults at the Nutley, New Jersey, Public Library read and reviewed new books for my department newsletter. Summer reading programs were opportunities for me to involve some of these young adults in a greater variety of reading and learning experiences. During the summer of 1994, I created an interpretive community, in which six young adults read and responded—both individually and collectively—to humorous books for young adults. The purpose of that program was to help young people develop critical reading and thinking skills. I was interested in working towards an understanding of the meaning-making process of adolescents and their ability to interact with texts.

After listening to debate over the Best Books for Young Adults list at various YALSA gatherings, I used the summer of 1995 to create a young adult BBYA committee. My primary interest was to ask young adults to begin making critical decisions about good and bad examples of literature, and to compare their findings with that of the "real" BBYA committee. I presented the young adults with the 1995 list, and the criteria that the committee used to select the titles. The criteria are as follows: "Fiction should have characterization and dialogue believable within the context of the novel or story. Nonfiction should have an appealing format and a readable text."

During my June school visit campaign, I talked up this program as the one to join for teens who loved to read. I promised the kids that we would write a response to the YALSA committee's list, and that their opinions might really affect what other young people around the country read. I met approximately 200 students during those school visits. Of these, fourteen kids registered for the BBYA program, and eleven of them attended at least two of our weekly discussion meetings and read at least two books.

Young Adult Readers

Nutley, New Jersey, is a small metropolitan Manhattan suburb. Approximately four square miles of residential neighborhoods and tree-lined parks make up this town of 27,000 residents.

Table One provides a brief description of the young adult readers involved in the program. Following the table is fuller description of each individual.

Table One: Young Adults

Reader	Age	Grade ('95–'96)	Favorite Book
Joe	16	11	*To Kill a Mockingbird*
Meaghan	15	11	*Naked Lunch*
Josee	13	9	*Wuthering Heights*
Katie	13	9	*It*
Regina	13	9	*The Magic Circle*
Dolina	12	8	*Fat Chance*
Sara	12	8	*I Hadn't Meant to Tell You This*
Matthew	11	7	*Treasure Island*
Jennifer	12	7	*Heart of a Champion*
Donnelly	11	6	*Kujo*
Daisy	11	6	*Number the Stars*

Matthew, grade seven. Matt has dreams of being a professional baseball player and says the best book he read this year was Carl Deuker's *Heart of a Champion*. He also loves karate, basketball and plays the trumpet and guitar. Matt reads about a book per week all year long.

Josee, grade nine. Like her brother Matt, Josee is athletic. She takes dance lessons and is proud of the progress she has made in pointe. Josee read more books than anyone else this summer. She is a quick and critical reader, citing *Wuthering Heights* as the best book she's ever read.

Meaghan came to me in 1993 as she was entering high school. Now, in her junior year, her tastes have developed and she is a fabulously interesting and smart young woman. When asked about her favorite book at the beginning of the summer, Meaghan couldn't stop talking about *Lost Souls* by Poppy Z. Brite. After a summer course in the literature of the Beat Generation, Meaghan doesn't leave home without her copy of William S. Burroughs's *Naked Lunch*. College was made for Meaghan, and she will probably be frustrated until she gets there.

Regina is a ninth grader who reads like crazy. She and I know each other well after having been neighbors for two years. She loves the morose and macabre, and I can never recommend enough books about subjects that quite frankly make me a little nervous. I am always pleased when Regina and I make a connection with a literary book like Napoli's *The Magic Circle*.

Donnelly, Regina's little sister, is a sixth grader and claims her hobbies to be television and sleeping. She was thrilled when she was finally permitted to join a young adult program officially. She reads more than ten books a month, and this summer she "graduated" from the *Goosebumps* series into some more sophisticated reading, and loved almost everything she read.

Dolina, grade eight, is intelligent and poised. When Dolina's verbal ability catches up to her intellectual precociousness, she will be a dynamo. She read the most sophisticated books over the summer and loved them. Aside from "interesting" she rarely had words to describe what made a book excellent, yet she could identify those that simply did not meet her standards. I hope Dolina doesn't get bored with school before the end of eighth grade.

Daisy, a sixth grader, is a quiet and thoughtful young woman. She reads fifteen books a month, but always has time for shopping. She claims *Number the Stars* as her favorite book of all times. Daisy came to every library program she could this summer and liked them all. She had a hard time getting words into the conversations because a lot of the other kids were more talkative.

Katie is a ninth grader who reads horror books and loves things about sick people. She wants to be a child psychologist or surgeon or... about a thousand other things, but each of them involves blood or brains. She loves horror movies, also, and spends a good deal of time reading books and watching the movies adapted from them.

Jennifer is a seventh grader who hasn't lost that wonderful quality of playfulness and androgyny that so many girls lose during adolescence. She is into everything from collecting comic books to pogs and bike riding. She loves R.L. Stine books but will read and love a more literary book once in a while too. This year she, like Matthew, loved Carl Deuker's *Heart of a Champion*.

Joe is a junior in high school and doesn't read unless asked to for a school assignment, or unless convinced by me. He joined the group because I told him how important an older male opinion was. Joe likes good books, but just doesn't have the time for them. He does, however, talk about *To Kill a Mockingbird* nonstop. Aside from hanging around the library, Joe is into his computer and likes to challenge opinions. He has been in the marching band, on the crew team, and in his school's dramatic productions.

Sara is in eighth grade and uses the library all summer long. She joins lots of programs and helps the children's librarian with the preschool summer program. She reads in the afternoon while she waits for her mother to come and pick her up. She likes almost anything I give to her, particularly younger YA titles.

Ground Rules

I asked the young adults to read as many BBYA '95 titles as they could, and then rate them on a personal scale of one to ten (ten being the highest). Each week through July and August we met for one hour, at which time they talked about the books they'd read the previous week. The first few weeks were slow, since no two kids had read the same book, but after three or four weeks, discussions started to get interesting, even heated.

All of the kids were given a copy of the guidelines that the real BBYA committee receives, and were asked to think about these as they read. I let them know that if they did not like a book, it was okay to put it down and pick up another one, since there was no way they'd be able to read over seventy books in eight weeks. Everyone was asked to respect each other's opinions and to hold their comments about a book until someone else was done talking about it.

Books, Scores, and Young Adults' Opinions

In all, seventy-five books were read, representing forty different titles. Given more time, the young adults involved would have been able to read all of the books, providing a clearer picture of their opinions regarding the entire BBYA list.

At our last two meetings, the kids began to talk about their favorite books. In fact, some good arguments developed when I asked the participants to work corporately to rank the books from best to worst. They ranked only those titles that had been read by the participants in attendance that day, but the list is interesting, especially considering some of the low scores that books high in the rank order received. This phenomenon speaks to the power of peer influence and the strength of a single person's argument to influence a group. The rank order is as follows:

1) *Shadow*, Joyce Sweeney; 2) *Coffee Will Make You Black*, April Sinclair; 3) *Catherine Called Birdy*, Karen Cushman; 4) *The Cage*, Audrey Schulman; 5) *When She Hollers*, Cynthia Voigt; 6) *Too Soon for Jeff*, Marilyn Reynolds; 7) *After a Suicide*, Susan Kuklin; 8) *No Effect*, Daniel Hayes; 9) *Deliver Us from Evie*, M.E. Kerr; 10) *Hannah in Between*, Colby Rodowsky; 11) *Billy*, Laura Roybal; 12) *Missing the Piano*, Adam Rapp; 13) *Oddly Enough*, Bruce Coville; 14) *Wish You Were Here*, Barbara Shoup; 15) *Owl in Love*, Patrice Kindl; 16) *Stranger at the Wedding*, Barbara Hambly; 17) *Driver's Ed*, Caroline Cooney; 18) *Letters from the Inside*, John Marsden; 19) *Something Terrible Happened*, Barbara Ann Porte; 20) *I Hadn't Meant to Tell You This*, Jacquelyn Woodson; 21) *Tell Them We Remember*, Susan Bachrach; 22) *Wolf Woman*, Sheryl Jordan; 23) *Am I Blue?*, Marion Bauer; 24) *Hearing*

Us Out, Roger Sutton; 25) *Those Who Love the Game*, Glenn Rivers and Bruce Brooks; 26) *Beyond the Burning Time*, Katherine Lasky; 27) *Something Permanent*, Cynthia Rylant; 28) *The Great Apes*, Nichols; 29) *Zoo Book*, Linda Koebner; 30) *Earthshine*, Theresa Nelson; 31) *The Glory Field*, Walter Dean Myers; 32) *Cool Salsa*, Lori Carlson; 33) *Celebrate America*, Nora Panzer; 34) *Toughing It*, Nancy Springer; 35) *Shakespeare and Macbeth*, Stewart Ross; 36) *Iceman*, Chris Lynch; 37) *Under the Blood Red Sun*, Graham Salisbury; 38) *Come in from the Cold*, Marsha Qualey; 39) *Gypsy Davey*, Chris Lynch.

For some titles, students never reached consensus regarding a book's status. They debated for over two hours to create this list of 39 titles in rank order, and still, a few young people were dissatisfied with the way it looked at the end. I gave them an opportunity to try to "talk" their books further up the list. The power of a young person's presence often seemed to positively influence a book's position, even if the argument they made had little substance.

The following books received at least one "no" vote, indicating that one or more readers regarded the book unworthy of the title "Best Book for Young Adults:" *Cool Salsa*, Lori Carlson; *Sarajevo*, Matthew Naythons; *Shakespeare and Macbeth*, Stewart Ross; *Driver's Ed*, Caroline Cooney; *Deliver Us from Evie*, M.E. Kerr; *Gypsy Davey*, Chris Lynch; *Iceman*, Chris Lynch; *Letters from the Inside*, John Marsden; *Billy*, Laura Roybal; *Under the Blood Red Sun*, Graham Salisbury; *Wish You Were Here*, Barbara Shoup; *Toughing It*, Nancy Springer; *Shadow*, Joyce Sweeney.

Young Adults' Recommendations to the BBYA Committee

After a summer of reading and thinking about good books, these teens have recommendations for other teens and for librarians who create lists of books.

Number One: Respect Us and Our Books.

Dolina perceives that her mother has little respect for young adult literature. "She doesn't see every book I bring, but most of what she sees she's not impressed with." When asked, Dolina elaborated and talked about *Deliver Us from Evie*, which she loved. She says that her mother doesn't seem to understand that some of the books she reads are actually very good. She presumes that much of what her mother thinks is "crap" (Dolina's word) is only because it is perceived as just like all the other stuff that young adults read. Other group members agreed, and talked about books by authors like R.L. Stine and Christopher Pike. They admitted that they like those books, and the V.C. Andrews books, but they also realized that those books are not "literary" as Meaghan says, and therefore that all young adult literature gets a bad reputation.

One of our discussions early in the summer might illuminate this point. After three people had read Sweeney's *Shadow* and talked about how much they loved it, I asked them to annotate the plot for others who hadn't read it (myself included). They explained it, and by description, it sounded like teenage pulp fiction. They differentiated between this book and others in the pulp fiction genre by saying that Stine's books are predictable and simple. This book was surprising and believable. It took them longer to read and understand, and held their attention better.

This relates to Meaghan's distaste for YA novels that "talk down" to a mature reader. She said, "there are some people who write, like Madeleine L'Engle. She just writes, and everyone can understand it and it's good. But there are some people who write for young adults and they talk down to them; I hate that. Like *The Silver Kiss*—I thought it really talked down. That could be because I really like that kind of stuff, like I've read *Salem's Lot* and stuff."

Number Two: Beware the Influence of Reviews and an Author's Momentum

Jennifer said during our last meeting that "one person said *Gypsy Davey* stunk, then everyone agreed even though only one other person read it, and that person gave it a seven." Jennifer refers here to peer influence in creating interest (or in this case disinterest) in a title. Josee referred to librarians when she responded, "Everyone says that Chris Lynch is a great author, but I think he stinks. Maybe it's because they keep using his book reviews, but nobody really reads the books."

This discussion continued and the students talked about books that they'd read and liked or disliked because of what they already knew about an author's work. Josee admitted that she gave *Driver's Ed* by Caroline Cooney a low score because she was comparing it to other books by Cooney that she had liked better. She was disappointed that Cooney did not rise to the level of her other works with this book. She admitted that it was a great book, but said it just didn't compare with her others.

Dolina referred to *When She Hollers* by Cynthia Voigt as an example of how an author's reputation might get them a spot on the BBYA list. She said the book was good, but she thought maybe it got on the list because Voigt's older works are so superb.

Number Three: Make Two Lists

Meaghan was frustrated with the BBYA list, particularly since it included so many titles for younger readers. She referred to the YALSA Outstanding Books for the College Bound list that she picked up last summer. "Now that I'm in high school," Meaghan said, "I'm hearing more about other books and stuff. This is definitely the list for junior high, not high school at all." She said that the Outstanding Books list is not like the BBYA list because BBYA recommends books that for the most part are interesting leisure reading. She views the Outstanding Books list as a college primer, and says she would never choose to read those books for pleasure; "those books are hard work, I don't read that kind of stuff and I know most people my age don't." She wishes there were another list like BBYA with only books for older kids.

Number Four: Use Real Criteria for Selection

These young adults were quite specific when they talked about what makes a book a best book. Some of their suggestions were surprising, particularly coming from a group of teens who read a lot and like reading. Jennifer started it off by showing the group Jacqueline Woodson's *I*

Hadn't Meant to Tell You This—certainly a sophisticated book stylistically. She enjoyed the short chapters and white space on the pages. Perhaps we forget that even the best readers like to get through a book quickly. Adolescents need immediate feedback and quick gratification, and a good book that can be read in a sitting or two is treasured.

Dolina cited humor as a most important criteria. Not everyone agreed, but most did. (Dolina was involved in the 1994 summer reading program focusing on humorous novels—she now has a critical eye for literary humor and appreciates it when it works.)

"This is going to sound really stupid but the cover has to be good. People say don't judge a book by it's cover, but it really is important," Joe said. Jennifer and Dolina both cited books whose cover art did them little justice. Jennifer showed the group Roybal's *Billy* and said that the front cover looks like a western, whereas the back cover looks like a book about a missing person. She said that more young adults would be interested in the missing person story than the western. Dolina talked about Daniel Hayes's book *No Effect*. She said that last year, no one read it on the humor project, because we only had the hard cover book which has a "terrible illustration." This year, we had paperbacks with photo covers of a good looking teenage boy. She didn't realize that the book was on last year's list until I brought it to her attention after she'd read it this year.

By far, however, the group decided that a book should be relevant to the teens who will read it. Dolina called this "interesting." Joe had a hard time articulating himself, but finally said that "like if there's a library in the middle of Harlem, I think you'd be better off with a book about black people." He cited McCall's *Makes Me Wanna Holler* as the only book like that, and then pointed out that no one on our committee read that or Maurice Jones's *Say It Loud: The Story of Rap Music*.

Meaghan referred to Voigt's *When She Hollers* as an example of a book with a relevant theme. "I think a lot of people can relate to it, I mean, because you hear about it [sexual abuse] on the Ricki Lake show and stuff so you are used to hearing about it so it's something you want to read about. You know how you hear about it on shows like Geraldo, about all these children being abused and stuff and you think its like funny because you hear it on these stupid talk shows and stuff, but *When She Hollers* is really serious so I think that people would want to read about that kind of stuff. . . . It has to be relevant to things that teenagers are interested in—like pertinent issues."

Number Five: Listen to Us

The young adults asked how the librarians on the committee were chosen. After I explained the process, they suggested that the list should be made by kids. Next they said that some combination of kids and librarians would be realistic "but not like those old fogie librarians." (I was pleased that they said I could be on the committee.) I was quick to tell them that YALSA meetings are by far the "coolest" ones to be at when attending ALA conferences, comprised almost completely of people that really like young adults and empathize with them. They thought that teens should be allowed to vote in selecting the committee, but realized that then groups of kids would vote for the only YA librarian they know—their own. Finally, Meaghan suggested that, "maybe teens should go to those meetings, like representatives of teenagers." That's when I told them they can, and that they ought to start reading now for next year.

So perhaps ten kids from Nutley will make it to Manhattan in July 1996. Certainly they'll be reading a good deal this year. [December 1995]

Teenagers Work Well in the Berkeley Public Library

Kay Finney in collaboration with Kim McCombs

Attention all librarians and library administrators:
Want to liven up your library?
Want to recruit talented, energetic people eager to contribute to their communities?
Want to honor your mandate to serve historically neglected constituencies? In 1991 the Berkeley Public Library found an elegant solution that simultaneously fills all three bills. As part of a specially funded two-year project, we hired three teenagers to assist young adult librarians.

Background of the Project

Designed as a kind of affirmative action for young people, the "Youth at Risk" grant (funded by the California State Library) distributed money to nine Bay Area library systems—charging each to devise or improve services to youth at risk. The grant provided each system with funds to conduct a thorough needs assessment. In Berkeley we hired a consulting firm, one with a solid track record in youth advocacy, to determine the status of youth in our community. Using this information, we hoped to develop a program that responded to the concerns of teenagers in realistic and concrete ways. Three players worked in concert to conduct the assessment: the consultants, the grant's project director, and a BPL Young Adult Librarian.

Needs Assessment Process

The assessors tried to determine what teens want and need in their public library by using a four-pronged approach. Through a number of

111

avenues, they talked with as many teenagers as possible. They personally questioned key informants, respected leaders who work closely with young people. They mailed surveys to seventeen youth services agencies. Finally, they compiled secondary data to paint a demographic picture of our community.

Youth involvement was the critical factor in the assessment; assessors reached out to students on their own turf. Since Berkeley has only one high school with a single offshoot, it made sense to conduct forums at the two school sites. Enticed by free food and the promise of being listened to, thirty students attended a discussion group held after school at Berkeley High. Assured a captive audience, we held a focus group during an English class at East Campus. Fifty students attended a forum at a local recreation center. This even took place in the evening during a regularly scheduled and historically well-attended evening program for teens. Again, pizza and soda helped retain the crowd.

Working with and building on the efforts of other youth services providers made assessment more efficient and more credible. For example, we took advantage of the "City-wide Forum for Youth," an event with two hundred participants. Organizers allowed the Library to distribute a questionnaire on library services to all participants. They made our task easier by making completion of the survey a condition for eligibility in a drawing for coveted prizes.

In an attempt to remove barriers to communication, the consulting firm selected young interviewers they felt teenagers could relate to easily. These interviewers conducted face to face, in-depth sessions with twelve young adults who were referred primarily by adults working in rec centers or other agencies. In other situations, students self-selected by responding to advertisement and word of mouth. What did we ask teenagers and youth services providers? We tried to design open-ended as well as specific questions to elicit responses. For example, what are the top five problems facing youth today? What programs would you like to see in the library? What types of information should be in the library? How would you improve the library? What activities would you attend if they were offered?

Creating a Service Plan

Continuing the effort to involve the community in the library's plans, a committee composed of youth, librarians, library administrators and representatives of other youth-serving agencies met to consider a course of action. Together, we reviewed the needs assessment report. In the course of working on the assessment and deciding on a plan for service, the library began building bridges to other youth-serving agencies. We discussed several options. Since employment—especially jobs for African American and Latino teenagers—ranked high on everyone's lists and fit the parameters of our institution, we decided to provide specialized library jobs for teens.

In 1991 Berkeley Public Library used a large portion of its share of the grant to enter into a partnership with another organization, the Real Alternatives Project. RAP, a consortium of city agencies, identifies young people considered to be "at risk" and provides tutoring, family counseling, social activities and employment services for those enrolled. The library provided three jobs at three different sites; RAP screened applicants through the employment component of their program. Each partner contributed $2,500.00, which allowed BPL to hire three teenagers to work for $5.00 per hour, ten hours a week for roughly ten months. We placed two workers in branch libraries in South and West Berkeley, areas of town where incomes are lower and that show a higher percentage of families of color. The third student worked at the Central Library.

Words—"Youth at Risk"

It didn't take long for the phrase "youth at risk" to catch on. The words fairly flew around conferences and meetings; it's common coin in the national media. Many library workers referred to the new student employees as the "youth at risk workers."

And that's exactly the place to interject words of caution. The term accurately describes social conditions; anyone who looks cannot fail to notice decline in the health and safety of young people. Because racial inequity persists in our country, young adults from families of color are disproportionately represented in "at-risk" statistics—in Berkeley, most notably in unemployment figures. Alarming evidence proliferates, and the Youth at Risk grant represents an innovative response by the Bay Area libraries.

But the words aren't useful as a label for individuals; they are not synonymous with "African American" or "Latino." Any child or young adult may be at risk due to a number of factors, including parental abuse, economic hardship, substance abuse in the family, etc. Here's what Kim McCombs, student worker at the South Branch Library (BPL) and a senior at Berkeley High, says on the subject. (The Youth at Risk grant and RAP provided funds for her salary.)

> The principle behind the youth at risk program is good. It opens doors to people who might otherwise have them shut in their faces.... To be labeled as someone "at risk" is very belittling to people. It gives a person a sense of being pitied, which may lower self esteem.

The Job

Primarily a training position designed for high school students, the job at BPL involved four components: public service orientation, clerical work, computer literacy, and outreach. Students worked closely with the Young Adult Librarian and, at branches, assumed responsibility for upkeep of the YA area.

The public service component, though somewhat nebulous, ranked first on this list because we try to impress students with the importance of courteous, equal treatment of all patrons. At the South Branch Library, patrons include people from many different ethnic backgrounds. Located very near a drop-in center, we also count many homeless people among our clientele. Many people with disabilities live in our neighborhood. We feel it's essential that all staff, including student workers, learn to feel as comfortable as possible with all patrons. While the students never worked a public desk, they did observe staff interactions and assisted with the summer reading games for children and for young adults.

Through the clerical component the student worker learned the basics of office work—filing, inventory, operating office machines, preparing mailings, and processing books as well as nonprint materials. As a rule of thumb, the student worker never performed tasks that would take work away from a "regular," i.e., permanent library employee.

Including a computer literacy component ensured that the student learned the rudiments of database manipulation, data entry and word processing. This, of course, includes learning how to search the library's catalog. Kim McCombs, student worker at South Branch, also spent some time learning database construction via Filemaker.

Some consider the outreach part of the job the most fun. Under other terms of the Berkeley YAR grant, Kim served on a committee (consisting of two other student workers and three YA librarians) who brainstormed, designed, publicized and produced the third annual BPL Rap and Poetry Jam. In the course of her work, Kim also represented the Library at community events including Cinco de Mayo, Juneteenth, and the South Berkeley Neighborhood Health Fair. As a panelist at a BPL system-wide staff training on interaction with teens, she spoke about her own perceptions and those of her peers.

Kim routinely assisted with special projects and graphic displays, and assumed responsibility for the bulletin board in the YA area. In her work with the sound crew, she got in on the nuts and bolts of library programming. All student workers, including Kim, traveled to other sites when special needs or requests arose. As a member of the Young Adult Advisory Committee, Kim advertised and planned the logistics of Cover to Cover, the Library's reading game for young adults. She also regularly provided support and assistance to South Branch's children's librarian.

We at the South Branch were lucky to work with Kim. She improved the quality of life at the workplace. Her presence and her opinions sensitized all staff to the special circumstances of being a teenager.

Successes and Mistakes

In retrospect, two things stand out as rough spots in the project. At one site the youth worker's supervisor worked a twenty hour week. The difficulty in synchronizing the two schedules turned out to be a problem, especially during the first few weeks of the student's employment. Since this particular student worker required close supervision, some confusion and inefficiency was inevitable. One of the challenges in working with student workers comes in the form of time management. It's very labor intensive; it's incredibly time consuming. To work successfully with student employees, one must rely heavily on the good intentions and support of co-workers. When a time crunch arises, or in the absence of the regular supervisor, an integrated, supportive staff that works as a team can make or break the experience for staff as well as for the student worker. Some students, highly motivated self-starters, respond quickly to training; others require more supervision.

Cementing relations with other youth service providers was the other area of concern. Even though we worked well with community groups during the needs assessment, many agencies still do not see the library as a player in the arena of youth services. We understand this as a symptom of the larger problem of library awareness. However, based on the competence of its student employees and the overall success of the project, BPL's director agreed to fund three permanent youth worker positions for the 1993-94 fiscal year.

Advantages for the Library

Clearly, the library stands to gain immeasurably by hiring student workers. We can't put a price on goodwill and improved relations with the communities we serve and the people whose taxes support us. In demonstrating that the library, as an institution, seeks to deeply immerse itself in the compelling issues of our time, we revitalize our institution. We have the opportunity to become part of the solution and to affect the lives of young people in a concrete way. By welcoming young adults to our staffs, we chip away at the all too common perception of the static, tradition-bound library. The student worker attracts young people to the library; in the meantime, we train a pool of life-long users and potential library workers.

Advantages for Student Workers

The student worker also benefits from this arrangement. Since holding the job is contingent on school enrollment, the job becomes an incentive to stay in school. Other obvious advantages include interview experience, developing job skills, computer literacy, absorbing the niceties of job etiquette, and practicing interaction with bosses and with co-workers. In some cases, students may enjoy mentor-type relationships with their supervisors. And of course the worker experiences the sense of pride and accomplishment that comes from confronting and mastering new situations.

Why Hire Teens?

Because they need jobs. They can use the money. They can use the training and job skills to prepare them for entry-level work. They can use the self esteem that all working people derive from a job well done.

Because they need to learn what it means to hold down a job. They need a supportive environment in which it's okay to make mistakes, that is, to grow and learn.

Because they make great co-workers. They question; they bring new ideas, fresh approaches, youth exuberance and a special quality of thought to every situation they encounter.

Because hearing what they have to say keeps us in touch with what our constituents want and need from a modern information center.

Because listening to their opinions improves the quality of our service and the quality of our collections.

Because, by the very fact that they work in the building, they help us break down the widespread stereotype that "library" means "old, white, boring, irrelevant." Because the library, as a public institution, has for a very long time been in the forefront of youth advocacy. Now is the time to focus on older youth—on young adults. After all, one of every four patrons is a teenager.

Suggested Reading

Information Is Empowering: Developing Public Services for Youth at Risk by Stan Weisner (0-922910-03-6).

America's Youth Are at Risk: Developing Models for Action in the Nation's Public Libraries by Judith G. Flum and Stan Weisner *Journal of Youth Services in Libraries*, Volume 6, Number 3, Spring 1993.
Berkeley Youth at Risk Project prepared for Bay Area Library and Information System by Moore Iacofano Goldsman, Inc.

Youth Enrollee—Library Services: Job Description 1993-1994

Definition

Under close supervision, receives training in entry-level clerical work and support services.

Class Characteristics

Primarily a training position intended for high school students, "student worker" is a special class in the library service support series. Under close supervision, incumbent performs a variety of support duties. At the same time, incumbents learn the rudiments of clerical work, public service and computer literacy. Although "student workers" are assigned to a permanent location, specific tasks may take them to various sites. This class is distinguished from "library aide" in that "student worker" assists young adult librarians in outreach efforts. Successful completion of student worker term prepares incumbents for entry level position.

Examples of Duties

1. Assist young adult librarian in a variety of special projects and services.
2. Assist young adult librarian in programming and outreach to teenagers.
3. Prepare displays and bulletin boards.

4. Understand Dewey Decimal classification system.
5. Sort and shelve library materials, periodicals, pamphlets, newspapers, microfilm, records and other library materials.
6. Spot check books and materials for incorrect shelving.
7. Straighten shelves.
8. Perform simple mending and repairs to materials.
9. Process books and non-book materials.
10. Lift and transport books and other library materials.
11. Perform basic clerical duties.
12. Maintain library reading rooms, stacks and periodicals area.

Knowledge of:

1. Basic principles of business English
2. Basic business arithmetic
3. Following oral and written directions

Other requirements:

1. Must be able to work a limited number of evenings and Saturdays
NO EXPERIENCE REQUIRED

Job Description 1992–1993

The position "Student Outreach Worker" has three components:

Training

1. Orientation to the library and to library services
2. Instruction on using the computer catalog

3. Instruction in the use of other library tools
4. Instruction on the Macintosh computer

Library Tasks

1. Overview of technical services and circulation
2. Mending
3. Shelving
4. Processing unaccessioned paperbacks
5. Maintenance of clip files
6. Maintenance of Young Adult areas

Outreach

1. Attend all meetings of the Young Adult Advisory Committee
2. Accompany library staff on outreach visits
3. Meet regularly with Young Adult librarians
4. Assist library staff in planning young adult programs
5. Publicize events
6. Plan and install displays
7. Gather and advertise information about local events of interest to teens [April 1994]

The Body in the Library: Who Dunnit?
Nancy Gorman

For a long time I had wanted to have a murder mystery day in the library. But I never was able to come up with a viable plan that would accommodate a large group of kids, would keep them moving, and would interrupt library services as little as possible. Even after I planned the program, I wasn't sure it would work. So, with fear and trepidation on my part, there was a murder in the library! Late Tuesday night during vacation week in February 1994, Michael, one of our librarians was stabbed through the neck with a card catalog rod. The Medical Examiner said he died quickly, judging by the amount of the blood on the body.

At 11:00 on Wednesday morning forty sixth to eighth graders came to the library to solve the crime. The body was discovered while they were milling about, and we studied the crime scene thoroughly. (The corpse smiled once or twice but that didn't seem to matter much.)

I gathered all the detectives together and took them to our community room to explain how this was going to work. They split up into ten teams of three or four on each team (any more on a team would have been unwieldy, I think). Each group was given a pad, a pencil, and an explanation sheet. The game worked this way:

Before the library opened that morning, I gave every staff member an envelope which had a scenario in it of what they did to, for, or with Michael the victim on Tuesday. Fifteen staff members got stories. The rest of the staff got statements saying that they didn't know anything because they had not worked on Tuesday.

The detectives were told they had to interview every member of the staff and take very good notes about their testimonies. They were told that they could discount anyone who didn't work the day before but that everyone who *had* worked would have a clue for them. There would be a keyword in these stories—the kids were to figure out what each keyword was, take the first letter of each word, unscramble the letters, and they would have the name of the staff member who killed Michael. When a team thought they knew who had done the dirty deed, they were to come to me with his/her name, get a pair of handcuffs from me, and arrest the perpetrator.

The program was wonderful! The staff had as much, if not more, fun as the kids. I chose the limited age group because I had no idea how it was going to work. If older kids had been involved I was afraid they might have taken over the whole game.

The murderer and I were the only ones who knew who did it—no one else—not even the victim, which made it all the more fun when the crime was solved. Michael Squillante, our dead librarian, was wonderful. He wore old clothes and sunglasses, and was slumped against a carrel in the back of the library with blood dripping from his neck, nose, and mouth. Prior to the arrival of our detectives we taped off his body and our custodian even found some yellow caution tape which we draped around the crime scene. Michael went back to work at the reference desk, but the taped outline of where the body was found stayed all day. The patrons loved it!

After an hour and half, I could sense the kids were getting a bit frustrated so I got them together again and gave them some hints. Fifteen minutes later a team came to me with the murderer's name and the mystery was solved. The perp was arrested, amidst great outcries and protestations on her part.

The program cost nothing. I borrowed the handcuffs from another staff member, the blood was left over from a Children's Halloween program, and the murder weapon was constructed by our custodian. Vinney bent one of our obsolete card catalog rods and padded it with duct tape. It was very effective. The only glitch was that my camera decided to misload that day!

I didn't give prizes. The arrest of the murderer was prize enough. Lorraine Tedesco, a children's librarian, was our murderer, and I chose well. She played the part to the hilt and was led away kicking and screaming.

The program took two hours. No patrons complained—actually the kids were very well behaved—I had told them they were not to interrupt anyone's work. The staff loved it; the kids loved it; I'll do it again. [August 1994]

Relieving the Junior High Jitters
Kathryn L. Havris

Do you remember what it was like on your first day of junior high? Were you one of those shy retiring types that peeked into classrooms and hoped you got the right one? Or were you one of those brash, arrogant ones (usually with an older sibling in the school) who knew what was going on and proclaimed it loudly, even though deep in your heart you were just like the shy type? Well, even now, those questions haven't changed and those feelings are still there for those entering junior high in the '90s. To help those current and future junior high students and their parents, the Mesa Public Library Young Adult Department has, for the past two years, presented a program called Junior High Jitters to help quell those fears and the great unknown of entering junior high.

Sparked by a presentation by Midji Stephenson of the Tucson Public Library at the Arizona State Library Association conference, we thought that a program to ease the transition from elementary school to junior high would certainly be worthwhile here in Mesa (our junior high school system in Mesa consists of grades seven through nine all on one campus). The programs were very easy to set up—all we did was coordinate and provide the refreshments. The two and one-half hour programs were conducted by psychologists who specialize in adolescence, and a person from the Governor's Office of Drug Policy or a police officer. These people were obtained for us by a contact in the Mesa Public Schools' Youth Placement Service, a department that has worked with us on many programs. Marjorie Walsh of the Youth Placement Service served as coordinator and facilitator for the groups and kept everything running smoothly. She found and contacted the presenters after discussions with us as to what the programs were to consist of, and we arranged for the room and did the publicity and sign-up. All the presenters worked for free and one has even done the program two years now.

We decided ahead of time to have someone at least touch on topics that we felt were universal to the junior high experience. Acceptance, peer pressure, popularity, friend selection, boyfriends/girlfriends, and alcohol and drugs were some of the biggies. Perhaps not so big but just as important were things like clothes, lockers, changing classes, showers in P.E., and dances—those little incidentals that buzz inside a new junior high student's brain. The presenters decided ahead of time who was going to cover what topics and in what order.

Both years we have been fortunate in obtaining opening speakers who were very dynamic and captured the audience's attention from the beginning. The first year, the speaker opened his presentation with the story of the wide-mouthed frog, which illustrates how not everyone is as they seem. He was a real showman and got the participants going with his imitations of various animals. The second year, the presenter was an extremely energetic speaker with an infectious laugh who used a variety of goofy hats to show the audience what kinds of attitudes young adults put on and how they appear to others. There was the crab hat for the complainers, the shark hat for the school bullies, and the grasshopper hat for the "don't bug me" attitude. Volunteers from the audience wore the hats and demonstrated the attitudes, which, as the presenter pointed out, took a lot of courage. He also used a Navajo word "wuzshe," which means "get ready to laugh," to teach the young adults to feel good about themselves. It also really got them involved in the presentation.

Both years the next speakers (who had a tough act to follow) did admirable jobs. Being former junior high teachers and parents of teens allowed them to speak with an intimate knowledge of what junior high was like. Using personal examples from teaching days, they illustrated things like thinking before judging another person or before jumping into a crowd that isn't right for you. The emphasis was on the many places there are to ask for help at school and not to be afraid to ask for help.

The final speaker each year handled the drugs and gangs topics. The first year, the person was from the Governor's Office of Drug Policy and she pointed out that people who do drugs don't hang out with people who don't do drugs. She also did an exercise with the group that showed how being confident and "centered" makes you a less likely target for gangs and bullies. The exercise had one group of students stand with two feet firmly planted on the ground, with the second group opposite, standing slightly off-center, they demonstrated how easy it is to push the

Potpourri of YA Programs

off-center person over using just a gentle shove with two fingers. New students remember these graphic participation exercises and take them along on their first days of junior high. The second year, our speaker was a police officer who is regularly assigned as the liaison between the schools and the police. He also emphasized that most students are not involved in drugs or gangs.

Right before the break, the audience was given combination locks and worked on opening them. The locks were borrowed from one of the junior highs and are the same kind the new junior high students will have to struggle with on their lockers and in P.E. It was a great participation exercise and forced the young adults to interact with one another for help because there were locks only for every two people. Refreshments were served during the break which was sorely needed by now. We supplied the cookies and soda the first year and the second year a local cafeteria gave sweet rolls and muffins as part of their community relations program. The break gave the participants a little more time to work on their lock opening skills and time to ask private questions of the speakers if necessary.

For both programs, the next phase was probably the most successful in terms of really helping the new students. The large group was broken into smaller groups, each headed by one of the speakers who was accompanied by a person who was either still in junior high or who had just finished. The older students were a reality check for these new students because their presence said, "if we could make it, you can too." Each speaker had a list of topics to be covered in these small groups but was free to explore anything that came up. As the kids stated what junior high they would be attending as an introduction, it gave others in the group a chance to meet a person they didn't know who was also going to their junior high. This gave them a forum to ask questions and voice concerns or fears that they had about these upcoming experiences. Concerns about taking showers, finding classes, being late to class, popularity, friends, homework, being teased, clothes, physical appearance (especially those short boys), and lunch break were all discussed using open-ended questions by the speakers to draw out the participants. It was amazing and reassuring to see how quickly the students felt comfortable enough with the crowd to ask the question that they personally needed to have answered. Hints like watching others for what you should be doing and just walking on by with your head up when you're being teased were just a few that came from the students themselves. Unfortunately for us as librarians, they defined a nerd in one group as someone who would rather read than play Nintendo or would rather read than go out for recess. We obviously still have a lot of stereotypes to shatter.

As an indication of how really scary the first days of junior high can be, one group started defining their ideal junior high. Besides getting all the usual recommendations for longer lunches and P.E. as an elective, one boy thought his ideal would be to have all his classes in a row with his locker opposite all those rooms. Another girl felt her ideal would include being allowed to have one person you know have exactly the same schedule as you. These suggestions show that the fear these kids have about getting lost and being alone are very real and sometimes all-consuming.

This year [1991], since parents were invited to the program, they also met with a presenter and asked questions about the program and about junior high. Parent participation came about because of a suggestion from the first year's panel that noted once children enter junior high they are not the same kids who have lived in the house for the past twelve years. The parents' presenter was our facilitator who works for the Mesa Public Schools and was familiar with the majority of junior highs in the area and so could help dispel parents' doubts. Many favorable comments about the program were received from parents during this time. By the way, they did not sit with their future junior high students during the program; that way the young adults could feel more comfortable during the presentation.

The program wrap-up was conducted both times by the dynamic first speaker. The first year, the speaker reminded the participants that junior high really can be fun and that it is a lot like the Junior High Jitters program where you come into a big room and don't know anybody and move from activity to activity. He also reminded them how there are always people who want to help at their school, whether they are counselors, teachers, or custodians. Even their parents want to help, and all they have to remember is to open their mouths and ask. As a closure activity the next year, our energetic presenter gathered all 100 future seventh graders around him and split them into groups of three. They were labeled "cowboy boots," "high heels," or "tennis shoes" and one was appointed boss and the other two were runners. Each boss had one minute to give each of his runners a positive comment to spread to others in the room. Each member of the group got to be boss for one minute. The purpose of the exercise was to show that you can find something positive to say about everyone. It was a noisy and confusing activity but everyone enjoyed it.

Our first year's program evaluation revealed that 97 percent of the participants thought that the program was either super or okay. The two most-liked parts were the wide-mouth frog story (for here was an adult willing to make a fool of himself in front of kids) and when they got into groups. Even though evaluations were neglected the second year, I feel that positive responses would have again come from the majority of the participants, including parents. Very few negative comments were heard and body language showed that the audience was pleased and inspired by the presentation. The panel of presenters, too, were enthusiastic and encouraged by the responses. The program was videotaped for later evaluation and study.

We submitted stories to the local newspapers about Junior High Jitters and announced it as an upcoming summer program during our booktalking visits to the sixth grades in the spring, as well as having our summer program flyer and library's summer calendar available. The first year's response to this program was so great that instead of our original rotation of 30 participants we had to double the number we would accept. Calls from irate parents whose children were not among those able to register in time for the smaller session prompted our enlarging the size. We even had one woman who called in, not to register her children, for they were all grown, but to compliment us on presenting such a program because she remembered how nerve-wracking junior high had been for her children. The second year we capped registration at 100 for young adults and 30 for parents and were completely filled. The success of the previous year's program was undoubtedly a factor in this high attendance as word of mouth is one of the best advertisements around.

As you can see, this program is an almost guaranteed success and doesn't take a lot of work on the part of the librarian once you find a contact you trust to be coordinator and facilitator. This will become a standard end-of-summer program for us until interest wanes which is not likely since there are always new seventh graders on the way. This is a program that fills a need and promises to be a rousing success every time. When you think back to your first days of junior high, you'll want to offer this too. [April 1992]

YAs Need TLC . . . Especially in the Summer
Lucretia Lipper

Summer. The word conjures up the image of long, sunny days swimming and hanging out with friends. The reality may not be so idyllic, however, to those teens in the 13 to 15 age group. They are limited by their inability to drive, lack of paying jobs, and ineligibility for day camp programs. Their plight can pose a real challenge to public libraries. How can we serve this hard to reach segment of the young adult population and encourage them to maintain the library habit?

Since 1980, the East Brunswick Public Library in central New Jersey has addressed this challenge with the Teen Library Connection, otherwise known as TLC. The Library Director, prompted by a phone call from a public library patron whose daughter was "too old for day camp and too young to work," asked the administrative staff for a response. The result was a volunteer program geared to this group, eighth to tenth graders.

The TLC program provides an opportunity for teens to work as library volunteers while enjoying some recreational experiences. Essentially, the volunteers work in various departments in the library under the supervision of particular staff members. Secondarily, the volunteers take part in social activities which make the program more appealing. In 1992, the program ran for eight weeks, considerably longer than the three weeks that were offered at TLC's inception. The increase in number of weeks came as a result of the large number of applicants we had for a limited number of volunteer slots. The TLC day has remained consistent over the years. Work is done Monday through Friday, from 9:30 a.m. to 12 noon with a half-hour break. While this year we were able to accommodate a record 66 participants, TLC sessions of whatever length have been completely filled each summer.

In order to maintain the success of the TLC program, several essential elements must be identified. They are supervision, recruitment, training, identification of projects, and evaluation.

Supervision

There are two levels of supervision involved. The Young Adult (YA) Librarian generally oversees the entire program, supervises the coordinator, and acts as liaison with the library staff. The coordinator oversees the program on a day-to-day basis. This position is one of the keys to a successful program, and the coordinator should be a paid employee, rather than a volunteer. All our coordinators have been college-aged students who have worked at the library as pages while in high school. They have all had previous knowledge of library operations and staff, which has proved to be enormously helpful. Since the coordinator is the person the volunteers will have most contact with, a mature college student seems to fill the bill quite well. The coordinator can function as friend and supervisor. The coordinator's duties include all scheduling of jobs with the department heads, training new volunteers and monitoring their progress, as well as administrative functions such as taking attendance and writing evaluations.

Recruitment

Planning for the program starts in early spring. Applications must be printed and delivered to the local schools by May 1. Since we accept volunteers who will be in grades eight through ten in September, we send applications to the appropriate schools, both public and private. Applications are available in the school libraries and in the public library. In addition, a publicity campaign is launched. Articles are printed in the library's newsletter and in local newspapers. Information about the program is sent to school librarians to post.

Applications are accepted usually by the second week of June. We give a specific date after which we will accept applications, and date them as received, since demand is high. Postcards notifying volunteers of the weeks they will attend are sent before the first week of the program.

Volunteers must commit themselves to a minimum of two consecutive weeks, and a maximum of four weeks total. Approximately twenty slots are reserved for each week of the program. If necessary, a waiting list is kept.

Training

As each new group of TLCers begins their service they undergo a general training session. A few ice-breaker games are played to enable teens of varying social skills to speak more freely with each other and the TLC coordinator. A two-page pamphlet is distributed, outlining general library rules and policies. An emphasis is placed on professionalism. We ask our volunteers to take their positions seriously. They are expected to be on time and to notify the coordinator if they'll be late or absent. All volunteers receive two "TLC" T-shirts, and an identifying name tag, which they're expected to wear each day. TLCers are given a tour of the various departments and are introduced to staff members.

TLCers fill out a work preference sheet and are asked to identify any special talent they possess (e.g. art or computer proficiency). An effort is made to match each volunteer with his or her preference; however, by the end of their time with the library, most teens have gotten a taste of all the jobs available. Each participant receives a written evaluation at the end.

Identification of Projects

Before the start of the TLC program, the YA librarian distributes job requests forms to all the departments. These forms indicate the type of work to be done, special skills needed, the number of TLC participants required, as well as due date. Department heads submit these forms to the TLC coordinator who assigns tasks and monitors progress.

Jobs range from small to large, individual to group, and one-time to long-term. For example. TLCers have aided in shifting entire sections of the collection in preparation for new shelving. This summer some of the jobs were data entry, genre labeling of books in the YA collection, processing paperbacks, and writing up postcard requests for pamphlet file information. Each year, TLCers prepare and perform a puppet show and flannel board performances for the Youth Services department. None of these replace the jobs of a paid staff member, but rather supplement the staffing during the summer when many seasonal programs are going on. Often, larger projects are saved for the summer when the volunteers will be working in the library.

The selection of appropriate jobs is one of the most important elements of providing a worthwhile experience for teens. The activities selected should not be too difficult for the volunteers to perform; but neither should the job bank be overflowing with too many really tedious tasks that have no apparent purpose. It is important to explain to the teens why they're doing a job and to give very *specific* instructions.

When asked to evaluate the TLC experience, teens often mentioned positively the opportunity to work with library staff members. This promotes a real feeling of belonging and seriousness of purpose.

One of the reasons for TLC's popularity is the chance to be with other teens. This past summer, three pizza and tie-dying parties were scheduled to accommodate all of the TLCers over the course of the summer. Blocks of time were scheduled on the library's Macintosh computer for TLC use on a weekly basis. Each day the teens were provided with a half-hour break for snacks, conversation, or a friendly card game. Most teens in the program became acquainted with at least one new person.

Evaluation

At the outset of the program, the volunteers are told they'll be formally evaluated. TLCers receive a copy of the evaluation and may discuss it with the coordinator. Evaluations are kept on file at the library in the event a reference is needed or the volunteer applies to the library for a paying job. Those TLCers with good evaluations receive preference in hiring for page positions; nonetheless, TLC participation does not guarantee them a job.

The teens get a chance to evaluate all aspects of the program and make suggestions. This feedback is very interesting and informative. One teen volunteer commented, "The TLC program is both an educational and fun experience." Another said, "Putting on a performance for the children of East Brunswick brought on a great feeling for *all* TLC members." We take all suggestions to heart and incorporate them in the program if possible. The TLC coordinator is usually very highly regarded by the teens themselves.. There have only been five TLC coordinators since 1980. This continuity has contributed greatly to the success of the program.

Costs and Benefits

The biggest item in the TLC budget is the coordinator's salary. Additional expenses are T-shirts, and the expenses associated with the recreational activities. In East Brunswick, the Friends of the Library generously fund the program.

The most obvious result of the TLC program is providing scores of township teens with an interesting summer activity. The volunteers gain work experience, have a pleasant way to perform community service, and interact socially with other teens. In addition, the amount of time the teens spend in the library increases their exposure to other library programs and material. In other words, there's always a chance they'll check out books. They also provide a pool of volunteers for projects throughout the year, as well as providing input on teen interests.

The library benefits directly from the many tasks completed by TLCers. Some activities, such as maintaining records for the summer reading club, would be much more difficult without the help of the TLCers. During TLC, the volunteers become familiar with library staff and operations, and as I said before, provide a ready-made pool of potential library employees.

Plans for the Future

TLC has been a functioning program since 1980, so it runs very smoothly. However, last summer's experience has made it necessary to change the format of the applications. We hope this will simplify scheduling.

Group size is another factor that will be dealt with differently in 1992. Experience indicates that for our library twenty teens is probably the optimum number. It would be better to have a group with less than twenty volunteers rather than a group with more. This keeps a group to a level where the TLC coordinator can get to know all the volunteers, and it makes easier the task of keeping the volunteers busy at meaningful activities. Since finding appropriate activities for the TLCers is one of the key ingredients for the success of the program, it is most important to keep the groups at twenty.

In the past, TLCers could volunteer for up to four weeks of service. The number of weeks will probably be decreased to three next summer for two reasons: first, to better accommodate all those who wish to participate; secondly, it seems that interest and energy level of individual participants peak at the three-week point in most cases.

More time needs to be allotted in the schedule for the evaluation process to allow discussion with volunteers about their performance rating.

We hope the changes will improve a vital, exciting teen program. Undoubtedly, the amount of planning and preparation is great, but the results have been well worth it. The large number of TLCers who wish to return each year testifies to its success.

REQUEST FOR TLC ASSISTANCE

TO: TLC Coordinator
Date: _____
From: _____
Project: _____
Number of participants needed: _____
Description of project/duties of participants: _____
_____
Skills required: _____
_____
Date and time participants needed: _____
_____
Supervisor will be: _____
_____
Other Notes: _____
_____

[June 1993]

A Library Where Silence is Banned
Cathi Dunn MacRae

"There's nae place to go." Decode the rich Scottish accent of Gary Russell for the classic lament of teenagers everywhere. I spoke with Gary, sixteen, in Johnstone, West Renfrewshire, in Scotland's industrial belt about twenty miles west of Glasgow. Johnstone is a down-at-heel town of 18,545 people who knew better days in the 60s and 70s, when thread manufacturing, engineering, and the nearby Linwood car factory brought prosperity. Chrysler's closing of the Linwood factory in 1981 caused "economic and social disaster," according to Renfrew District's then Chief Librarian Joseph D. Hendry.[1]

That same year, having long noticed that teenagers were not attracted to its public libraries, the district conducted a survey which showed library use decreasing as teens grew older, especially among "non-academic" secondary school students. Even libraries with "teenage collections" had little effect, and those which drew teen interest through programming often alienated older patrons, who found boisterous adolescent presence in libraries a nuisance.

These results are old news to librarians everywhere who struggle to meet young adult needs. But what this one library district in Scotland did to counteract the situation is big news indeed. Faced with shockingly high youth unemployment, widespread truancy, and school suspensions due to youths' "real despair and bitterness, cynicism and apathy,"[2] they opened J.I.L.L., Johnstone Information and Leisure Library, in February 1984. As this article goes to press, J.I.L.L. celebrates its twelfth anniversary. When Gary Russell complains of "nae place to go," he is not talking about himself, but of those who have not discovered this library dedicated strictly to teenagers.

"J.I.L.L. has changed the way I think," Gary confesses on a bright September morning while relaxing at one of J.I.L.L.'s small round tables. When I ask how, Gary's enthusiasm sparks a torrent of impenetrable lists of activities he enjoys at J.I.L.L. Reminding Gary of my slow American ear, we rewind and translate more carefully. Without J.I.L.L., admits Gary, he might be among the crowds of young people out in the streets taking drugs, drinking, sniffing glue, and fighting. "There should be more teenage libraries like J.I.L.L.," he declares, winding up again. "They should be in all the places where trouble happens. People would feel better if they could be in the library socializing, meeting new people, and getting educated instead of arrested."

Gary is a student at Reidkerr College, in a course training him for work in a daycare center. He spends much of his leisure time at J.I.L.L. What kind of library could change the way a sixteen-year-old boy thinks?

A Tour of J.I.L.L.

Many of J.I.L.L.'s twelve hundred registered members, aged twelve to twenty-five, have never used a library before. They come from all over Renfrewshire, often traveling miles to this unremarkable white building trimmed with red brick on Collier Street. This revitalized 1935 branch library is just thirty yards from Johnstone's town center, and a mere three-minute walk from the "regular" public library branch, the second largest among twenty-four Renfrew District libraries. J.I.L.L. is a branch just like, and unlike, any other.

Unsuspecting youth with preconceptions about quiet libraries do double takes when entering J.I.L.L. Stereo loudspeakers reverberate non-stop with popular music of listeners' choice. "Down in Collier Street, silence is banned," promises J.I.L.L.'s manager Christine Storie, in an article for a local high school newspaper.

On one side of this spacious high-ceilinged room lined with bright movie and music posters, the top twenty single song hits are prominently displayed for checkout, their covers decking the walls. Banks of compact discs and audio tapes beckon, their covers facing out. Three huge shelves of computer games—35 percent of J.I.L.L.'s entire stock—fit three different types of computers, including Gary's favorite Genesis, Omega, and games for the Sega master system games consul, which can be reserved for half-hour sessions. A high wall-mounted VCR plays videos for the whole room. Computer games circulate, while videos do not. Because J.I.L.L.'s audiovisual fund is twice the size of its book budget—attempts are underway to increase and separate the computer budget—the array of nearly four thousand media items is what a newcomer notices first. But there is much more to grab one's attention.

On either side of the front door are large bulletin boards labeled "What's On" and "Information and Advice," crammed with local events and resources from nature reserves to poetry competitions and alcohol advice centers. A door-sized poster appeals for submissions to J.I.L.L.'s own magazine. Additional community resources are available online on Strathclyde Regional Council's Viewdata Service, listing job vacancies, health and welfare information, educational opportunities, organizations, recreational facilities, and a way to leave messages for local councilors. As of late 1995, the Internet had not yet arrived at J.I.L.L., though its surf is expected to crash on its computer-savvy shores soon.

At least thirty popular magazine titles on pop music, fashion, computers, film, and cars are displayed face out, mixed among books arranged by subject on burgundy shelves. Yes, J.I.L.L. does have books, over three thousand of them, 90 percent in paperback. But in revolutionary user-friendly style, J.I.L.L. abandons the sacred Dewey classification system for its own broad subject categories. Shelves are labeled as humor, graphic novels, comics, space and fantasy, spinechillers, lucky dips, romance, hobbies, pop and rock, sport, and show biz. Spine stickers sport pictorial symbols for each category—rockets for space, skeletons for spinechillers. But horrors! There are no call numbers, no alphabetical order, and fiction shamelessly rubs shoulders with nonfiction. Adult and junior novels sit side by side, with nontraditional items such as fanzines and annuals intermingling.

"This deliberate policy," asserts librarian Christine Storie, "attempts to lure in the reluctant reader and saves them the effort of wading through acres of shelves of books. Flexibility is an important issue both in the kinds of stock we buy and in the way it is promoted and displayed." Bookstore-style merchandising is everywhere apparent; face-out covers "sell" both books and media, and are arranged to accommodate the way young adults spontaneously browse.

An ever-changing display case previews forthcoming purchases which can be reserved ahead. During my September 1995 visit, an unauthorized Michael Jackson biography was advertised, along with

Michael Crichton's *Congo*, the latest R.L. Stine, *Sweet Valley High*, cassettes, and CDs. "Currency is our watchword," declares Storie, who purchases materials "almost weekly to keep the stock bang up-to-date." Great effort is devoted to processing new acquisitions quickly while still in demand. Storie reports hot items as YA novels by British author Pete Johnson, Christopher Pike, and various horror series, football (soccer) bios, computer magazines, Star Trek and Star Wars books, new biographies of Blur and Oasis (two bands vying for the top), and heavy metal, rave, and dance scene music. Graphic novels and comics have been enormously popular forever, Gary's favorite superheroes being X-man, Batman, and Spiderman.

Instead of issuing library cards, J.I.L.L. uses the British method of registering "members," ages twelve up, who sign forms after showing name and address identification. Then they are given ten tickets, six for books and four for audiovisual materials, which they exchange for items to be borrowed for a month, including computer games, the heaviest issues (circulators). There is no upper cut-off age for patrons; J.I.L.L. welcomes "anyone who can stand the noise."

A "token" reference section in an alcove contains books and vertical file boxes on topics for personal information rather than school research (which can be done down the street at the other library). A key to identifying trees, budget travel guides, books on social skills and drugs share space with atlases, *The Guinness Book of World Records*, and pamphlets on education, housing, transport, women's issues, and money. A small traditional card catalog lists this nontraditional collection in drawers labeled for various media, from sheet music to CDs, with computer game types organized as Amiga, Sega, and Megadrive.

Upon request, board games from Pictionary to Monopoly to Star Trek, as well as role-playing games, are retrieved from a huge pile in the staff office, to be played in the library in any of the comfortable lounge areas. The Tuck Shop (snack bar to us) has a soft drink machine, crisps (potato chips) and sweets (candy) for avid consumption right there in the library. The informal social ambiance inspired by snacking, playing games, listening to music, or watching videos together is the key element in what makes J.I.L.L. work. Members come because they are comfortable and accepted there. "Teenagers want a place of their own," says Storie, "a place where noise is the norm and behavior that might be

Potpourri of YA Programs

unacceptable elsewhere can be tolerated."

Echoing Storie, Gary reveals what he likes best about J.I.L.L.: "good music makes the atmosphere warm and inviting, keeps people coming back to meet friends and have a chat. It's a place to stay. After school's out, J.I.L.L. is jam-packed. Hanging out here, it's like a happy family. Nobody's left out, and everybody's welcome."

Gary appreciates how the friendly, open attitudes of the three full-time staff members create the climate he likes at J.I.L.L. As Young People's Services Librarian, Christine Storie oversees Madge Scott, Senior Library Assistant, and Norah Cassidy, Library Assistant. Having moved from the children's department in Renfrew District's library headquarters to setting up a teenage area in another branch, Storie was pleased to come to J.I.L.L. four years ago. "It suits my personality to work with young people," she says. "It's great fun." In a 1992 report on J.I.L.L., Storie wrote: "Probably the single biggest reason for the continued success of the project is the quality of its staff. They need to have a particular temperament, commitment, attitude, and tolerance level. The job requires a lot of one-to-one consultation with young people, which is labor intensive and makes great demands on the staff's abilities. Such commitment has its rewards, however, and watching troubled adolescents develop and improve their skills and confidence is just one of them."

The staff's effectiveness is evident in the camaraderie shared with young patrons. During my visit, Madge Scott shared her lunch hour with several young men watching the MTV Awards she had videotaped the night before. Her companions seemed unmoved when Hootie and the Blowfish won, confessing to me that they had never heard of the band. With so many American authors, artists, and products crowding J.I.L.L., I needed the reminder that Scots' youth have their own culture, and their favorite music often varies from ours.

Because J.I.L.L.'s young patrons feel a sense of ownership, they usually police their own behavior. They know the staff accepts noise levels, crude language, and horseplay that would not be tolerated elsewhere, and they also know the limits. The Sega computer system can be turned off. Troublemakers can be asked to leave. Storie notices peer pressure being used to resolve conflicts, usually before staff has time to intervene. Even overdues are handled by youth themselves, who urge friends to return items they want: "If you've got it, I cannae have it." Vandalism and damage to library equipment is negligible because its users take care of valued property which belongs, they feel, to them. They clean up their own food spills, monitor their own computer time. The rewards of cultivating this sense of ownership among youth are proven by statistics: J.I.L.L.'s stock loss rate is lower than that of other district libraries.

How Did J.I.L.L. Happen?

After the Renfrew Library District analyzed the results of its 1981 survey of teen library use taken during the bleak atmosphere of Johnstone's economic decline, they applied jointly with the Strathclyde Region's Social Work and Community Education Departments for a grant from the Scottish Office in Edinburgh. Provoked by the whopping 82 percent youth unemployment rate (which left out sixteen-year-old school-leavers not yet eligible for benefits), in 1984 the Urban Aid Programme funded 75 percent of a range of new education and social services including an experimental teenage library. The local authority supplied the other 25 percent of funding for the first three years. J.I.L.L.'s portion of the grant totaled about 26,000 U.S. dollars.

When the teenage library opened in a twenty by thirty-foot classroom in an old school building, its founder, district Chief Librarian Joe Hendry, and its first librarian Monica McBride, had no blueprint to follow. Hendry's concept, expressed in his official opening remarks, was unique: "to give working-class kids—who have left school and who may never work—the chance to listen to their music, read their kinds of books. And in the long term, to think, to ask questions and to get the information they need for their lives, and on their terms."[3]

Targeting sixteen-to-nineteen-year-olds, J.I.L.L. succeeded beyond anyone's wildest dreams. Within six months of opening, the small room was bursting at the seams with enthusiastic regulars like Frankie Stevenson, who called the library magic. "It's far better coming here to read or play games than just hanging around with nowhere to go and nothing to do. I've become a really keen reader by coming here."[4] Another success story was Eddie, inspired by music workshops at J.I.L.L. to forsake a career in shoplifting to start his own band, eventually attending college after failing in high school.

Overgrown J.I.L.L. moved to its current location in March 1985, just one year after opening. Six months later, J.I.L.L. boasted nearly 6,500 registered members, circulating 5,000 items monthly. It also offered an impressive array of programs from breakdance and computer clubs to welfare rights clinics, creative writing classes, and talent competitions. Field trips went to plays, camps, and leisure centers to broaden members' outlooks. Facilities for teens' own rock band practice were used even when the rest of J.I.L.L. was closed.

Showing a video about the library made by its young users at a library conference in 1985, J.I.L.L.'s librarian Monica McBride gave an impassioned speech in support of what we recognize as youth participation: "It is not enough to organize things for teenagers to do. You have to motivate and interest them too—get the ideas from them. We don't believe in spoon-feeding them. We take them so far down the road and then get them to think for themselves. The staff are there to give them the back-up and support that is necessary. . . . we get much more of a response if the idea has come from them originally."

In November 1985, J.I.L.L. received the Library Association's prestigious Robinson Medal, for "the most imaginative innovation in British Librarianship," which helped spread news of its success, attracting international visits from as far away as New Zealand. In 1987, when the national grant expired, Renfrew District Council took over J.I.L.L.'s entire funding, treating it as a full-fledged library branch in this district with the most patrons in all of Scotland.

J.I.L.L. Today and Tomorrow

J.I.L.L. continues to flourish, though not so headily as in its early days. Factory closings halved Johnstone's population, so J.I.L.L.'s circulation and membership reflects this decrease, though book circulation, separate from media, increased a dramatic 33 percent between 1993 and 1995. Its target audience has changed from original ages sixteen to nineteen, to the broader range of twelve up. Unemployed youth are still a visible portion of J.I.L.L.'s 60 male and 40 percent female users.

Storie's mission continues to be "to provide comprehensive library service for all teens in Renfrew District." She sees her newest challenge as convincing the local council to expand hours (and therefore staffing) so the library is open on evenings and weekends when most needed. Currently open weekdays, J.I.L.L. stays open only two nights a week until eight o'clock. Though no longer sharing a government grant, J.I.L.L. continues to participate in a local interagency youth group, with representatives from careers, education, social work, and health departments who coordinate youth services in the Johnstone area.

In February 1995, J.I.L.L. launched a "roadshow" promoting its materials and services, an exhibit which traveled among schools and sport centers (recreation centers) over several months. Storie personally addressed all second-year pupils, aged thirteen and fourteen, when teachers brought classes to hear her in the school libraries of surrounding towns.

At the core of J.I.L.L.'s service is the Users' Committee, six library users elected by J.I.L.L. members to serve with two staff members for a year's term. Like Young Adult Advisory Boards in American libraries, they consult staff as to youth preferences in activities and stock, plan and run programs, and raise issues of policy or discipline.

The Users' Committee has revived an older J.I.L.L. magazine *Chat 'n' That* through various incarnations *Power Blast* and *Super Power* to the current effort, *Spill the Beanz*, containing "moans," poems, reviews, stories, essays, jokes, quizzes, personal messages, cartoons, even an "agony aunt" advice column if contributors respond. Recent issues gave music and computer game reviews much more weight than books. That perennial teen pastime of spoofing or faking news events a la *Saturday Night Live* appears in items such as *Reincarnation Riot at Teenage Library* in the July 1995 issue, reporting that during the Queen Mother's visit to J.I.L.L., "she went looney tunes." Proclaiming herself the reincarnation of both Elvis and Cleopatra, she sang *"Return to Sender* wearing only an asp and a pair of blue suede shoes."

Through fundraising efforts such as raffles, car washes, scavenger hunts, and drink can recycling, the Users' Committee donates to charities chosen by vote among J.I.L.L. membership, sending sixty pounds to Oxfam's Rwanda appeal in 1994, and more recently, a hundred pounds to a hospice. They also run the Tuck Shop.

The Committee suggests stock purchases, and actually goes to the comics shop to pick thirty titles each, which circulate much better than those selected by staff. "They're the experts," acknowledges Storie. Committee member Gary Russell enjoys his senior status over younger thirteen- and fourteen-year-olds. "They always run their ideas by me first," he claims proudly. "They all look up to me. They're learning from you," perfectly demonstrating my own cherished principle of combining senior and junior high YAAB members.

The Users' Committee sponsors many activities, events, and separate groups such as Gary's favorite, the Dungeoneers Club, which meets regularly for role-playing games including Dungeons and Dragons, Advanced Hero Quest, and Dark Worlds. Gary and his brother Ian are pictured with Spiderman at another J.I.L.L. event, a visit from A-1 Comics Shop staff, who brought life-sized superhero figures and loads of comic books for sale. Comics were awarded as prizes to superhero quiz whizzes. The Committee has also sponsored a Megadrive computer tournament, T-shirt painting, and a week-long Star Trek extravaganza featuring Trekkie collectors' items and a visit from Klingons. To support such activities, J.I.L.L. owns both a still and video camera, camping gear, musical instruments, a sewing machine, and a karaoke machine.

One of Britain's most popular young adult novelists, Pete Johnson, included J.I.L.L. on his March 1995 publicity tour, autographing many of his eleven realistic and humorous titles which accurately reflect the lives of his young fans. For each of his novels, from his first *Secrets from the School Underground* to *Ten Hours to Live*, his most recent story of first love from a male viewpoint, former English teacher Johnson consults his own teen panel of manuscript readers, keeping a waiting list of many who send letters asking to join. Johnson is also popular in Germany, noting during a visit there that "there is nothing uncool about going to the library on a Saturday night—and the young people get all dressed up as if they were going to paint the town red. It was quite a revelation."[5]

Will Pete Johnson hit the American YA market? I am unable to judge. Having never heard of Johnson until seeing J.I.L.L.'s display, I was disgruntled by not finding a single one of his original paperbacks, published by the Mammoth imprint of Reed Children's Books, in any of five bookstores scoured in the three Scottish cities of Stirling, Edinburgh, and St. Andrews. Instead, teen horror series hogged young adult shelf space, as they do in too many bookstores here. Librarians on both sides of the ocean know that horror is not the only reading teenagers do.

Unfortunately, one of our worst American plagues has infected the very town which boasts such enlightened young adult library service. Scotland has had little need for policies to cope with rare book censorship, until 1992 when a single Johnstone High School board member succeeded in removing all post-1970 adult novels from the school library, due to what he deemed offensive sexual references in a few titles such as Alice Walker's *The Color Purple*. My study of a dozen contradictory newspaper reports of the situation from all over the U.K. failed to reveal the final outcome. Since Britain has no written constitution, and since its politics and education are more intimately entwined than ours, it is difficult to judge such a case from an American standpoint, without further research. Yet Christine Storie's outrage when she told me about this "appalling" book banning incident was identical to mine.

How Can J.I.L.L. Inspire Us?

Finding a fellow YA librarian soul in Scotland, who faces the same problems we do, with a similar youth participation philosophy which results in unique solutions, makes me more convinced than ever of the necessity for increased communication among librarians who serve young adults, including young adults themselves. The "American Day" J.I.L.L. celebrated for the Fourth of July, 1990, featuring our burgers, comics, music, and football, proves Scottish teenagers receptive to their American counterparts. Some of my Colorado YAAB members have been happily penpalling with members of J.I.L.L.'s Users' Committee, and that's a start.

What most perturbed me, in my delightful discovery of J.I.L.L., was how few British libraries have followed its example. Storie knows of two others in Scotland, the Yoker Youth Library in Glasgow, and the Petersburn Library/Youth Drop-in Project; and only one in England, the Exchange in Bradford, West Yorkshire. (In a 1982 research project, I found two more English teenage libraries in Walsall, West Midlands, and Lincoln, Lincolnshire, which are unfamiliar to Storie and may no longer exist.)

With Bradford's Exchange librarian Chris Binns, Christine Storie appeared in a 1994 debate sponsored by the Youth Libraries Group of Britain's Library Association (the equivalent of ALA's ALSC and YALSA combined), during a weekend conference "Sex, Violence, and Heavy Metal: Teenagers and Libraries." The two intrepid young adult librarians opposed the proposal "This house believes separate provision for teenagers is out-of-date and patronizing," against two speakers supporting it, one a chief librarian. When Storie read the motion, she was "so incensed" she determined to brave "the horrors of British Rail to Wales" to defend J.I.L.L.'s philosophy.

"Who won the debate?" I asked.

"We did, of course," said Storie triumphantly. The principles of their generalist opponents were no match for the passions of young adult librarians. "I got mad and banged my shoe," said Storie, a gleam in her eye as she recalled her moment of glory. It was only a moment, for though her conviction and impressive experience seemed to convince the audience attending the debate, no new teenage libraries have yet appeared.

I would like to begin a column in *VOYA* that can become a forum for exchanging ideas about serving young adults in libraries, among both librarians and youth. How do you react to this description of J.I.L.L.? Has it sparked you to jot down a list of questions, changes, things to try in your own library? Here are some of the issues I have been pondering since visiting J.I.L.L.

How can I use YA library space differently?

Can I possibly find a separate enclosed room or facility for young adults?

Could a teenage library be its own library branch in my community?

How exactly could I advocate for a separate library service for teens, as opposed to integrating them within the rest of the library? How do I see the opposing view?

What if all the old rules of discipline and quiet in the library were changed?

Would young adults really self-police their behavior and respect library property if we made it feel like theirs? Could we actually circulate computer games?

What if librarians said yes to teenagers more often than they said no?

How could my library network more effectively work with other youth-serving agencies, for cooperative funding and expanded, integrated community youth services?

Are there any libraries like J.I.L.L. for teenagers in the United States and Canada?

When I returned from Scotland, I excitedly showed my photos of J.I.L.L. to my library director. We have been puzzling over what to do to increase usage of our Young Adult Hideout, next to Adult Fiction. Young adults hanging out in the Hideout are often accosted by enraged adult patrons who insist on quiet, even when teens are merely speaking at normal voice levels. Needless to say, such adult intervention is a real turn-off to teens using the space we provide.

As my director shuffled through the photos, she did not hesitate. "We could do this here in Boulder," she stated. "If other agencies would cooperate, we could move the Hideout and treat it as another branch. Hasn't the Youth Opportunities Advisory Board been talking about opening a teen center? We could get in on it."

Great minds think alike. I am already discussing the teen center with three other community groups. I will keep you posted. Thank you, J.I.L.L.

Notes

1. J.D. Hendry, "J.I.L.L.'s Pure Brill'—Johnstone Information and Leisure Library: the Development of a Project," *Library Association Record*, February 1986, 78.

2. Ibid.

3. Ibid, 79.

4. Hugh Dougherty, "The Kids are Reading," *The Times Educational Supplement*, 1984 [month unavailable].

5. Jennifer Cunningham, "Words of Wisdom for that Difficult Age," *The Herald*, May 2, 1995. [April 1996]

Romancing the Young Teen
Mary Maggio

When I was hired as a children's librarian at the Mastics-Moriches-Shirley Community Library in Shirley, New York, I knew very little about this part of Long Island, and even less about this particular community. Just as I knew little about my new surroundings, I also knew next to nothing about young teens. Now I am hooked on them. Yes, that age group that terrifies some, disgusts others and drives almost everyone else crazy. How did I get so involved? All I can remember is that one day I traded my job of keeping the vertical file up-to-date for the job of Young Teen programming. In retrospect I must admit that I questioned my decision many times during my first year with them and at times I still question my sanity, particularly after a time-consuming project or program. However, now I wouldn't trade them for anything and I almost always find them to be a delight and constant source of inspiration.

What is a Young Teen? He or she is a student in sixth, seventh or eighth grade, who is too mature to fit nicely into the traditional public library's Children's Department. In this library they are still very much a part of the Children's and Parents' Services Department, but we have added additional materials, sources, services and programs that are specifically designated and designed for them. Of course, they are still welcome to participate and use any and all of the resources found in the Children's and Parents' Services Department.

In 1987 Kathleen Deerr, my Department Head, decided that this age group should be targeted for service. It had come to her attention that they were not coming into the library for programs or materials. That was when the Young Teen Advisory Board (YTAB) was born. It started as a small group of young teens who met once a month in the library to plan programs that kids their age would come to. They also provided input on the purchase of materials such as audio cassettes, CDs and videos that would appeal to the young teen audience. They started having some dances that were not very successful. Kids brought their own cassettes and approximately thirty to forty young teens attended each one. Cassettes were getting stolen, the "cool" kids hated the dances and attendance was poor. Another major problem was that there wasn't one specific librarian who was committed enough to this age group to really get things off the ground. We all had plenty of other work to keep us busy and we weren't used to making young teens a priority.

Although the dances were not the success we had hoped, the YTAB sponsored several talent shows that were very popular. These shows were open to anyone in sixth, seventh, and eighth grade, and they demonstrated all kinds of talent from magic acts to dancing to lip synching. The YTAB came up with judging criteria, and local celebrities performed those duties. There were fifteen to twenty contestants for each show and their parents and friends loved watching them perform. From 1987 to 1989, the YTAB concentrated on the programs mentioned above and on expanding their membership.

In 1989, the YTAB was the responsibility of one librarian, Berna Eich, who would oversee their meetings and activities. She discovered that one of the adult reference librarians was also a disc jockey. Dawn Triche generously consented to DJ the next Young Teen dance for a very nominal fee. The YTAB publicized that the next dance would feature a "live DJ" and this greatly increased the popularity of the dance. Over 100 tickets were given out and about seventy-five kids attended the dance. The young teens who were at the dance were ecstatic about the DJ and we hoped that word of mouth would increase our numbers even more the next time. That summer, we expanded our Young Teen Programming to include a book discussion and lunch program called "Brown Book It." Berna Eich was the moderator and found it frustrating. The kids kept coming back, but they weren't very interested in discussing books. We decided that they were interested in the free food. This was a useful discovery, since we know that teens enjoy themselves more if they are eating! That September, Berna accepted a job as a school librarian, and the rest, as they say is history. I made my fateful switch, and became the proud, if tentative, librarian in charge of Young Teen programming. My predecessors had made a good start, but I wanted to show the staff, patrons and the young teens themselves that this group would respond if given the opportunity to express their needs and wants to someone who would listen to them, advocate for them, and then help them turn their ideas into viable library programs.

My first challenge was to get the monthly YTAB meetings under control. I observed that the students who were coming each month wanted more of a "club" atmosphere than a serious meeting where ideas and concerns would be addressed and solved. There had always been food served at the meetings but that became disastrous as more and more teens attended the meetings. By the time I took over kids were throwing food at each other during the meetings, spilling soda and not cleaning up after themselves, which, of course, led to total chaos. I felt that emphasizing size for the YTAB itself was a mistake. This group started as a small planning board and had grown into a large group of disruptive individuals who were looking to come to a social hour once a month. My first big decision for change was to eliminate food at the meetings. This worked very well. I was left with a small group of concerned teens who really wanted to plan programs for the library, which was our original intent. We also stopped having meetings every month. I found that it was not necessary, so we only met when there was specific planning to be done. Some of the kids still wanted to meet once a month, but I wanted to hold firm on this at least for a while.

Young teens tend to be very grandiose in their ideas, so one challenge I've had to face is having to scale down their plans, so they are workable. Yet I don't want them to think I am copping out on them. During the 1990-91 year we were looking to add another Young Teen program. I called a YTAB meeting, and listened to ideas for awhile, some of which included a beauty pageant and a trip to New York City, and some others I don't remember. None of them were feasible and I was trying to let them down easy, when one of my eighth grade boys said, "how about a game show?" Now, I know a good idea when I hear one so I immediately starting promoting this idea to them. The more we talked, the more we all liked the idea and we even decided to invite WBLI, a local radio station to attend, and we would ask Berna Eich, the former Young Teen librarian, to be the MC. So there it was, a program that was grandiose and scaled down at the same time.

We decided that "Win, Lose or Draw" would be a good choice for a game show, since it required relatively few props, and we could use book titles for drawing choices. The radio station was very cooperative and said they would bring small prizes for everyone as well as some T-shirts and CD's. They were also willing to send one of their morning disc jockeys. This was going to be our biggest program so far and I was hoping to attract at least 100 young teens. I felt that getting that many kids to attend something that was not a dance would be a great accomplishment for the Young Teen Advisory Board. I called a meeting to discuss the logistics, and it was decided that we would give out tickets to all those who were interested in being on the drawing teams. The audience would consist of the people who just wanted to watch and kids who were waiting for their turn to draw. Teams would be chosen by the luck of the draw. Fliers were made up and distributed to the schools where, hopefully, they were handed out in the homerooms. This is an effective method of publicity, and I still believe it is the best way to get the word out to the majority of kids. Everyone at the library and the YTAB was very excited about "Win, Lose or Draw" and it really lived up to our expectation. The people from the radio station were great, the kids who participated and the kids in the audience had a wonderful time and we had an attendance of over 150 young teens. I, of course, was ecstatic and felt that I and the YTAB had proven that you can get that age kid into the library, if you plan the right programs and have enough publicity.

Because of this success, I was ready to forge ahead and do lots of Young Teen programming. Unfortunately, this age group is not very popular and it is only after several years of my advocating for them that I can get other librarians to see their merits. Anyway, back then, there was very little history of young teens being reliable about attending programs, and we weren't used to spending program money on this age group. So I concentrated on getting the attendance up at the dances and nurturing the YTAB. At the dances we started serving pizza, which was donated by our local Domino's Pizza, and giving out candy and cassettes as raffle prizes. During the dances I would talk to the kids I never saw in the library at other times to see what their likes and dislikes were. I discovered that even the toughest looking kid loved to share his or her opinion and little by little I started to see some of these kids in the library at other times. It was decided that we would have two dances a year, one in December and one in June, to celebrate the end of the school year and the beginning of summer programming.

In addition to dances we were starting to have more and more

Potpourri of YA Programs

successful programs. Teens in the community now knew that the library was a place they wanted to be and that they could go in and talk to Mrs. Maggio if they had any ideas for programs or materials. I knew we were reaching them the summer the Young Teen programs filled up faster than the preschool programs! Our Young Teen reading program has gone from about seventy registrants per summer to well over 200 completing the program. Each summer we have a different theme but we do something special halfway through the summer to remind them that they are supposed to be reading and to get them into the library. One of the more popular midsummer programs was a "Lost in Time" party. We borrowed costumes from a local theater group, had the kids dress up, then we took "professional" pictures of them which we put in cardboard frames and let them keep. The teens had a great time trying on all the clothes and hamming it up for the camera. Of course, food was served as well. That summer the reading club was a huge success, and we had more young teens finish than we ever had.

This library is very fortunate to be enthusiastically supported by our community. Because of overwhelming support, we have moved into a beautiful, newly expanded and renovated library. The Children's and Parents' Services Department is in the extension and it has been designed to accommodate every age group. Because of the rise in attendance at Young Teen programs and the obvious need for services to this age group, we were able to successfully lobby for a space in the room just for young teens. It is far away from the early childhood room, and it has been designed for and by young teens. On a snowy Saturday eighteen young teens met with my department head and me at the library to discuss decorating and furnishing the room. They decided to call it "The Place—for Young Teens."

"The Place" consists of a large open area with an alcove off to one side. A quiet study room is next to the alcove and there is a bank of computers outside the quiet study room just for use by young teens. The teens decided to decorate their space with a black wall in the alcove highlighted by neon-painted footprints traveling up that wall. Opposite the black wall there is a mirrored wall with a cabinet along the length of it. The cabinet houses CDs and cassettes, CD and cassette players, headphones, video monitor, VHS tapes, and software and CD-ROMS for the computers. The open area of "The Place" has a tackable surface on one long wall for posters, announcements and displays, a futon for comfortable seating, several coffee tables for magazines and six video chairs which can be moved between the two areas as needed. Sounds great doesn't it? They requested neon lights which I thought would be no problem until we looked into the cost. We felt, however, that it was important to go to bat for the kids about the lights to prove to them that we are on their side, and as a way to truly define "The Place." My department head went to the board of trustees and made a wonderful case for the neon lights based on our success with this age group and the need to keep them coming into the library. As I am writing this, neon lights are shining over "The Place" as a welcome to all sixth, seventh, and eighth graders who come into the library. "The Place" is designed to look like a mall. The paperbacks are on metal shelves similar to those found in clothing stores that cater to this age group, and as I add the finishing touches I always try to remember how important marketing is.

The new Children's and Parents' Services Department has been open since early July. I am happy to report that after school and on weekends there are always young teens in "The Place." They are on the floor, lounging on the futons or doing homework in groups. In an effort to continue marketing "The Place" articles continue to appear in our newsletter and we invite young teens to come in and check it out. We asked the teens what they wanted and we gave it to them. Now it is up to them to take advantage of it and to communicate to me any additional wants or needs that they have.

"The Place" is important to our young teens in so many ways. It shows them that their community and their library care about their needs enough to design a space they can call their own. It also shows them that the library staff and trustees listen to them. I have every confidence that "The Place" will serve the young teens well and that they will treat the equipment and materials there with respect. I am not worried about vandalism or graffiti. As I stated in the beginning of this article I am hooked on young teens, but more importantly I have faith in them. We listened, we showed them that they are important to this library and they are returning that sentiment by using our wonderful resources to their fullest. [February 1996]

"Are You Afraid to Die?" 7th Graders Confront AIDS

Arthur S. Meyers

The questions come without hesitation:
"What did your family say?"
"What did your friends say?"
"What did your coworkers say?"
And from group after group:
"Are you afraid to die?"

* * * * *

The 7th graders are on the carpeted floor of the community arts center. Sitting on a tall stool, 39-year-old HIV+ Curt begins with the facts. He lists the ways we can get AIDS. Knowing so much and yet so little, the kids are shocked to hear that a mother's milk is one way the virus is transmitted. They didn't know.

They are uneasy when Curt asks them to call out what they like to do and their plans after high school, once they have AIDS, and then listen to his responses:

"Read." Forget it, with a $2,000 monthly drug bill.

"Sing." You will be too depressed.

"Swim." How can you have the physical energy? Besides, nobody will want you to go into a public pool.

"Military." That's out.

"College." You will die before completing it.

"Car." Not only can't you afford the insurance and gas, you're losing the sense of feeling in your fingers and toes. You will no longer be able to drive.

"Teach." What parents will want you to be with their kids?

There is no second chance, Curt tells them, you are going to die. The 12–14-year-olds are very quiet.

* * * * *

Since 1994, centered around World AIDS Day on December 1, a collaboration of organizations and committed individuals have come together in northwest Indiana in a project for life. The goal is to raise the awareness of 7th grade students on the human face of the AIDS crisis. The focus is to learn the facts and human dimensions of HIV and AIDS directly and to view panels from the AIDS quilt.

Curt has been a marvelous teacher in the process. He is articulate, passionate, and knowledgeable. He talks about the "blood brothers" ritual, in which kids share blood cuts to show their loyalty. He lists the facts: 8,000 new cases in Indiana, 80% of whom are 13–19 years old, 1,000 reported cases in Northwest Indiana, with 250 persons already dead. He tells them the actual rates are much higher as many people go into Chicago, which adjoins Hammond.

Young women are the highest sources of new transmissions. "Young ladies," he pleads, "I'm not saying it's fair but you have to protect yourself. HIV takes a piece of you at a time, it robs you. You lose everything that's important to you."

He asks two students to stand. Through role-playing, he shows that a single sexual encounter is at risk from previous partners, and partners further back, who did not know they were affected. Fairly quickly, still role-playing, twenty students are standing in the group of 75. The risks of being sexually active are stark.

For Curt, too late for him, abstinence is the best choice. "I was not responsible. If you think it can't happen to you, I'm living proof that it can."

After the discussion with Curt and a video on the NAMES Project AIDS Memorial Quilt, the classes are divided into small groups. Adult volunteers walk with them around the art gallery, talking about the Indiana panels on display, viewing other exhibits in the gallery, and looking at a special display, "A Day without Art." The latter consists of black frames with the names of creative and well-known persons we have lost to the illness. The students also talk informally with Curt.

In 1995, building on our first program with Hammond 7th graders, we invited suburban and nearby Illinois school districts as we knew the information was needed by all kids. A committee representing Hammond and Lake County library systems, Hammond schools and PTA, local AIDS support groups, Arts Association, Hospice, health agencies, and

Potpourri of YA Programs

religious organizations planned the format, set the days and times for the school groups, and trained the volunteers. During the weeks before and after Thanksgiving, 1,600 students from ten districts arrived on school buses. Financial support came from individuals, organizations, businesses, and the school sytems. A vital part of the planning and implementation are individuals who know firsthand the human toll of AIDS.

For 1995, we also wanted to expand adult awareness and invited the Hammond PTA Council to hold its November meeting at the arts center. The school board president, superintendent, and other administrators came to the Parents' Night. Each adult that night and each teacher during the two weeks of programs was given a packet of PTA and Red Cross brochures, information on local AIDS services, and a list of books and videos in the Lake County and Hammond public libraries.

After each program, we gave the teachers evaluation forms. The written responses showed clearly the impact. One teacher described the prelearning activities of an information unit by the science teacher and banners and posters for the school hallway. Afterward, the students completed the unit. These students also made paper quilt squares on "Celebration of Our Lives" and held discussions. "Many of them felt that the demonstration of how AIDS is spread from sexual contact with only one HIV+ person was the most significant part of the program."

After the program, one group did worksheets, saw a video, and discussed the disease more thoroughly. "My students all responded favorably to the program. They thought the program was excellent." Still another teacher noted that the reading and science teachers were teaching units on AIDS before the program, including excerpts from Ryan White's book. Ryan was the Indiana teenager whose family was hounded out of their community. He was in the display, "A Day without Art." "The students were touched as well as informed by the program. Do not change a thing for World AIDS Day in 1996."

Curt's impact came through in the evaluations, as he related so well to the students and they responded to him. "I felt a speaker with HIV was extremely effective for 7th graders." One teacher wrote, "*Please* get all school systems involved." Another reported, "Many positive comments were made in later discussions and students remembered important facts." All of the evaluations showed 7th grade is the right age group. One teacher added, "Parents should be as informed."

For World AIDS Day in 1996, we displayed Quilt panels in the Lake County Public Library and Hammond Public Library. Educational programming with the 7th graders in Hammond included learning how to access information in the library's electronic sources and elsewhere in the collection.

We face many challenges in libraries and make decisions on our time and resources. We also know that kids make choices and they are scared to die. The AIDS crisis clarifies the decision-making for libraries. [February 1997]

The Wall of Shame
Nancy Moore

Sometimes in the dead of winter when summer seems an eternity away, teenagers, teachers, and librarians need something dynamic and invigorating to warm up those long "after the holiday" months. Last year Base Line Middle School was a part of a very warm adventure that spread throughout the district and state. My name is Nancy Moore. I have been the media specialist at Base Line in Boulder, Colorado, for over ten years. Before that, I taught third, fourth, and fifth grades and also taught college classes. For four years, I was a librarian at a large Denver high school. No matter which level of education I found myself in, February always seemed to be a time to look for new ideas. Last year particularly, Base Line was ready for innovative projects and programs. After forty years as a junior high school, the school board announced that we would become a middle school. Many of our teachers were therefore new, and over one third of the student population of 350 were now sixth graders. The parent/teacher advisory groups in the school district had written a goal that stated the schools would work very hard to provide multiethnic educational experiences for the students. Multicultural book lists just weren't going to do it. Even though booktalks are my great love and specialty, this time individual reading was just not enough. No teacher had time to read all the books on the lists. The lists just seemed too impersonal to them. Everybody was too busy revising curriculum.

I had heard about an exhibit at the University of Colorado's Norlin Library created by a historical librarian there named David Hays that was causing quite a stir. So one cold frozen afternoon, I trudged over to the university to see the exhibit for myself. University students were crowded around five or six display cases of cartoons, war posters, advertisements, and a few articles and headlines ranging back from the late 1800s up to the present. They pointed out, as nothing else could, how common stereotypes have been over the last hundred years. There were splashy sports pennants and baseball hats interspersed with cans of food covered with questionable logos to brighten up the entire display. Eye catchers turned out not to be needed though as the outrageous combined with the subtle to stop the students in their tracks. Various professors at the University had added their thoughts and explanations which had been neatly printed and placed at strategic places in the exhibit. As I watched the faces of the students studying the exhibit and listened to their comments, I excitedly began to envision reworking the exhibit to present to middle school students.

The University exhibit followed many ethnic groups through the last century. I decided to pick five of those groups which were represented in our school population. The majority of students at Base Line are from white middle-class families. We do have a group of about fifty of our 350 students who are members of a group we call STEP or Students To End Prejudice. Many of the students of color belong to that group. Looking at the makeup of STEP, I chose to focus on Black, Chicano/Chicana, Native American, Asian, and Jewish people.

Having decided that, I made an appointment with Dave Hays. He very graciously offered to copy material from his collection for me to keep and use as a base for a new exhibit. He believes strongly that such exhibits are a powerful educational tool. He also believed that it would be better for each exhibit to start from scratch. Each exhibit would then have ownership built in from the effort it takes to create each project. Don't despair. I will give you some clues soon on how to do just that after a little more explanation.

Remember when you were fourteen? A year was an eternity! A decade was a lifetime! One hundred years could only be described as ancient history along with Trojan horses. It was very important to me that the exhibit focus much more strongly on today than the university exhibit did. Today would hook middle schoolers. To look at the caps on their heads, the T-shirts on their chests, the movies on their videotape recorders, the cassettes and CDs attached to their ears would, I felt sure, be quite an experience for them. I had no idea then what an impact the exhibit would have and how right I was.

I began with Dave's exhibit divided into the five groups. I made placards with what I hoped were probing questions strategically placed. There is a paper called *Klanwatch* published by the Southern Poverty

Law Center that prints hate crimes committed the previous year. I cut some of those out and tacked them to the wall at random. The exhibit was called That Was Then This Is Now, but somehow in the time it was up, it came to be known as the Wall of Shame. On one long wall entering the library were materials from the past. As the students walked along that wall and turned into the library, they found themselves face to face with the This Is Now wall. This wall I think you will find the most interesting, because it took me almost a month to find all of the materials, and because this wall had students constantly glued to it. Everything on it was from the last year. This was my contribution to Dave's original exhibit. This exhibit would help the students question their world a little more. This wall was fun to build. Once I started looking for things that somebody said "hurt," those things were everywhere.

My first stop was the local video rental shop. I explained what I was doing to the manager of Video Station and asked him if he had a poster of *White Men Can't Jump* for a discussion of "positive stereotyping" that I could borrow. He immediately "jumped" into the project with two films I had never heard of but which had great posters. One was *Hangin' with the Homeboys* and another that starred Pat Morita and Jay Leno was called *Collision Course*. As the manager said, "Everything that comes from Hollywood is a stereotype." If he was right, it didn't matter if I knew the film or not. All we had to do was look at the posters and ask questions like "Who is the smartest?" "Would you like to spend time with these kids and why?" "Who is dumb but strong and emotional?" It turned out that the students had seen the films and said in amazement after the questioning, "That's just the way it was in the film!" I am very grateful to the manager of Video Station who let us keep the posters.

The next stop was the local record shop where that manager was just as supportive, and gave me some wonderful record covers. Next was the sporting goods store. No freebies here but they did, after some discussion, allow me to photograph the backs of jackets, sweatshirts, and caps. When I color copied those photographs at the corner copy shop, they made striking posters. The grocery store let me do the same thing with some labels. Cartoons and newspaper articles as well as ads jumped out at me. An old magazine called *Life* (not the *Life* magazine of today) is a treasure house of stereotyping. Posters and articles from World War II are also easy to get your hands on. *Doonesbury* featured a series of cartoons in July 1992 about Asian students and the belief that somehow they have an intellectual advantage over other students. Those worked well in the exhibit.

Of course there were examples of sports logos such as the Washington Redskins, Kansas City Chiefs, Fighting Irish, Florida State Seminoles, an article about a Colorado team called the Savages and how they wanted their mascot seen in a positive light. I asked the question of the students, "Is it possible to see the mascot savages in a positive light?" Then we played with inserting other groups' names to see how our new logo would sound. The Washington Whiteboys, the Kansas City Rabbis, or the Florida State Blacks just didn't have the same ring as the existing names. We thought about the Jeep Dakota or the Jeep Cherokee and substituted other names. There was a wonderful cartoon where a man is buying a bumper sticker that emphatically states that ethnic groups are not mascots, which he proudly puts on his Jeep Cherokee. We looked at food and drink labels. From singles ads to serious articles, ethnic groups were continual targets. There were covers of magazines, newspaper articles, flyers, and magazine articles with such subtitles as "He's witty, intelligent, creative, energetic, and slightly neurotic. Oh and he's Jewish!" that left the students with their mouths hanging open. There was a section of the exhibit at the end titled Whom Have We Left Out? One article there was on the top women newscasters in America and insisted that their "credibility is undermined by hair stiff enough to withstand a tornado." There were rap music articles and record covers, posters for All You Can Eat Taco Night with "great art work," comments about the Barbie who says that she hates math, Bill Cosby asking why blacks are always portrayed as fools on television, flesh colored Band-Aids, and a *Far Side* cartoon with two Indians looking at a head buried in the sand with the caption "Little Bear, you know a watched head is never eaten by ants."

All that had to be asked to collect things was the question "Does something bother you here?" Soon all of my library aides were bringing in things they found, and even their mothers and fathers joined in the search. It became a serious game that spread by word of mouth. Before long we had about sixty pieces which was enough to begin.

The This Was Then part of the exhibit had about one hundred pieces. To begin a discussion using it, there was really only one question that needed to be asked over and over, and that question was "Somebody said this hurt. Why do you suppose they said that?" I never answered the question "Why did you put that there?" but always changed it to the first question. The exhibit became one huge Socratic Seminar. In the month that it was up, there was always someone reading it or touching it.

To introduce the exhibit, I invited parents, teachers, and community members from each ethnic group portrayed to speak in the library. They read from books that had been important to them when they were twelve to fourteen years old. They talked about what it was like to be that age and from that ethnic group. Teachers signed up by classes to hear different speakers. Each hour for two days was different. Each personal story was moving.

The teacher response was overwhelming. Eighth grade history and language arts teachers assigned short stories from each ethnic group. Then they asked the students to respond to the stories with posters which they created. One poster that a student who does not do well with the written word made showed the Constitution with a huge teardrop over it. The art teacher had the students do copper etchings since she said many of the parts of the exhibit were visual. The images that the students came up with actually moved me to tears. We had a large art display of the 150 entries the following month. The eighth grade teachers also did an assignment tracing each student's ethnic background. The last part of this immigration assignment was to find the stereotypes that each group had faced. The seventh grade language arts teacher created an assignment on the lyrics of protest which had songs from the past and present. The students read about and saw the videotape of the Nazi/Skokie conflict and studied First Amendment rights. They were very aware of Martin Luther King marches and the simultaneous demonstrations of the Ku Klux Klan here in Denver. They wrote their thoughts and opinions and wrote some more. I realized as the more than 200 responses began piling up on my desk that there was going to have to be some recognition for their soul-searching. The principal offered $50 for the best response, $25 for the second, $15 for the third, and $10 for the fourth place responses. We only have 350 students in our school, and still the entries came pouring in. A team of teachers helped to choose the top four entries. It was very difficult, but we looked for those students whose opinions really seemed to have changed from beginning to end.

We could not compare the written entries to the visual ones however, and so a soul food dinner was prepared to pay for prizes for an art contest. It was so successful that there was money left over. We used it to bring a famous dance troupe started by a black dancer in Denver to the school.

When the sixth graders came with their classes, we just sat in front of the wall with them and talked and talked. The students drew pictures and wrote. In fact, one of the sixth grade boys wrote a poem that won an award. There is so much to tell you about this project that really took off and flew. If any of you would like to ask me questions about it, I would be happy to talk to you. If any of you would like one of the programs that gives copyright information on the pieces in the exhibit, I will send them to you if you send me two stamps. Now I would like the students to share with you some of their thoughts on the exhibit.

Eric Mitton—6th grade

The wall is about many things,
But all things are about racism.
Cold-hearted, cruel, racially injust things . . .
All on the wall
Even a doll's voice or a truck's name,
Even these can be offensive.
People don't like being put to shame,
So don't put them on the defensive.
You may not think it unjust,
but look at this wall!
From ads to comics to articles, it's all here,
On this paper-covered wall.
All of these things we're
Used to seeing as we walk along a hall.
However, now alert
to anything that is not right
It might be just one woman being called a "skirt,"
But still, who can call it right?
This question, I ask you,

As you look upon this wall
What is right and what is not, I ask you,
The answers are upon this wall.

Ian Armstrong—8th grade

A sheet of white is covering America
Covering every little pebble.
The white tries to melt away,
But more white falls.
Covering it in a sheet of white.
But now some pebbles
Pebbles of different shapes
Pebbles of different colors
Some pebbles,
Not all Pebbles,
But some pebbles are seen in the White.
And the White, again, tries to melt away.

Ethan Magee—7th grade

Ethan ends his paper with this paragraph:
But all this makes me think. Am I a little bit prejudiced even though I don't know it? Are there ever times that I look down on people because they are mentally ill, fat, or bad drivers? I don't know. But at least I think that no matter what skin color, religion, or beliefs, we are all created equal and that is how it should be, forever.

Justine Rice—7th grade

This was a great experience for me and I assume for the whole class. I learned a lot about how upsetting name calling can be. Hazel said to ask what people want to be called instead of naming them. I totally think that is right. I never realized how hurtful stereotyping is and how much of it there is in our society today. I thank Ms. Moore for this display.

I think that it is disgusting how people still in this day and age discriminate and stereotype people. I would think that people would look at what is inside people instead of what is different from themselves. How come we still have teams named after different races of people. How come there is a Ku Klux Klan that protests on Martin Luther King's birthday. Is it all right to call a different group of people stupid? Is it all right to hurt feelings intentionally? I don't think so. Our teachers taught us not to and we get punished if we do. How can grownups do what we are taught not to do? Why don't they get punished like they should?

Eric Nordwall—8th grade

[Eric] points out that he never wears a feather sticking up in his hair and that according to Warner Brothers cartoons, his people are so stupid that even a rabbit could outsmart them.

Ben Sukow—7th grade

Speaking of stereotypes, I thought that the library display's stuff was really really horrible. It was outrageous. In my opinion, the "That Was Then" board was by far the worst. It's pretty hard to imagine that this stuff was in Boulder within the last hundred years. One of the items was an ad for Gold Dust. It showed a picture of two black twins. Cleans pots and pans and their motto "Let the twins do the work." Another thing that was on the board was a comic. It had five or six bulldogs on it, each one had a name. The Hebrew dog had a long corn like nose. The Yankee dog had a big droopy slobbery mouth that reminded me of beer. The Irish dog was smoking a pipe and looked like a sailor. Even though I'm not one of these races, the thing that offended me the most was a *Time* magazine article that said how to tell a Japanese from a Chinese.

The This Is Now part of the display was a lot more subtle. You really had to think to see the racism. One example of what I just said is the movie *White Men Can't Jump*. The movie was a comedy but the title is still a racist remark. One thing was very obnoxious. It was the cover of a *Time* magazine "Teens and AIDS; Krista Blake had a basic white-bread American life until an older boy gave her HIV. She was 16!" Big Deal! Lots of heterosexual people have AIDS and this white bread #@**&# is really dumb. Big Deal!

Let's end with Brooke McCarthy—8th grade

Why is it necessary to use Native American Names for sports teams and cars? Why do people constantly degrade Native Americans by calling them all wild, scalping savages?

In Summary

These are questions that can only show the ignorance of our society. If the American culture can't get past its false beliefs, stereotypes, and ignorance then it will stay far behind where it could be as a culture and as a society.

The Wall of Shame is not finished. It will be a wonderful day when it is no longer needed, but for now there are no signs that it will be finished in the near future. As it travels throughout Colorado, it will be added to and expanded upon. It has been a tremendous lesson to me on how such a project will capture the minds and hearts of many people if allowed to do so. Such displays belong in media centers, and often we have ignored this powerful medium.

Our superintendent of schools, Dean Damon, began the project with his guidance to the community to explore multiethnic possibilities in education. David Yeager of the curriculum department of the Boulder Valley schools called evenings and threw himself into the project helping with legal questions. Jim Williams, the assistant superintendent of schools, made the physical possibilities of moving the exhibit a reality. Hazel Marable, a parent of students at Base Line, gave her energy and fire to the students and other parents as a leader in the Reading Against Racism opening. Teachers Sam Donelson, Tom Trujillo, Harriet Boonin, and Maureen Dolan as well as many others made it work at school. Local businesses were very pleased to be asked to help and participate. School board members came on their own to study the wall. The local newspaper followed its development and *The Denver Post* featured it on their front page which was one of the first times I remember education making it to the front page of a large city newspaper. Always, there was the quiet originator David Hays supporting and encouraging the use of a method that has been one of the most successful projects in Colorado. [February 1994]

Sleuths in the Stacks
Merry Beth Oliveto and Sharon Vincent

Good evening, I'm Inspector Oliveto. I have been assigned to investigate the kidnapping of Stretch Cunningham. You are suspect in this crime. You can prove your innocence only by helping to prove someone else's guilt. Please enter the crime scene, but do not touch any of the evidence.

This was the greeting given to twenty-four young adults as they entered the Farmington Community Library, Saturday night after hours. They came to participate in the Solve-A-Mystery Party. The participants solved the mystery of who kidnapped the star basketball player Stretch Cunningham by playing the roles of the suspects, visiting the scene of the crime, and by going on scavenger hunts in the library to earn additional clues to the mystery. The players were divided into seven groups. Each group represented one of the suspects in the crime. We found that three to four participants per mystery suspect is a workable number. The solving of the mystery was divided into three separate rounds. Each round began with a scavenger hunt to earn information needed to solve the crime. All members of the groups took turns in the role-playing of the suspects. The Solve-A-Mystery Party was a success with both the participants and their parents. Many expressed an interest in next year's mystery. We found the party relatively easy to plan and well worth the effort.

Development of the Mystery Script

We attended a workshop on planning mystery parties at the Michigan Library Association's Fall 1994 conference. The workshop was hosted by Sally Weber, Assistant Librarian, Chelsea High School. At the workshop, several librarians role-played characters in a reenactment of an actual mystery party. The solving of the mystery and the role-playing of characters was so enjoyable that we decided to host a similar party at the Farmington Community Library. What better way to get young people in the library!

We found that it was not necessary to compose our own script. With Shelly's permission, we used the script presented at the workshop and adapted it to our local setting. There are a variety of other sources that can be used for script ideas and we have listed those sources at the end of the article. All can be adapted to local personal needs. Using the names of your own library, streets, and schools makes the mystery seem more realistic to young people.

The mystery scripts should use characters that are larger than life and situations that everyone can identify with. For example, one character, Mike Megabucks, is a college basketball recruiter who is materialistic and egotistical. He will generally do anything for money. This type of character is easy for young adults to portray. In the first round, each character is described, and each team member is then encouraged to act out how they think the character's personality would be. The script is also essential in the establishment of motives for the crime and the participants use the motives to accuse other suspects of the crime.

Evidence and the Scene of the Crime

It is important to provide props that connect each suspect with the crime scene. For example, a memo with the address and time of the crime was left to incriminate Mike Megabucks. Each piece of evidence should be as realistic as possible—the memo we used had an actual University of Michigan letterhead. Go to you local police station and beg for some *real* police crime tape to section off the scene of the crime.

Caution: choose an area without other pieces of potential evidence! The crime solvers will notice *everything*. We used an area of the library that included the magazine rack and the paperback book section. One young man wondered if the curled down corner of a magazine's cover was significant to the crime. Another young man was asking about titles of paperbacks and how they could tie into the mystery. We definitely underestimated the observation skills of these young people. Many of the young adults did not want to leave the crime scene. They were fascinated with searching for clues.

Scavenger Hunts

Each round in the mystery solving was preceded by a scavenger hunt. The scavenger hunt involved a variety of tasks: searching for young adult fiction titles by using the computer, finding a book with a specific word in the title, and searching for a particular author. All of these scavenger hunts involved using the library in some way. All of the groups were having fun while learning to use the online catalog—what a painless way to teach library skills!

Promotion of the Mystery Party

We found that networking with school media specialists and promotion in person were the most effective means to publicize this event. Mention of the mystery party was made during the annual winter visit to all the area middle schools. Flyers were left for posting to announce the program. We also called the media specialists at a time closer to the event to remind them to make the announcements to the student body.

At our library branches, we promoted the party through posted fliers, a description in the program booklet of library events, and through word of mouth with our young adult patrons. We have found that young adults talking up an event is the best way to promote a program for this age group. One group of girls even planned this event as the entertainment for their slumber party.

In addition, we sent a press release to the local newspapers, radio, and television stations. These promotions resulted in twenty-seven young adults registering for the program. We scheduled this program as an activity during our local schools' winter break. This provided a fun activity for those students with no travel plans and kept participants to our desired workable number of twenty-four.

Ideas for Future Mystery Parties

Due to the success of this party, we anticipate a greater number will want to participate in 1996. This will involve using a different mystery script with a greater number of suspects. We also discussed having two separate mystery parties, one at each of our branches. We also would like to try to get the community more involved in our party by soliciting donations for food and prizes. This year we provided pizza for after the party, and a paperback mystery for each participant.

This program was a definite success! Not only did the young adults tell us how much they enjoyed it, but the parents made a special effort to thank us through phone calls and one-on-one compliments. The young people had fun sharpening their deductive reasoning skills, broadening their library knowledge, and went home with a new mystery to read and solve!

Mystery Script References

Books

Warner, Penny and Tom Warner. *A Deadly Game of Klew*. St. Martin's, 1986.
___. *Greetings from the Grave*. St. Martin's, 1986.
___. *Secrets of the Bitter Sweets*. St. Martin's, 1986.

Penny and Tom Warner can also be contacted for mystery scripts written specifically for libraries. The cost is approximately $150 for each script, but a sliding scale can be applied to your library's special needs. They can be reached at 710 Sinnet Court, Danville, CA 94526. Telephone: (510) 837-7089.

Games

Lombarde Marketing, Inc. has developed a series of mystery game kits titled *Murder a la carte: Host Your Own Mystery Party*. Call toll-free 1-800-874-6556 to contact them. [October 1995]

Programs with Boys and Girls Together
Frances Plesser

How do you get boys from eleven to fourteen years of age to participate in Young Adult programs? How do you prove that the moon is blue? It is just that hard to convince boys and girls to coexist happily in an ongoing program.

In October 1993 our small but Ready for Prime Time YA Department thought it might be fun to show a mystery movie made for young teens and shine up this short feature with clues that we jotted down as we previewed the film. Gotten from the Nassau Library System, link to member libraries, the movie was *Haunted Mansion Mystery*. The film was almost a clinker, but we managed to elicit ten good questions out of it. To add interest we scheduled the movie in the evening from 7:30 to 9 p.m.

June Steuer, my assistant, went to buy fifty detective hats and fifty Dick Tracy Pins. Now we could name it "The Detective Club"! After purchasing three prizes we announced that there were to be points given to the growing group of sleuths who attended the movie. We were in the detective business.

The next day we dragged out a small bulletin board and posted the full names of the participants along with the points they won. One important note—we took pictures of the players with hats and pins on; developed them quickly and then posted them on this busy bulletin board.

An interest in points and the other magic word "competition" has been the secret of the success of the Club. When the young detectives came to our desks we suggested that they could amass points by picking out hidden Waldo-like characters in a puzzle book we found in a dusty drawer. More points!

The summer arrived and we planned to use a large part of our yearly budget on leisure time activities related to our new baby. The date of August 11th, was chosen to air another movie called *The Murders* which was adapted from a paperback book of the same name.

We imitated ourselves and wrote more and harder clues. After asking the kids to wear their hats and badges (more pictures) they came to *The Dollhouse Murders* in large numbers. Some came for the first time because we made it worthwhile to win points in our competition. No conflict of interest.

Now that we were percolating, we announced a mystery writing contest. Here we set rigid ground rules. A murder must take place at a circus. Writers must use certain characters, i.e. Strong Man, Trapeze Artist, etc. Characters in the audience were Detective Sam Austen and his niece and nephew. The murder weapon could be a knife, sand bag, or poison. All participating writers would get fifteen points.

On August 25, 1994, the Department held an End-Of-Summer awards dinner. We asked Harriet Edwards, Assistant Library Director, to judge the contest and what a good judge she was. To the best murder mystery story she gave a small cash prize, and to all the writers we promised to bind their stories into a book and distribute this private printing to the fifteen writers, the East Meadow Public Library and the schools they attended. The detective with the most points during the preceding contest got a substantial prize. Everyone in the competition got certificates of participation. The YA staff knew we had a winning program.

To complete the circle, we got what we wanted. At least half the teens in the Club were boys. The ages ranged from ten to fifteen and for the first time, age wasn't of primary importance. The Detective Club is a great leveler.

The Young Adult Mystery Festival was our way of building further suspense and interest in our Detective Club. We picked a weekend in the fall of 1994, and on the first evening we taught the club members to make a cipher wheel. They exceeded our expectations by learning quickly and then dashing to the YA Department to solve the questions. Points for the winning team were given. On the next night we showed a 3-D classic called *Creature from the Black Lagoon*. The audience were given the 3-D glasses.

Last, we enlisted a group of theatre players who presented a Murder Mystery Theatre that included a crime scene and four live suspects. Our members threw themselves into the solution of the mystery and the winning team got more points.

Potpourri of YA Programs

Nothing could be sweeter than the pleading of parents asking for more programs! So far, we have invited a Nassau County detective to explain how a crimie is solved. We have showed two more movies with clues and points.

Now—if you read this whole article, award yourself fifty points and full permission to form your own Detective Club! [April 1995]

The Empire Summer Puzzler
Carol Shama and Lindsay Ruth

The New York State summer reading theme for 1992 was "New York Is Reading Country." Our challenge, as young adult librarians at two small upstate New York libraries, was to develop a program that would appeal to teens using this rather broad theme. A number of brainstorming sessions held over plates of Chinese food and bags of donuts, produced the Empire Summer Puzzler: a reading and trivia game. For every book read, program participants would be given a clue having to do with a person, place, event, or "thing" in New York State, and they would be challenged to outsmart the Puzzler by answering the clues. Some sample puzzlers included:

> My short stories set in the Hudson Valley may make you "sleepy." Who am I?
> My name means "Thunder of Waters." What am I?
> I was the first capitol of the United States. Where am I?

Teens would have the choice of guessing the answer, researching the information, or submitting another book they had read to receive another clue for the same puzzler. We decided that teens would be limited to three clues per puzzler, but could solve as many puzzlers as they wanted. In addition, we decided that teens could read books of their choice to receive clues—the books certainly did not have to relate to New York.

Preparation for the game involved developing the puzzles (26 of each type, each requiring three clues), a time consuming process which greatly enhanced our knowledge of New York State. At the end of this process we were still excited about the program, but weren't so sure that teens would share our enthusiasm. Would an adolescent be willing to use the reference collection during summer vacation to do research on the first potato chips, or to find out what village is the birthplace of

Memorial Day? Keeping our concerns to ourselves, we created flyers, T-shirts, and press releases to advertise the program, and we went into the schools in our communities to promote it.

To our delight we discovered that the game had teen appeal: well over one hundred middle and high school age readers signed up to outsmart the Empire Summer Puzzler. They read voraciously and armed with their enthusiasm and a short bibliography of reference works, they spent hours sleuthing in the library. Since we both share reference responsibilities in addition to young adult responsibilities, we took particular pleasure in seeing teens discover the libraries' reference collection. They were impressed when *Famous First Facts* yielded the story of the first potato chips, and they found new respect for atlases when one yielded the name of the city they were seeking. It was a pleasant surprise to find out that the clues and the promise of prizes were tantalizing enough to motivate teens to do library research, and to keep them coming back for more.

The success of the program established that given some incentives and adequate promotion, teens will actively participate in summer reading programs, even if these programs require some "work." The Empire Summer Puzzler proved to be an excellent tool for promoting reading and fostering research skills—all in the name of summer fun. [August 1994]

What a Summer We've Had!
Joan Stainforth

Introduction

In the June 1988 issue of VOYA *we printed an article by Lynn Eisenhut entitled* Teen Volunteers *which was subsequently reprinted in* The VOYA Reader. *What follows is the report Joan Stainforth, a Library Assistant at the Chapman Branch of the Orange County (CA) Public Library wrote to inform the administration about the success of the 1992 program at her branch. We print it here as an example of what a report should be: filled with the excitement and delight that conveys the very essence of a successful program.*

A Success Story

What a summer we've had, every lassie and lad, it's the best we have had in a while. Volunteers such as these, they delighted to please. It's no wonder we closed with a smile. [Editor's note: Sing the preceding paragraph to the tune of Lerner and Lowe's *It's Almost Like Falling in Love.*]

Yes, we had a truly outstanding group of youngsters this summer. Some were returning from previous years, some were up through the ranks of preschool story hours and summer reading programs. Some were brand new walk-ons. How fortunate that in a summer when we lost about twenty-six hours of extra help, after the first week we had a group of competent, intelligent, delightful and funny young people who have saved what could have been a difficult summer and made it into one of our most successful ones. These kids were workers! The two thousand plus hours they gave were true working hours. Sure, they giggled a lot, but what a pleasant sound it was to hear and it was usually followed by a much louder chorus of "shhhhhhhhhhhhuses" from the gigglers.

The volunteens quickly signed up to help at the summer reading program desk and began to practice skits and songs and stories for the "Gather Rings" (the weekly school age programs) and preschool story hours.

For the first several weeks we were lucky to have a former volunteer give up hours of her summer vacation to organize and present an "Orange Peel Puppeteers" production of *The Wizard of Oz*. Shannon Koenig, now a twenty-hour clerk here at Chapman and sophomore at Fullerton College, helped the volunteens to make puppets, make scenery, rehearse and present a charming program for a "Gather Ring."

Meanwhile, other volunteers chose skits and plays to present, helped at preschool story hours and did hours of stamping and other clerical tasks. They took upon themselves the task of typing author labels for all the books that didn't have them. They relabeled the pamphlet file. They typed their fingers off. Some were flamboyant and some were quiet, but there was very little they didn't attack with pleasure. Do I seem enthusiastic? How nice to come in and hear that on a frantic understaffed Friday, volunteers had been able to assist patrons with the catalog, tell mothers where the picture books were shelved and politely assure patrons that a staff member would be there to help them as soon as possible.

When the puppet show was over, the 20th annual volunteer melodrama moved into high gear. Casting took place, scenery was designed and rehearsals started. What talent! When the heroine was on vacation, she memorized all her lines. While she was gone another girl generously stood in for her during rehearsals, then continued herself in a smaller part. In fact, everyone took turns being stand-ins. Hours were spent painting the sets. If something went wrong, and it did, they just started all over again. At the final "Gather Ring" *Lilly of the Label Dept.* played to an enthusiastic and enchanted crowd. An even more enthusiastic and vocal audience of families and friends enjoyed the evening performance.

All this time, these youngsters were also working at the summer reading program desk—helping the younger kids with their books, typing, practicing for other skits, telling stories, learning and leading songs . . . and in this hottest of summers, returning from lunch gasping with laughter that they had skipped all the way back from Pizza Hut and were ready to go back to work!

We had our 20th summer of Chapman Branch Volunteers and our

Potpourri of YA Programs

20th annual Chapman Branch Volunteens Orange Peel Players melodrama. We finished with our 20th annual hot dog roast and baseball game to express our thanks to this great group of kids. *They* should be on the front page of the newspaper. Chapman's summer reading program would still go on without them, but it would be a different and less enjoyable one.

Several times during the summer a former volunteer, Tony Rose, came in to visit and help and advise on the melodrama. During his time as a volunteen he not only acted in the plays, but he also wrote or helped write several. His brother and sister were in this one and I know he coached them and other players. Before the performances he kept the actors quiet—he even had them meditating to quell their butterflies. I'd like to quote from his comments on a thank you card the volunteers gave me but was directed to all the Chapman staff. (By the way, Tony is now a senior at San Diego University and considering a career in law and diplomacy.) "What can I say—*This library and its staff* have given me eight years of happiness, joy and endless opportunities. . . . and words cannot express what I feel. Thank you for everything." Tony would also like to write the play for next year. Already has a plot in mind. What more can we say? Except thanks to the volunteers of '92 from all the staff. "What a summer we've had. . . ." [February 1993]

Locked In and Loving It!
Janice T. Ungar

Press Release:

"Spend the entire night in a locked building and live to tell the tale. Sixth and seventh graders are invited to sign up for an overnight at the Farmington Branch of the Farmington Community Library on Thursday February 18, 1993 from 7:00 p.m. to 7:30 a.m. New friends, games and a storyteller await those brave enough to come. Parents are invited to ransom their children by attending a free breakfast on Friday morning."

Yes, I really did it. I subjected myself and our other Young Adult Services Staff member, Sharon Vincent, to twenty-five young people with a lot of energy for twelve hours. Not only did I live, but I had a ball! Planning ahead was the key to a successful evening.

Planning

The planning phase of this event involved several steps. The initial idea was to give middle-schoolers who were not going away during the winter school break something to relieve their boredom. It would be a stress-free method of exposing them to the library and also a good source of public relations with the community. Holding the event on a Thursday night gave the young people something to look forward to during the week. The timing of the event was also critical. No one would be eliminated from attending due to having working parents. A 7:00 p.m. start time allowed for parents to come home from work and the young person to eat dinner before attending the event. Having the event end by 7:30 a.m. allowed time for parents to pick up children before going to work the following morning. Also, our custodian was able to do any cleaning and setting up of the library auditorium before the library opened on Friday. A proposal was written describing this and the activities planned with costs (both described later in the article) and given to our director, Beverly Papai. She submitted it to the Friends of the Library and they agreed to underwrite the cost of the event.

As plans progressed, it came to light that it was necessary to check to make sure that we could actually host the event due to city ordinances. It was unclear if it was considered a non-conforming use of the building and special permission of the city council was necessary. A letter written by our director to the city manager revealed that it was considered to be part of programming and no special permission was needed. The city manager did suggest that we have the area the group was to sleep in inspected by the building inspector and fire marshal. Their inspection revealed several helpful safety tips. These included moving a large bulletin board which partially obscured a fire exit, showing the attendees where the exits were, placement of some extra, temporary, smoke detectors, and having the sleep area arranged in aisles so no one would be trampled in case of an emergency. All of the suggestions were easy to comply with, but probably would not have been done without their suggestions. Two other safety measures were necessary. One was an emergency form for each of the young people including contact phone numbers and any health problems we should know about. It also included a statement that if the individual was destructive to any other participant or the building that the parents would be called at any point during the evening to pick up their child. All parents were made aware of this form when they signed a child up for the sleepover. The last safety concern was adequate staffing. Both Young Adult Services Librarians were there for the entire evening with additional help offered by our branch head, one teenage library page, and the teenage daughter of one of the librarians. Two adults needed to remain in the building at all times in case there was an emergency and one of us had to leave for any reason.

The last and, from the participants' point of view, the most important things planned ahead were the events for the evening. The busier the young people could be kept, the more likely we could maintain order. Also it would tire them out so that the last thing they wanted to do, sleep, could actually occur. Once this final step was in place, promotion of the event was needed.

Promotion

Promotion took several forms. At the same time we were advertising the sleepover, we were conducting booktalks in the public and parochial schools to introduce another program: Battle of the Books. At the end of the booktalks a plug was put in for the sleepover and fliers given to the students to take home. Fliers and posters were placed at the schools and in both branches of the library. In addition, the press release at the beginning of the article was sent to the local paper. As a result of the promotion, twenty-nine people signed up from various schools within the two cities served by the Farmington Community Library. The night of the program twenty-five showed up.

The Sleepover

The overnight began with a short explanation of rules and expectations for the evening. These included showing the participants the fire exits, discussing where to meet in case of fire, demonstrating that, yes, the alarms really do go off if anyone goes through the emergency exits. It was mentioned that the library would be locked at 9:00 p.m. and to please not leave the building. Further, they were asked to please not go into the work areas unattended so that any projects being worked on would not be disturbed. On a personal note, I asked them to leave any feelings of dislike for each other at the door. I explained that we were all there to have a good time. This was done because the first two girls that came in saw the sign-up list and immediately told me that they did not like a person on the list. All of the young people obeyed these requests.

Many of the young people did not know each other before the overnight. After the rules of the evening were explained, two ice breaker games were played. The first is called human bingo. Instead of using numbers there were squares with different characteristics such as "has a library card," "has read an R.L. Stine book," or "has been to Ohio." Each participant could sign one square on his or her own board and then find a person who matched a characteristic and have them sign that square. In order to complete the board, each would have to talk to twenty-three other people (including persons staffing the event). After they had completed this, we played bingo with the names, and small prizes were given out to winners.

The second game was a shoe game. All of the participants were seated in a circle on chairs. They were asked to remove their right shoe. They were then asked a series of questions and then had to move to the right or the left based on their answers. Example: "move three to the left if you like prune juice." This resulted in many young people sitting on each others laps. The object was to make it all the way around the circle and back to their shoe. After these two games all of the participants seemed comfortable with each other. They were then given a short bathroom and drink break.

The next activity was a professional storyteller from Ann Arbor, Barbara Schutz-Gruber. She told a variety of stories including string and scary stories for one hour. My personal favorite was a modern telling of *The Three Little Pigs*. She held the audience's interest and did a fantastic job.

The participants were then given snacks. These included Famous Amos cookies, a variety of chips and pop. They appeared to be well received as noted by the fact that there was hardly anything left.

The final portion of the evening was a mini-Olympics. This involved dividing the group into teams of five and having them do a series of events. They included:

1. Face painting—Fifteen minutes to paint each others' faces and come up with a team name.
2. Magnetism—A facial tissue passing game with straws
3. Word Search—Teams had to find ten things that one could find in a library.
4. Orange pass—Passing oranges under the chin.
5. Song game—An elimination game where teams had to think of songs with the word love in it and sing them.
6. Paddle bouncing—Participants had to bounce the ball four times and pass it to the next person. The last person had to bounce and then chew two crackers and whistle.
7. Brady Bunch—Teams had ten minutes to think of as many Brady Bunch episodes as they could and write them down.

Two of these events had slight problems. One was the Brady Bunch event. One team said that no one on the team had ever watched it.

Potpourri of YA Programs

However, all the other teams were able to come up with between ten and twenty-four episodes. The other was the song game. Two teams dropped out quickly and the remaining teams came up with an extraordinary number of catechism songs which we did not have the knowledge to verify. Individual events were scored with three points for first place, two points for second place and one for third place. The winners were given the paddles to keep. Overall, the mini-Olympics was a success and the young people enjoyed themselves immensely.

One other game went on throughout the evening. This involved the group being given pins with colored tape on them. They were not allowed to say the word sleep or any variation of it or they would lose their pins to the person who caught them. The young person (there was a tie) with the most number of pins at the end of the evening won a prize. The "s" word took on a whole new meaning.

After the Olympics, they washed the paint off and got ready for bed (approximately 11:30). Many of them went into the library to get books to read. One of the hardest parts of getting them to settle down was that they were extremely enthusiastic about finding reading materials. Lights went out at 12:30 and most of the group, other than a few die-hards, were asleep or trying to go to sleep by two a.m. Everyone was awakened at 6:50 a.m. and parents began arriving at 7:00 a.m. Breakfast consisted of muffins, milk, juice, fruit and coffee. All children were picked up within five minutes of the designated time.

Feedback

Feedback from this program was terrific. Parents were asking when we were doing it again. Unsolicited, several of the parents said that they would be willing to pay to have their children attend. They said it really gave their children something to look forward to on vacation. Several participants said to one of the youth librarians that they had an absolutely wonderful time and hoped that we did it again soon (very soon). Approximately two-thirds of the young people attending were not signed up for our Battle of the Books reading program so that in addition it brought many people into the library who might otherwise not have come.

Cost

The total cost of the evening, excluding staffing was approximately $250 with the largest amount ($150) going to the storyteller. In an attempt to keep other costs low, prizes were purchased at a 99-cent store and all food was purchased at PACE, a bulk warehouse store. The expense for the items needed for the events were negligible.

Ideas for the Future

If the program is repeated in the future, a few changes may be made. First while twenty-five came, we would have accepted thirty-five. Once the sleeping bags were out, for safety reasons, I would not allow a group larger than thirty to come next time. Also, moving the storyteller to later in the evening would mean having a quiet activity to wind down the energy level. When planning the sleepover, I had checked into showing a movie but the licensing fee was prohibitive ($175 to show *Beethoven*). If more money could be found this would also be a viable alternative.

Don't hesitate to put on a sleepover. The rewards in smiling faces will come by the dozens. Just don't, as the two librarians staffing this event did, forget to bring your glasses if you wear contact lenses. [December 1993]

Tapping Teen Talent in Queens: A Library-Based, LSCA-Funded Youth Development Success Story from New York

Barbara Osborne Williams

The Setting

The Central Library of the Queens Borough (NY) Public Library System is located in Jamaica in the heart of a business district and bustling downtown shopping area. The library is within walking distance of three New York City public high schools and two private high schools. The library also sits at the connecting point of a major mass transit system for teens traveling to and from various high schools outside of the downtown Jamaica area. One block from the library is the 165th Street Mall, a major shopping strip of the downtown Jamaica shopping area. Shops along the mall cater directly to the teenage market. On any given day teenagers can be found browsing or purchasing clothing, footwear, audiotapes, CDs, electronic equipment, personal care items and fast food. Many teenagers spend time standing in groups talking or purchasing audiotapes, clothing and jewelry from teenage street vendors. Teens gather at the mall to hang out with friends, meet people and add to the energy the area exudes.

Local teenagers use the library as a meeting place to socialize with their peers and to meet potential girlfriends and boyfriends. On average, approximately 300 minority teenagers pass through the Central Library during after-school hours. Many teens generally stop by and/or settle in the Youth Services Division (the section of the library with staff specially trained to provide services and programs for children from preschool through high school). These groups of young adults often do not use the library for its intended purpose. The majority of them are not registered members, do not borrow materials or use in-house resources for leisure reading or academic course work.

Identifying the Need

While these after-school teenagers are generally well mannered, there is occasional rudeness and disruptive behavior. The librarians assigned to the Young Adult Room spend a generous amount of time developing a friendly, caring rapport with them. When conversations revealed their deep need to have adults who would take the time to share in a conversation—someone who would just take a moment to say hello, ask them how everything is going, and then listen for an answer, I developed a deep concern and need to find a way to provide them with growth opportunities. They were already in the library with so much of what they needed but didn't take advantage of. There was a wealth of information at their fingertips, a specially trained and caring staff and an organization with a youth centered philosophy. How could we begin to guide them to the resources in a meaningful but "hip" way, really let them know we care and demonstrate a tangible example of the Queens Library's "youth centered" philosophy? We needed to develop a program somehow which would attract them, provide them with solid growth opportunities and help them to see the practical use of the library as a life resource.

Getting the Idea

I did some personal brainstorming and then spoke with Carol Sheffer, Head of the library's Programs and Services Department, about my concerns and possible solutions. After pondering several possibilities, I found that money would attract teens, opportunities to develop and to practice leadership skills would provide them with growth opportunities and if I could somehow tie these ideas to the library, I would really have something. Carol encouraged me to write an LSCA grant proposal, gave me the packet of proposal information, and the rest is now history. I came up with the idea of teaching teenagers to become library program presenters. They would be trained by adults to present library programs for children and/or their peers.

The LSCA Proposal

The project was called "Tapping Teen Talent." The goal was to build teenage self-esteem by encouraging the development of individual talents, interests and apparent potential. The participating young adults would be selected based on their desire to participate. They would have to agree to participate in unpaid training sessions and accept a nominal honorarium for planning and conducting programs. The proposal was written specifically for teenagers 14-18, since this age range corresponded with age eligibility requirements for working papers. Teenagers would be trained to levels proficient enough to plan, implement and evaluate programs for their peers and younger children, and guided toward an awareness of the relationship between goal setting, preparation and planning and its effect on the outcome of task performed as evidenced by measured levels of success. The program would seek to provide a congenial learning and working environment with mutual respect and cooperation among all participants regardless of age, sex and academic proficiency. There would also be an informal focus on career development by helping teens develop an awareness of their natural and developed abilities and career choice and preparation.

Written to incorporate these project concepts and goals, the LSCA proposal requested eleven thousand, eight hundred dollars ($11,800) broken down as follows:

One information session-refreshments.	$200
36 Professional one-hour training sessions @ $100.00.	$3,600
28 program presentations by teenagers	$2,000
Supplies	$2,000
Library materials	$4,000
TOTAL	**$11,800**

The grant was issued for $10,000, just $1,800 below the requested amount. The library materials portion of the budget was reduced by eighteen hundred dollars.

Recruiting Participants

I met with the library's Public Relations Department to discuss a design for a flyer to advertise the general information session. The flyer read "Tapping Teen Talent, Queens Library seeks teens with varied interests, we'll show you how to teach, perform, perfect your skills, plan and lead programs." The flyers were placed in the library and taken to local high schools. Fifty-nine teenagers attended the general information session held on a Friday December 16th at 4:00 p.m. The overall response and the response to the program concept itself was quite overwhelming. Teens were fascinated and pleasantly pleased to find a program where they would be given the opportunity to assume a leadership role. They were also impressed with the idea of having a program which deemed them important enough to have their interests and ideas as the focal point and primary aim. They would be in a position to share in the total design and implementation of the project.

Teens completed a general application form which included basic information such as name, address, telephone number and high school. Interested teens were then scheduled for individual or small group interviews to discuss their areas of interests and determine the methods of training. The interview questionnaire asked them how they found out about the program (flyer, newspaper, at school, or other), library membership and the status of their borrower's account, the branch they used, how often they came to the library, if they considered themselves a reader, what types of materials they read and finally the most important question, their interests. The majority of the teens found out about the program from the flyers at the library and conversations with Youth Services staff. Seventy-five percent had library cards with one-third of them unable to borrow books due to delinquent accounts. They all considered themselves readers and read materials ranging from the sports pages to black history, and from magazines to American classics and poetry. The answer to the question addressing their leisure interests varied from "Chill, talk to girls on the phone" to reading and writing poetry. Teens were involved in sports, rapping, reading, watching TV, going to the movies, hair braiding and hanging out with friends. They found the library to be a "hang-out" where they came to "chill" with friends and/or read some books. One teen voiced feelings about the attitude of the library staff towards teenagers. "The young adult staff is basically cool; however other staff needs some working on."

Teens shared feelings of frustration as a result of their inability to communicate with adults because of an invisible wall created by the adults' inability to see them as individual persons. "Adults seem to see all teenagers the same." "They put you in a group and that's it." The general sentiment was that adults do not have confidence in their ability to make the "right" decisions or assume leadership positions. Adults are basically not trusting.

Teens expressed interest in working with children in craft sessions, story hours, and storytelling. One of the young adult males shared a recent work experience where he assisted in a Summer Day Camp Program. He accompanied children ages five through seven on trips to Flushing Meadow Park, the Bronx Zoo, on picnics and to other cultural facilities. He read them stories, ate lunch and snacks with them and shared some really nice times. His work with children made him aware of how his behavior affects theirs. He was quite surprised to see that these kids watched him and wanted to mirror his actions. At that point he and I were able to share the idea of how he was a role model for those younger children. He loved the idea of being a role model, someone the children looked up to. He also expressed deep concern for the responsibility which comes with working with children.

The interview conversations left me with a deeper commitment to develop my project concept. These teens possessed hidden qualities masked by society's stereotypes assigned to inner city youth. They were more than just teens who came to the library to "hang out." These young people wanted a chance to show how they could make a valuable contribution. The interview sessions with teens were followed by a search for adults who would agree with the concept of the project and also possess the character to serve as role models. It was important to employ both men and women of varying educational levels, occupations, ages and life experience. I combed the library's program files and spoke with program presenters and adult customers from the community. A meeting was scheduled to formally discuss the project. The final adult training team was comprised of me, six women and two men. This meeting was followed by a meeting with the teens to share the news and set times for the training. All project participants agreed on a training schedule and time frame which was best suited for the teenagers. Teens accepted the responsibility for final scheduling decisions with the full understanding that they would be held accountable for lateness and absences.

Adult Training Sessions

The actual training sessions began in January after the holiday season. Adults would teach teens creative arts, crafts, storytelling and techniques in program planning, implementation and evaluation. The training took place during the week and on several Saturday afternoons, starting with three sessions of reading and discussion. Teens met with an African-American man who has a passion for the history and contemporary plight of black people. In his mid forties, this gentleman is quite inspiring because he is a high school graduate who is an avid reader, possessing phenomenal advanced knowledge of black history. He ran a biweekly book discussion group at a local church and he and I often shared conversations about areas of black history.

He chose *From the Browder Files*, written by Anthony Browder, a collection of twenty-two essays on the African American experience. Teens read the essays of their choice independently and met each week to share what they read. Conversations were always interesting and thought provoking. These sessions helped the teens get acquainted. One of the other adult members of the training team also joined us for these training sessions, which were designed to develop critical thinking and verbal presentation skills. There were really no right or wrong answers, just an opportunity to get to know each other, learn a little, and share ideas from both an historical and contemporary perspective. The teens really enjoyed the sessions. They even requested that they be lengthened from one to one and a half hours. This training was then followed by sessions conducted by artists, storytellers, and self-taught crafts people. Teens learned the art of jewelry making, clock making, peanut butter-making, stenciling and T-shirt designs, mask making, and storytelling. I conducted training workshops on book-based programming and held generalized sessions on program planning and design.

The Programs

The first workshop presented by the teens took place on May 20th. The program complemented the Queens Library's major exhibit on the life and times of Lewis H. Latimer an African American of numerous accomplishments, one of which included the perfecting of the electric light bulb. Teens planned and conducted an afternoon of workshops titled "Celebrate the Lives and Accomplishments of Four African American Men of Science and Invention." Children ages six to twelve years old enjoyed hands-on workshops, film discussions and read-alouds to learn about Lewis H. Latimer, Benjamin Banneker, George Washington Carver, and Granville T. Woods. Workshops consisted of T-shirt stenciling (stencils were make by teens), clock making (teens learned how to make real working battery operated clocks from CDs in one of their adult training sessions and taught the craft to the children), and peanut butter using fresh roasted peanuts in a blender. All sessions included a story and discussion. One hundred and ten children attended the program. The teens were encouraged.

Branching Out

The training sessions conducted by adults and the success of their first program gave the teens the confidence to form training sessions of their own. The young adults assumed a true leadership role when they decided to be responsible for their own training by setting up peer training sessions. Some of them conducted training sessions based on personal skills, while others read books from the library's collection to train themselves first and then to train each other. Altogether, the teenagers trained themselves to conduct twelve programs, just about 50 percent of all the programs conducted by the teens for the LSCA project. They planned workshops in fabric painting and created decorative pillow cases using a stenciling technique. Clay, cardboard, paper and other objects were used in another workshop to make original board games. The teen participants also planned and conducted workshops using clay to teach basic techniques for creating pinch pots, wedging and building coil pots, as well as weaving on cardboard looms using yarns, ribbons and other objects. They taught themselves origami and paper-maché. A major highlight was planning and delivering a program designed for toddlers and their parents, "Toddlers Play and Paint." Toddlers and their parents enjoyed informal play and explored creative arts. They painted with sponges, brushes and their fingers. Families enjoyed the three-part workshop series.

In addition to these programs, the young adults planned and conducted sessions in mask making, decorative photo albums, basic drawing using oil and chalk pastels, pencils and felt marker, and storytelling. They planned an all-day "Say Good-bye to Summer" program consisting of face painting, workshops in lanyard weaving, magnet making and play dough, with storytelling and ice cream for everyone.

Teenagers also planned and conducted a session in jewelry making for teenagers who were seventeen and eighteen years old. This was a rather interesting and rewarding experience for both the teen leaders and learners. I too gleamed greater insight into the minds and spirits of teenagers as I watched the interaction. Teen leaders were shown a great deal of respect from workshop participants who remained attentive and totally involved in the jewelry making. They addressed the teen leaders as "Miss" when they asked a question or made a comment. Teenagers who are often accused of being disrespectful even to their peers, demonstrated great respect and admiration for their peers in a position of leadership, and those leaders felt good about the respect shown them by their peers.

The teen program presenters played a crucial role in summer programming by planning and conducting twenty-five independent programs and assisting librarians with regularly scheduled programs. By the time summer ended, the teens had provided programs for 1,286 children. The "Tapping Teen Talent" LSCA project provided an avenue for twelve teenagers to assume a leadership position in the library. They also began to formulate positive views concerning the possibilities for teen participation in the library as a workplace. The teens brought fresh ideas and great enthusiasm. Their programming proved far superior to that of librarians. They chose interesting and challenging themes and crafts and advertised them with some exciting titles. Their training prepared them to plan effectively and conduct themselves in a professional manner. Their program evaluations were realistic and offered constructive criticism which was graciously accepted. Their mere presence created an atmosphere where librarians were forced to work harder and closer to perfection. The professional accountability of librarians became an issue as teens could tell when librarians were unprepared for programs, were not able to "think on the spot" to resolve unexpected occurrences, or were unable to maintain order and the children's interest and attention during programs. Librarians, who at first exhibited cynicism towards the project's goal of training teens to become program presenters, became transformed after they witnessed the teens' level of competency and problem-solving abilities. [August 1996]

FOCUS ON ADULTS

Books for the Beast: A Maryland How-We-Did-It-Good Self-Training Success Story!
Mary K. Chelton

In 1990, while driving home from a retirement party at my training ground, the Enoch Pratt Free Library in Baltimore, it occurred to me that I was then the last Margaret Edwards-trained young adult librarian still working in a Maryland public library. Margaret Edwards, the founder of young adult services at Enoch Pratt, was one of the great pioneers of American public library youth services history.

The library I was working in, though, did not then (nor does it now), have any young adult front-line staff, but such are the vagaries of needing employment in an imperfect world. What it did have then (and still does now), were lots of young adults using the place, served by a dichotomized adult/children's staff, most of whom did not participate in either ALA or local associations. Group training time was scarce and demands on it competitive from all parts of the organization. My position was split between adult and young adult services, with major collection development and generic systemwide programming responsibilities in an administrative environment that precluded the dedicated attention to YA services training common in previous positions. There were, however, (and still are) enormously talented front-line people there interested in helping kids beyond homework support, if only I could find a way to teach them how to do it. From this need and frustration, *Books for the Beast* was conceived.

Proposal and Training Design

I used a training design similar to Velma Varner Day at the now-defunct Columbia University library school in New York City, in which participants were asked to register for two peer-led thematic discussion groups of books for youth chosen by a planning committee of local librarians. A notable professional speaker, box lunch, and wine and cheese social rounded out the day. *Books for the Beast* differed in two respects. Instead of a professional speaker, I wanted an author as a draw who was authentically young adult, as opposed to someone who wrote primarily for middle school. Authors who write for the middle school audience are inevitably invited as a compromise to appeal either to an exclusively children's or to the combined children's and young adult audience common at state and regional association programs. This is not to say that middle school kids are not part of the young adult clientele, but they are not the *entire* young adult clientele, as many programs and a fair amount of annoyingly self-serving professional rhetoric would have us believe.

I went after Ron Koertge because he was from the West Coast, most people had not seen him in Maryland, his books were hilarious, and also because the adolescent sexuality and sensibilities of his books made them quite distinct from books for children, but they were still a part of the juvenile publishing that many non-children's librarians and generalists serving young adults did not know about.

The second difference was that I wanted the discussion leaders to include library generalists and librarians with adult services job titles, so that the preparation to be a discussion leader would become an intensive participatory training model in and of itself.

I tentatively confirmed Koertge (pronounced Ker-chee), explaining to him that I was going after grant money, thought it would all work out, but to tell me if he got a better, less tentative offer, so I could switch gears if I had to. I then asked Julia Losinski, the recently retired and distinguished YA Coordinator from the Prince George's County Memorial Library, if she could help direct the project, and wrote a proposal to the Margaret Edwards Trust for funding. The Trust was set up by the terms of Margaret Edwards's will to fund projects that promoted reading and books to young adults and/or trained young adult librarians.

My proposed objectives were: 1) to expose Maryland public and school librarians serving young adults to the following on a regular basis—authors and titles of interest to young adults, the implications of adolescent development for library services, and young adult services concepts as pioneered by Mabel Williams, Margaret Scoggin (both of the New York Public Library and YA services pioneers), and Margaret Edwards (on the optimistic assumption that *Books for the Beast* would only be the first of an annual or semiannual event), and 2) to create a structural opportunity for Maryland public and school librarians serving young adults to read, discuss, and critique literature of interest to young adults through preparation for and participation in thematic book discussions.

I did not ask for an outright grant, but a loan, speculating from experience with a similar program in Virginia, that I could probably make the event pay for itself but that I also needed seed money to assure payment to the author in case I did not. I estimated 150 people at a registration fee of $15.00, (which later proved optimistic and had to be revised to $35.00). This was to pay for the author at a minimum $500 honorarium (I think to offer less is insulting) plus expenses, printing and postage. I used the Friends of the Library in Montgomery County as the 501(c)3 tax exempt organizational conduit for the money.

Organization and Planning

Because Margaret Edwards's career had been spent in Baltimore, we felt it was appropriate to locate the workshop there if we could find a place, and asked Jo Ann Davison, Upper School Librarian at the Gilman School, if they could host and cosponsor it. (I had met Jo Ann working on a program for the MLA Intellectual Freedom Discussion Group.) While this made an enormous amount of work for the ever hospitable Jo Ann, it also gave us multiple classrooms for the breakout discussion groups and a free site. Jo Ann also provided free on-site helpers as well as a student participant who proved invaluable to the success of the day, found the cheapest and tastiest deli box lunch in history, and provided the names of all local private school librarians for publicity.

Besides Julia, Jo Ann, and myself, other pivotal people we identified for the planning committee included Deborah Taylor, Youth Services Specialist at Enoch Pratt, for her invaluable book knowledge and training skills; Sandy Owen, Anne Arundel County Public Library, to represent the co-sponsoring Public Services Division of the Maryland Library Association, who not only had experience running similar programs for adults within MLA, but also proved to have formidable organizational and group process training skills (she could also add and subtract, unlike yours truly); Pat Costello, *VOYA* reviewer at Enoch Pratt, also representing PSD, (with Bonnie Willen at Baltimore County as alternate); Frances Sedney, Children's Services Coordinator in Harford County, to represent children's staff who worked with and cared about young adults, who gave us the program title; Wanda Van Goor, YA literature teacher at Prince George's County Community College where we had first thought of holding the event; Nisa Merritt, Specialist in the Public Library Services Section from the Maryland State Department of Education's Division of Library Development and Services, who got us state library co-sponsorship and access to several school library mailing lists; and Dolores Maminski in Carroll County, a former Pratt YA librarian and VOYA reviewer, to represent that area of the state.

James Liesner at the University of Maryland's College of Library and Information Science was also included, not only to involve CLIS, but also because of his evaluation expertise and ties to the school library media specialist community. He provided a supervised student evaluator, who designed and summarized our evaluation instruments and attended several planning meetings, all training sessions as well as the workshop itself.

Since Maryland is also part of the District of Columbia suburbs, we also invited and got co-sponsorship and representation from the DCLA Children's and Young Adult Services Roundtable in the form of Elizabeth Elam, an experienced YA Librarian from Prince George's County, and a DCLA member. The only weakness in the planning committee was the overt omission of a public school media specialist representative, although Merritt and Liesner helped, and both could meet during weekdays when we held the planning meetings at either Gilman or a nearby Enoch Pratt branch. Julia Losinski was also in touch regularly with the Baltimore County School Library Media Services Coordinator.

The first meeting was held March 8, at which a laundry list of major tasks to be accomplished was drawn up, including primarily how to go about identifying, selecting, and training discussion leaders, which thematic categories of books would be used for discussion, the issue of titles in print as well as circulating availability in local school and public libraries, publicity ideas and access to various relevant professional groups, author support, how to organize a book sale of the author's books, and the evaluation of the workshop. No meeting, including this one, ever ended without everyone being assigned a task to be accomplished by the next meeting date. (In retrospect, this meeting should have taken place in January for an October program because of the necessity of getting publicity to school librarians before school let out for the summer. We also should have established an overall timeline by which all relevant tasks would need to be completed, but we were consumed with book titles and discussion leaders at this point.)

One of the more interesting issues discussed at this point was whether the discussion leaders should primarily be specialists or generalists. Julia felt that generalists could not do justice to a literature in which they had no background. I countered with the fact that training them was an objective of the workshop, that many of them were fine literature discussion leaders already and just needed exposure to these books and their audience appeal for adolescents. We wound up with a mix, partly because a mix was available within the state, and partly as a compromise of views on the issue of book background.

By the next meeting in April, we had a schedule for the day set, a preliminary list of themes and books the committee had chosen for discussion with the provision that the leaders could have the option of adding one or two in-print or widely available favorites we might have omitted, a list of expectations for the discussion leader pairs (one for content and one for process), a draft letter of invitation for possible discussion leaders, decided to lock Ron Koertge immediately into the best fare we could get for budgeting purposes, decided to add a panel on how to promote YA books, and established a registration deadline. (We moved the fee up to $35 because everyone felt that $15 was unreasonably low to meet anticipated costs, all of which were not in the original proposal—like paying for the lunches of the discussion leaders and presenters.) We also established a timeline, thanks to Sandy Owen's reminder to do so. (We should have done it at the first meeting.)

The final book categories were humor, multiculture, real life, fantasy, and suspense. We had an interesting discussion over whether *Arizona*

Kid would go into humor or real life, finally putting it into humor at my urging. (It is important to remember to include the guest of honor's book in the discussions at a program like this, something we almost forgot once in Virginia.) We also discussed whether Annette Curtis Klause would either be embarrassed herself, or make other people embarrassed to discuss *Silver Kiss* if we asked her to be a leader. (Annette is a Maryland librarian and an expert on SF and horror literature. She wasn't embarrassed and didn't make others uncomfortable.) We also divided the books under each thematic category into three "core" titles that everybody would be expected to read, and three "optional" titles that they might read.

By May 1, news releases were drafted. These were mailed to *SLJ*, *VOYA*, *Booklist*, and local association newsletters and calendars identified at our May 17 meeting. Copies were also carried to the annual Maryland Library Association conference. By early June, a self-mailing registration brochure had been designed, printed, and mailed to every school librarian, public library director, and professional library association mailing list in the Maryland and DC areas. (The co-sponsoring organizations made their membership lists on labels available to us as a co-sponsorship contribution. Every brochure emphasized that this was a *discussion* program and that the more books participants read, the more they would enjoy it. We wanted to make it clear that this was not lectures and note taking masquerading as a workshop.) The discussion leaders were confirmed and a training session set for September. Besides the suggestion of additional titles for discussion, each content leader was asked to prepare a supplementary bibliography for his or her theme that would be copied for every participant in the workshop, whether or not they participated in that particular session.

Later in June, form letters went out to every mass market and trade publisher who sells YA books or science fiction and fantasy (labeled "YA" or not), all library vendors selling YA books, all ALA units dealing with YA services, materials and issues (YALSA, AASL, OIF etc.), all relevant journals (*American Libraries*, *VOYA*, *SLJ*, *Booklist*, and *Kliatt*), pertinent nonlibrary organizations (Center for Early Adolescence, ETR Associates, etc.), including the brochure and asking for giveaway copies or single display copies of promotional materials in the YA area. I also asked Tom Riggin, our local Baker & Taylor representative, if he could arrange to have the three B & T YA paperback dumps available for display and then raffled off to participants. He also offered donuts for the coffee and registration period and cat photo shopping bags which I gratefully accepted.

At our August 16 meeting, we assigned registrants, whose registrations had been date stamped in the order received, to their discussion groups so confirmation letters could be sent. Everybody got their first choice, and most their second. Everyone was asked to specify any group they did *not* want under any circumstances as well as to prioritize choices. Some people only wanted one group in either the morning or afternoon which was relatively easy to do, depending on when they registered. We were adamant that no group would be more than twenty people to keep the groups manageable. Each discussion was repeated once in the morning and afternoon to accommodate the size restriction. A waiting list in order of receipt was established beyond the 150 ceiling, which we made relatively easily. (This proved valuable later when several people asked to cancel—despite our "no cancellations" pronouncements—for solid reasons.) We also made it very clear in our confirmation letter that people were expected to go to the groups they had registered for, not just hop around among groups. We wanted to protect the integrity of the discussion from unnecessary interruptions as much as possible.

The August meeting also dealt with final details about registration logistics (we decided to take possible walk-ins at the full registration fee, but not give them lunch or a choice of assignments), who would acknowledge the Edwards trustees who decided to come, the book sale setup, Koertge's introduction and dinner for him the night before the program, who would unpack the display materials when, how many vegetarians we were getting for lunch, the morning coffee and afternoon wine, cheese and fruit set ups, a final review of the evaluation forms, and the status of author care and feeding.

One committee member's sole assignment was to "take care of" Ron Koertge, including picking him up and delivering him to the airport, seeing that he got his honorarium check before he left, making sure he showed up where he was supposed to be, getting and paying for his hotel room, and providing tourist guide and transportation services as needed. The idea was to make him use as little personal money as necessary, make sure he got what he needed, and leave him alone the rest of the time, without abandoning him. Dolores Maminski of the Carroll County Public Library did this admirably and efficiently. It helped that Ron is a lovely human being.

Evaluation Design

In between these formal meetings, I met with Jim Liesner and Elizabeth Wetzel, our MLS student evaluator, to discuss the evaluation design for the project. Elizabeth was recruited at a presentation to Jim's YA Services class that spring. She was working as a paraprofessional law librarian, liked kids, and felt that this would make an interesting independent study to explore public library work around the edges, and learn a little about evaluation. We discussed the objectives of the proposal and the training sessions, what level of evaluation was possible and appropriate, given limited resources of labor and time, as well as the various evaluation perspectives that were needed to get a full picture of the day. Successive evaluation instruments for both participants and discussion leaders were drafted, critiqued, and revised at least three times. To make her independent study experience a good one, I made sure that Elizabeth always knew which were my needs as codirector of the project, and Jim made sure that she reflected on what she was learning about evaluation and instrumentation. It helped enormously that she was a conscientious self-starter and well worth the time investment for both the project and for developing a new colleague to the profession.

Discussion Leader Training Session

After a final review at the August Planning Committee meeting, the session was held for all discussion leader pairs at an Anne Arundel County branch meeting room on September 11 from 1 to 4 p.m. The session included introductions and time for the discussion leader pairs who had not previously met to talk with each other, a generic presentation on "How to Facilitate a Discussion" by Sandy Owen and Michael Gannon from Anne Arundel County, followed by information on how to prepare to discuss the content and appeal of the books from Julia and me. We told them to research the author, be familiar with reviews of all the books, keep discussions of political problems separate from literary ones, and stress what about the book appealed to some adolescents (no book needs to appeal to all of them). We also gave them background material to read such as *Literature for Today's Young Adults*. We also reminded the adult services leaders that many YA books were a genre themselves, and should meet genre standards of excellence, rather than constantly being compared with adult notables, for example. The issue of general versus special reader audiences was covered, and some attention was given to science fiction as an "adult" genre with intrinsic "adolescent" appeal. We also explained why certain books had been chosen and categorized the way they were and possible problems they might encounter explaining our choices, gave them a list of possible discussion starters to get past that awful silent moment, and ended by asking them to call us with questions and to please stay healthy until October 26th! (We did have one backup pair among the planning committee, but there was only one dropout and subsequent substitution prior to the training session.)

The Night Before the Big Day

We arrived at Gilman to unpack and set up all the promotional materials that had arrived since the June appeal, leaving room for Greetings and Readings, the local bookstore handling the book sale. Jo Ann had made directional signs and arranged custodial help to get tables. I had delivered checks for the lunches and reception food to her the day before. (The Friends of the Library treasurer was most accommodating.) Dolores left to pick up Ron, check him into his hotel, and tour the Pimlico Race Track at some point. He owns part of a race horse and that was the only tourist attraction he wanted to see. After unpacking tons of stuff (publishers are very grateful to have a target market event pointed out to them), we walked through all the rooms and left to meet Ron for dinner at a nearby restaurant, a "perk" deliberately built into the schedule for the planning committee with his agreement.

The Big Day!

To say that this was as near a perfect day as possible is a vast understatement. We were worried because the weather was dangerously foggy in the morning, but luckily, other than some hair-raising tales of getting there, 132 people did, excluding discussion leaders, planning committee, Gilman staff, etc. One disappointment was that Que Bronson from Montgomery County, who was going to talk about merchandising on the expert promotion panel, called with the flu to beg off the night before. (I stood in for him.)

Memories include Baker & Taylor's great donuts, Ron reading his poetry, the general air of excitement and camaraderie throughout the day, especially for our evaluator, the welcome delight of Sara Siebert, Margaret Edwards's successor at Enoch Pratt, who represented the Edwards Trustees at the event, teenage Adam Borden's advice on how to get boys involved in reading projects (invite girls), and a testimonial from James Ulmer, President of Enoch Pratt's Board of Trustees, whose teenage daughter had been a participant there in Cathi MacRae's (now Deborah Taylor's) Young Adult Advisory Board.

That just about everyone had a great time was more than confirmed in the evaluations. Nobody from the 117 respondents disliked the program, and 104 wanted to see the program repeated. Best of all, 110 reported that they had read four books or more to prepare for the discussions. One hundred six people would recommend Ron Koertge as a speaker to other groups, and the one thing 12 people would change is more involvement by young adults in the day. The discussion leaders liked being paired, wanted more time for discussion among themselves, and generally liked the training, although it was obvious that, except for those already specialists, it was too superficial. A zip code analysis of those registered showed that we drew an audience from almost all parts of Maryland, the District of Columbia, and northern Virginia down to Loudon County. All discussion leaders and committee members, as well as Ron Koertge got copies later of the evaluation results, which included the participant ratings of their own sessions.

Everyone got a thank you letter within two weeks, with information about proposing future projects to the Edwards Trust. (For information, write Margaret Edwards Trust, c/o Julian Lapides, Esq., 807 Cathedral

St., Baltimore, MD 21201-5281. Phone: (410) 752-4518.) Best of all, the Edwards Trust got their $3000 loan repaid in full, to the amazement and dismay of their accountant. As a result of the good evaluations, the repayment of the loan, and obvious interest in a repeat of the program, I proposed establishing it with money routinely set aside as an annual or semiannual event to be directed by Deborah Taylor with some minor modifications to increase the involvement of both young adults and inner-city librarians. This idea was approved by the Trustees at their June, 1992 meeting, and has been a continuing success story under the leadership of Deborah Taylor.

While I no longer work in Maryland, with thanks to the perfect planning committee as well as the competence and hospitality of Gilman School personnel, I hope that we have made sure that Margaret Edwards's legacy lives on there in this project. She was my teacher during my Rutgers MLS program, and her wonderful successors trained me. *Books for the Beast* is a very small repayment for many kindnesses from my Maryland mentors, as well as an ongoing commitment to Maryland's young adults for the staff that serve them.

APPENDIX

Genres

Humor

Anthony: *Blue Adept*, Gilmore: *Enter Three Witches*, Jones: *Howl's Moving Castle*, Koertge: *Arizona Kid*, Korman: *A Semester in the Life of a Garbage Bag*, Pinkwater: *Snarkout Boys and the Avocado of Death*.

Multiculture

Crew: *Children of the River*, Dorris: *Yellow Raft in Blue Water*, Soto: *Baseball in April*, Spinelli: *Maniac McGee*, Staples. *Shabanu*, Taylor: *Road to Memphis*.

Fantasy

Butler: *Kindred*, Donaldson: *Lord Foul's Bane*, Klause: *Silver Kiss*, Lackey: *Arrows of the Queen*, Pierce: *Darkangel*, Sleator: *Interstellar Pig*.

Suspense/Horror

Avi: *Wolf Rider*, Duncan: *Don't Look Behind You*, King: *Shining*, Koontz: *Watchers*, Littke: *Prom Dress*, Pullman: *Ruby in the Smoke*.

Real Life

Carter: *Up Country*, Crutcher: *Chinese Handcuffs*, Mazer: *Silver*, Myers: *Fallen Angels*, Peck: *Princess Ashley*, Voigt: *Izzy, Willy-Nilly*.

Schedule of the Program Day

9:30 a.m.	Registration and Coffee
10:00 a.m.	Ron Koertge
11:15 a.m.	Discussions
12:30 p.m.	Lunch
3:00 p.m.	Book and Reading Promotion Panel
3:45 p.m.	Evaluation
4:00 p.m.	Author Reception

[August 1993]

Teens in Transition: A Workshop on Teen Sexuality and AIDS for Youth-Serving Professionals

Mary Alice Deveny

"AIDS is the sixth leading cause of death among 15 to 24-year-olds. AIDS cases among teens and young adults have grown 62% in the last two years alone!" (*Sex, 50 Things You Should Know Now*, by Kathy McCoy, *'TEEN*, December 1992, p. 30+).

The Beginning

A group of us librarians from southwest Florida sat around meeting room tables about a year ago, voting on the topic we most needed in a continuing education workshop. We chose teen sexuality and AIDS. Our State Library Consultant, Carole Fiore, received a Library Services and Construction Act grant to fund the workshop, "Teens in Transition: Teenage Sexuality and AIDS," at a site in Sarasota County.

As the site hosts, we sent invitations to everyone we could think of. Librarians, HRS staffs, public and private school teachers and guidance counselors, school board members, youth organizations staff, church and religious leaders, psychologists and counselors. We talked, we planned, we prepared bibliographies, media lists, lists of speakers, resource people and organizations. We gathered pamphlets and handouts and prepared displays. We cut lengths of red ribbon. We handled registration forms and luncheon checks. I pleaded, "What will change as a result of this workshop? Will we have an action plan? Will we leave knowing what we need to do to make a difference?" Nobody was answering those questions.

January 29, 1993

I walked into the Holiday Inn early to do my shift at the registration table. An hour and 109 people later, the program began. We were greeted. Our purpose was the same, "to make a difference." So what will be different, I wondered. Dr. Marilyn Volker, sexologist and sexuality educator from Miami, began speaking. Totally engaging, direct, communicating with the audience on many levels. "Search your heart," she said. "What is your own personal fear about HIV? Our helplessness about the behavior is our common ground." She has that right, I thought.

If you're going to "do education," she said, find your common ground. Spend time with people to understand where they're coming from.

We learned the difference between safe and safer. "The word 'masturbation' should be rolling off our tongues with the word 'abstinence.' Before a friend of mine died, she told me, 'If I had been touching myself instead of other people, I would be living longer.'"

How much fear do we have about getting up in front of a group and saying things like this, she asked us. "Ask yourself, 'Can I stand up to my peers?' and know how teens feel standing up to theirs. Be sure you know what label is going to get you. Be very clear about your goal."

"Then look at your beliefs. If you're not sure about kissing and spit, and the kids ask you, you're going to waffle. Third graders want to know about boogers and snot. Always find out what *they* believe so you'll know what page of paper you're starting on. The real test in life is that, when someone says something, my next words either open doors to intimacy or close doors to intimacy. I'd like to know more about what you believe and may I share with you what I believe. Now we have an honorable process. Listen to yourself, watch out for the judgments."

Dr. Volker showed us different types of condoms and "dental dams." She told us how she took her own teenage son to a drugstore to buy a package of condoms. A parent in the audience expressed disapproval with the explicitness: "You should be preaching abstinence, not showing them how to use condoms. Abstinence isn't getting the same play as drugs and alcohol."

Marilyn Volker responded. "Parents are our primary sex educators. But look at the belief system. Teens believe rock stars and movie stars and sports stars before they believe their parents. If they don't believe

Focus on Adults 213

they can get it, no amount of talking will change that. Do you want your kids to come to you or to go to someone else? There is an art to teaching. It's interactive, personalized. This is a dance we're doing. I'd rather you be embarrassed or offended than infected or reinfected. Who do teens believe most? Other teens. Their peers. We ought to be training peer educators. Teenagers will ask three types of questions, about fact, feeling, and resources. Collect the questions teens are asking. Have a box for anonymous questions on slips of paper in the library, in schools. Put these questions in front of the school board. Ask if we should answer them individually or have a curriculum. The best curriculum is collecting their questions. And remember to not always put things in a heterosexual sense if you want to have a sex education program for your entire community."

At a break, the chairperson of our local school board asked Dr. Volker, "Do you ever do presentations for school board members?" (Quick nodding from the speaker.) "This is fantastic. It would be good for us." "Here, take my card."

I asked Dr. Volker to speak to librarians, specifically, about what we can do. She said, "Librarians have a very powerful voice in the community by what they have on the shelves and what they don't, what they're avoiding, and by their ability to bring people together, like this, to address HIV issues. Librarians can provide meeting rooms for dialogues between PWAs (Persons With AIDS) and community leaders. Librarians can affiliate with local AIDS projects that might need materials for PWAs and their families, such as your on-line computers. This is not only about prevention. It is about being supportive of individuals in our communities."

An old friend of mine said, "She's wonderful . . . . But I hope she doesn't want us to all go back and do what she's doing, or we would all be fired. Especially after the censorship problem we just had at our library with an AIDS book. I wish I could."

After the break, Dr. Volker stated the HIV Education Program Goals: 1) Increase adolescents' awareness of HIV infection and factors that put them at risk for infection.

Fifth grader to Dr. Volker after a school presentation in a junior high school: "Ms.-Volker-my-boyfriend-says-if-we-butt-f—k-I-won't-get-pregnant-what-do-you-think? (breath)"

Marilyn: "(She asked for my *opinion*, thank God.) 'Your boyfriend's right, you won't. Now may I ask you some questions; you don't have to answer. O.K.? Have you and your boyfriend ever talked about AIDS? No? Did you know that butt-f—king (use their language) is one of the easiest ways to get the HIV/AIDS virus?' I have one shot at getting the information to her. Otherwise who is she going to go to for her information? Her boyfriend, that solid rock of information? I gave her a hotline number and she wrote it on her arm. Always have hotline numbers by your phone."

2) Describe how HIV is transmitted and what can be done to prevent transmission. "We must honor all parts of our body. Name them, accept them. Prevention is absolutely the common ground. Be safe."

3) Dispel myths about transmission.

"You believe AIDS is God's punishment for certain sexual behavior? Did you know that the social group that has the lowest amount of HIV is lesbian? Then you must believe that God approves of lesbianism. Back off, back off, back off."

4) Motivate adolescents to change behaviors that place them at risk with HIV. "We talk about driving and driving values to our kids long before they are ready to drive. We tell them about driving safety and we give them a test to see if they are ready.

"Where to kids get self-esteem? Black kids get it from the black community. Hispanic kids get it from the Hispanic community. Gay and lesbian kids, where do they go? To the bars, the streets, the bushes. Gay and lesbian youth need a place to go, to talk, to develop self-esteem. They are ten percent of our population."

5) Discuss ways to support community members who live with HIV/AIDS and their families.

Marilyn Volker told us she had just gone to her 120th funeral in ten years. "How do you feel? What do you hold about them in your heart?" These are questions that can be asked in a group setting, in a library. She will send a list of questions to use with groups of kids.

"Because of 120 people I know, I've stepped out into a risky place. It used to be lonely. Thank you, those of you who were there. You were supporting me. Someone had gone before to lead and to hold out a hand."

After the session, she told me the Clinton administration has been

Focus on Adults

asking AIDS projects and educators to come up with information regarding HIV prevention education. She has been asked, along with others, to make suggestions to the Clinton administration, so "a number of us are meeting together to make suggestions."

At the Lunch Break

Christian School teacher: "I have a fifteen-year-old son. Teens are not getting the message. They think condoms are safe, not *safer*. They think oral sex is safe. The handout literature is not as specific as she (Volker) is. It needs to be."

Girl's, Inc. staff member:
"She said, 'Find a challenging place to stand and put yourself in it.' Or something like that. I wrote it down. It was a challenge to us all, I think, professionally and personally, to take a step into an uncomfortable place and go forward with this important program. Because we have more information, it is our responsibility to do something with it. If we disseminate information properly, it can be used within any belief system. We are sexual beings. That is a fact."

Carole Fiore, Florida State Library Consultant: "Relationships are being forged here today between libraries and other youth-serving organizations. It is so important that we go out into the community and work with the people who work with the kids."

Break-Out Sessions

Counselor in my group, from a family counseling service: "Do you know your counterparts in Pinellas County?" (Yes, I did.) "Are they here today?" (Yes, they were.) "Maybe you could point them out to me."

"Come on, I'll introduce you."

Request from the floor: "Could we have a mailing list of the participants here today, for networking? Or start a list around?"

Response from the floor to a series of questions including who of us knew PWAs (almost everyone in the room was standing): "I felt ashamed for even wondering how he got it."

Example of group discussion questions; this portion of the program was moderated by the Education Director of the regional Planned Parenthood office: "A teen with whom you are familiar through your work exhibits behavior which you believe may be severe depression. The teen inquires about books on the subject of suicide, specifically *Final Exit*. What do you do?"

Groups chose spokespersons to report the results of the small group discussions to the group at large.

Suggestion after one of the scenario discussions:

"If you have complaints about having sex information pamphlets in the library, you could put out a survey to determine strategies, create a forum of a cross section of the community to discuss it."

A Play by the Source, A Teen Drama Group Sponsored by Planned Parenthood Association of Southwest Florida, Inc.

"The First Time Club," four preteen girls, meet together the first night of every month, to do things they've never done: pierce their ears, sneak into a movie, smoke cigarettes. They pledge their loyalty to one another by cutting their fingers with a razor blade and joining fingers: "My blood with your blood, bonded in friendship, adventure, and blood." Things begin to change when they reach the ages of 13, 14, 15. Boyfriends and then sex enter the picture. When Allison's boyfriend is diagnosed HIV positive, Allison gets tested and finds she is infected. The last club meeting is in her hospital room. They don't use the razor blade this time.

Sponsor:

"Teachers have told us that they've done AIDS units sometimes for three days with no response. Then the play comes in, then everybody's talking about it. We've got to talk, especially about AIDS. Any kids who become HIV positive, that's wrong. It could have been prevented."

"It's our future. It's our lives we have to save. That's why we're doing this."

A Week Later

I receive a phone call at the library from a parent. After a reference interview, I discover that she wants books with "facts of life" information for her fifth grade son. She tells me she's been evading his questions for some time now, indicates that she's fearful about having to do this. I ask her if it might be because of the way the information was presented to her as a child. She says she was told nothing. I say, "If he doesn't hear it from you, he'll hear it from someone else." She says, "He did use the word 'condom' the other day, and I said, 'Where did you hear that word?' He said, 'On the playground.' I said, 'What do you know about *that*?' and he said, 'Nothing.' I don't know if he really knows nothing or just isn't saying." She wants nothing explicit, just basic information on reproduction. Her husband will be bringing home some library books shortly, but she isn't sure she'll like what he brings, because when she looked before, she couldn't find anything she liked. I say, "And will you want something on AIDS, too?" She says, "I don't know. He knows about that. A family friend just died from it. But they don't talk to anyone about it." I say, "You know, that gives you a perfect lead-in to this conversation. You could buy a box of condoms at the drugstore and show him what they are." She says she has to go and she'll call me back.

I think about the pamphlets in the workshop packet on *How to Talk with Your Young Child about Sex*, and *How to Talk with Your Child about AIDS*. I make copies for her. I see the Planned Parenthood stickers on the backs of the pamphlets. I remember previous conversations with this same parent, who has had objections to various types of materials on children's library shelves. I know something about her belief system. I wonder if she'll object to these. I send them anyway. Tomorrow I'll keep looking, even if she doesn't call me back. I want to give her the best material I can find for her, something she'll feel comfortable using with her son, so she will use it. And if we don't have it, I have lists and catalogues. I know where to find more.

I think about what I said to her, about how I used what I learned. I wonder what she'll say to him. I think about how people can change through education. How do we educate? The same way we learn, one by one by one. "It's a dance we're doing." That's how we'll make a difference. [October 1993]

A Matter of Time: An Overview of Themes from the Carnegie Report

Jane Quinn

The Library and Information Science Department of the Rutgers School of Communication, Information and Library Studies held an invitational, federally funded institute called "Toward a Nation of Readers: Community Partnerships for Fostering the Reading Habit in Childhood and Early Adolescence" directed by Jana Varlejs on March 3-5, 1994. Twelve community teams from New Jersey, New York, Pennsylvania and Vermont received training in collaborative community reading partnerships. Each team invited consisted of a public librarian, a school librarian, and a community-based youth worker. The idea for the institute came from the 1992 Carnegie Council on Adolescent Development report, **A Matter of Time: Risk and Opportunity in the Nonschool Hours***, which each community team received as part of its training. The institute keynote speaker was Jane Quinn, who directed the Carnegie project which produced* **A Matter of Time** *prior to her present position. The following text is her keynote address. Copies of the report are available for $13 (single copies) from the Carnegie Council on Adolescent Development, PO Box 753, Waldorf, MD 20604. Phone: (202) 429-7979. —Mary K. Chelton*

Introduction

Good morning, fellow youth advocates. I have been asked to talk with you today about the report on American youth organizations entitled *A Matter of Time: Risk and Opportunity in the Nonschool Hours*. Recognizing that the title of this conference is *Toward a Nation of Readers*, I want to start out by assuring you that I don't intend to read a speech. What I do intend is to tell you about three things: *how* we conducted the *A Matter of Time* study, *what we learned*, and what I see as the major *implications* for librarians and their community partners.

This study, which was published in December of 1992 by the Carnegie Corporation of New York, examined the state of America's youth organizations with a focus on two major issues: how well current services address the needs of young adolescents (ages 10-15); and how effective they are in reaching and serving young people growing up in high-risk environments. The staff and the Task Force that guided the study were charged by Carnegie President David Hamburg with producing a report that offered recommendations in three areas: program, funding, and policy. Our report not only offered such recommendations but also provided a comprehensive description and analysis of the terrain of contemporary community-based youth development programs.

How We Conducted the Carnegie Study

The study examined the following five sectors of community programs for young adolescents:

(1) Private, nonprofit, national organizations that serve youth (including organizations that are primarily or exclusively youth-serving in their focus—such as Boy Scouts, Camp Fire, Boys and Girls Clubs—as well as multiservice organizations, such as the YMCA and YWCA, that offer substantial service to youth); (2) Grassroots youth-development organizations not affiliated with any national structure; (3) Religious youth organizations; (4) Youth programs run by privately sponsored adult service clubs, sports organizations, senior citizens groups, and museums; and (5) Youth programs run by selected public sector institutions, including libraries and parks and recreation departments.

Since all of you in this audience are knowledgeable about youth issues and services, you have some idea of the immensity of this undertaking. According to the National Center for Charitable Statistics, an arm of Independent Sector, there are 17,000 youth development organizations in America, and that does not include many of the religious groups (which are counted in a different category for their purposes), sports programs, libraries, municipal services, or the youth programs sponsored by adult service clubs, senior citizen groups or museums. How then were

Focus on Adults

we going to wrap our arms—or, more accurately, our brains—around this huge universe?

We decided to follow the dictate of Jane Addams who advised social workers to keep "one foot in the library and one foot in the street." We knew that a literature search would quite naturally be a part of our study; but we also knew that, by itself, a literature review would constitute an inadequate data-gathering mechanism in a field like youth development where knowledge is based as much on *experience* as on research. So we attempted to combine the best of both worlds—the *practice* world and the *research* world—by employing nine different methods in our study design:

(1) We started by convening a twenty-six-member Task Force to guide and oversee the project. This group was composed of national policy makers, researchers, youth organization executives, local and national funders, and other civic leaders. The Task Force met six times during the course of the research phase, participated in research interviews and planning subcommittees, and in many rounds of reviews of its final report.

(2) Next, we conducted focus groups with young people in the age range that was of interest to us (young adolescents). In all, we conducted sixteen groups that were then separated by race, gender, and age. We talked with these young people about how they spend their non-school time, about activity preferences during the non-school hours, about the characteristics they do and don't like in adult leaders, and about how they would design an ideal youth center.

(3) We did conduct an extensive literature review, combing through research and practice literature, both published and unpublished. As we conducted our review, we were interested in building both the theoretical and empirical cases that youth development programs can and do make a difference in the lives of young people.

(4) We commissioned twelve papers, researched and written by specialists in various aspects of youth development, on topics ranging from adolescent time use to the funding of American youth organizations to cross-national perspectives on youth development. All of these papers are available free from the Carnegie Council in Washington, DC.

(5) Members of the Task Force and I interviewed scores of youth work leaders, including the board presidents and executive directors of the

twenty major national youth organizations. Other key informants were local youth work practitioners—including direct service workers, agency administrators, and volunteers.

(6) A major challenge in this study was how to learn anything coherent and systematic about the hundreds of independent, grassroots youth development organizations that exist in cities and towns across America. We decided to conduct a national survey of these groups, using the Independent Sector database as a means to identify them.

(7) We consulted with other national experts, inviting researchers and policymakers to meet with the Task Force.

(8) Staff and commissioned paper authors visited programs and communities, in an effort to learn at the ground level about exemplary program practices and about models for comprehensive community-wide planning of youth services.

(9) Finally, we held two consultations—one-day meetings with practitioners and researchers—to discuss the urgent and important issues of program evaluation and professional development of youth workers. In both cases, we were seeking to establish a consensus about the current state of the art and about recommendations for improving those states. Both of these consultations have resulted in written reports that are available *free* from the Carnegie Council.

Themes of the Final Report

In synthesizing the results of these various analyses, the Task Force saw ten clear themes emerge. I would like to outline these themes and tell you briefly about each one.

Theme #1: Building on Current Strengths

Many strengths characterize today's community-based youth development programs: tradition, commitment, credibility, diversity, and an extensive reach to millions of young people nationwide. The magnitude of this reach is documented in several places—probably nowhere better than the 1988 National Education Longitudinal Study, which found seventy one percent of its nationally-representative sample of eighth graders to be involved in at least one type of organized, out-of-school activity.

Another strength is durability. Many national youth organizations are nearly 100 years old. They must be doing a lot that's right. And many of the local, grassroots groups that we surveyed have existed for several decades, often in the face of seemingly insurmountable odds; again, there is much to learn from their resilience and experience.

Theme #2: Responding to the Needs and Wants of Young Adolescents

Many youth programs are not responding as fully as they might to the needs and wants of *young adolescents*. Most current youth development programs are *planned, led, run and controlled* by adults. This strategy works much better with five-year-olds than with fifteen-year-olds, who want and need a bigger piece of the action. In our study, many types of youth organizations—including sports programs, recreation departments, religious youth groups, and a number of national youth agencies—reported difficulty attracting young people after the age of twelve or thirteen.

Yet young people—in our own focus groups and other surveys—consistently report that they want *places to go, things to do, people to care about them*. They drop out of after-school activities for a good reason: there's a mismatch between what many youth organizations offer and what young adolescents want.

For example, teenagers want to know about human sexuality and they want to know how to avoid violence. But many youth organizations avoid or water down discussion of these topics. The reasons? Such issues are often seen as too controversial—not by the young people, but by adult leaders, donors, or board members. (Librarians know about this.)

Another example: while adolescents want to be useful and involved, many youth agencies offer insufficient opportunities for young people to participate in organizational decision making. Young people serving on boards of directors and program advisory committees should be *commonplace*, not *unusual* as it is now. (Think about where you work.)

The *voluntary nature* of youth agencies suggests that young people should have a great deal of autonomy in structuring and selecting their own activities. When they don't, many frustrated teens understandably "vote with their feet."

Theme #3: Reaching Out to Young People in Low-Income Areas

As we pieced together existing data from several sources, we observed a persistent pattern: that many youth programs are failing to reach out to *young people in low-income environments.*

For example, the 1988 National Education Longitudinal Study confirmed that only seventeen percent of eighth graders from *upper-income* families *do not* participate in organized out-of-school activities, while fully forty percent of lower-income youth report no such involvement. When you look at the array of existing surveys of parents and adolescents, it's difficult to conclude that this differential is based on a lack of interest. Rather these studies point out clearly that youth in low-income areas don't participate because they can't afford the fees and dues, they can't get to programs safely, or the programs *just don't exist* in their neighborhoods. Expanding services in low-income areas will require individual and collective action at both the local and national levels. Community programs for youth (and this includes libraries) should view themselves as actors in a network of services, and these networks should engage in systematic planning and coordinated decision making. We should be thinking about a *web of support* or a *richly woven tapestry*, not a *safety net*. Youth and community needs, rather than organizational concerns, should remain at the center of these efforts.

Theme #4: Addressing Economic and Employment Issues

Young adolescents consistently name *economic and employment issues* as a priority for them, yet few organizations deliver. Approximately twenty percent of fourteen and fifteen-year-olds work for pay outside the home, often in jobs that are routine, boring, and devoid of positive interaction with adults. Some of these jobs are physically dangerous as well. Both common sense and research tell us that there *might well be* more constructive alternatives to sweeping floors at McDonald's or selling T-shirts at The Gap.

Youth organizations, including public libraries, have many positive ways to respond to these issues. The Bay Area Public Libraries came up with a solution—they listened to teens, and then hired some. [See Finney article, p. 108] Other youth organizations offer a career ladder of sorts that begins with voluntary service in the agency, then moves in stepwise fashion toward paid part-time employment.

In addition to offering employment when possible, youth organizations should capitalize on the interest of young people in the world of work by providing career awareness, pre-employment training, jobs skills training, and internship programs on an ongoing basis.

Theme #5: Responding Pro-Actively to Competition from Youth Gangs

In general, programs do not adequately acknowledge the benefits that teenagers get out of belonging to *youth gangs*, and they do not actively compete with gangs for youth membership. American society has witnessed several waves of youth gangs throughout its history, and we know a lot about their formation, organization, and functioning. Youth gangs intuitively understand young adolescents' developmental needs and cater to them. They provide safety, status, meaningful roles, income, and a sense of competence and belonging. One researcher, James Diego Vigil, has correlated the rise of youth gangs in Los Angeles over the past fifteen years with the dismantling of social programs for youth. He discovered, for example, that the city of Los Angeles sponsored 130 inner-city teen centers in the 1970s and by the early 1990s, only *five* such centers remained.

Youth development programs can compete successfully with gangs for the time, attention, energy, and commitment of young people. Promising initiatives—for example, the Gang Prevention and Intervention Program of Youth Development, Inc. in Albuquerque appear to be directed not toward disbanding youth gangs, but toward discouraging younger teens from joining gangs in the first place and toward providing constructive, nonviolent activities for current gang members.

Theme #6: Intensifying Program Efforts to Meet Program Goals

To respond to the needs of today's young people, many community programs will need to *provide service more often and over a longer period of time*. Once-a-month assertiveness training is unlikely to prevent drug abuse, and a one-hour session on how to dress in the workplace is not going to arm any teenager, even the most eager, with the skills that he or she needs in order to succeed in a first job.

Research evidence is growing that, to be effective, community-based interventions—particularly those designed to serve young people from less advantaged backgrounds—must be *deeper* and *more sustained*. This by no means indicates that every program or service must be *comprehensive* and *intensive*; rather, young people should have access to an *array* of services that meet these criteria.

One youth worker summarized the situation quite eloquently when he observed: "I think our program is on the right track, but sometimes I worry that *the touch is kind of light*."

Theme #7: Increasing and Stabilizing the Funding Base

One of the most striking features of America's youth development organizations is the *precariousness of their funding*. Many organizations are forced to spend *inordinate* amounts of board and staff time on fundraising simply to keep the agency in business. In our research, the struggle to survive was repeatedly cited as an ongoing reality. One of America's most successful youth organizations, The Door in New York City, juggles 130 funding sources at the same time.

The Task Force identified four major problems: (1) the inadequacy of the overall level of support; (2) the instability of that support; (3) the tendency of funders, especially public sources, to support *remediation*, treatment, and control rather than youth development and primary prevention; and (4) the tendency to fund *categorically*, by problem area, rather than comprehensively. In *A Matter of Time*, we offer specific suggestions to local United Ways and other federated campaigns, national and local foundations, businesses, and government agencies about how to rectify these problems. We advocate *focused, predictable, sustained* support.

Theme #8: Investing in Adult Leadership

Youth-serving agencies, religious youth groups, sports programs, parks and recreation services, and libraries all report that the adults who work with young people in their systems, whether serving on a paid or pro-bono basis, are *the* most critical factor in program success. Yet the quality of adult program leadership in all of these systems was consistently cited as inadequate.

Improving the quality of adult leadership involves recruiting and retaining a more diverse group of youth workers in the first place; it involves more adequate training programs for staff in colleges and universities before they begin work; and it involves more systematic on-the-job training. Our report offers specific advice in each of these important areas.

Improving the quality of adult leadership also involves the thorny issue of inadequate compensation. Low salaries, coupled with paltry or nonexistent benefits, lead to the burnout and high staff turnover that typifies the youth development field. In the mid-1980s, I met a full-time Program Director in a youth agency who was earning $4,000 per year. I'd like to think that this situation has changed dramatically—as it needs to—but I've seen no evidence that it has.

Theme #9: Documenting and Evaluating Services

The Task Force was dismayed to find that many programs and organizations do not collect even the most basic information about the youth they currently serve. Many national organizations do not know the age, gender, racial, ethnic, or economic backgrounds of their current service populations.

Local youth organizations are more likely to have at least some of this data, in part because United Way and other local funders have come to require it. Ideally, all youth organizations would keep *accurate, regular, and consistent information* about service demographics. Armed with such data, organizations can conduct more effective planning, and can develop joint efforts to reach underserved youth.

A related problem that plagues the field of youth development is the *poor state of program evaluation*. Many programs have unclear, unspecific, or unmeasurable goals and objectives, and therefore have no reliable basis for claiming that their services are effective. This vagueness undercuts individual agencies' ability to solicit funding, and it hampers collective efforts to advocate for expansion of services. The Task Force recommends that some type of assessment mechanism be built into every community program for youth, and that the level of the assessment or evaluation match the needs of the sponsoring organization and the state of the program's evolution.

Theme #10: Formulating Youth-Friendly Public Policies

Local, state, and federal policies all play a critical role in supporting, or in failing to support, healthy adolescent development. Current U.S. youth policy has a decided orientation toward treatment, remediation, and control of problems. But healthy youth development has a different focus. It strives to help young people *develop the inner resources and skills* they need to cope with pressures that might lead them into unhealthy and antisocial behaviors.

An ideal set of public policies would be *integrated* at all three levels—local, state, federal; would be firmly committed to the concept of *youth as resources*; would focus on increasing support for basic youth development services; would target services to areas of greatest need; and would give priority to *locally generated solutions*. In *A Matter of Time*, we further outline the principles of such youth-supportive public policy, and cite examples of enlightened policy at all three governmental levels.

Well, What Are the Implications for Libraries and Their Community Partners?

To oversimplify, I would say that there are three major implications to the Carnegie research: young adolescents need libraries, libraries need young adolescents, and libraries need community partners if they are to meet the real needs of contemporary youth. Let's take these implications in that order.

Young adolescents need libraries (and librarians). There is no question, from the original research conducted by the Task Force (such as our focus group study with young teens) or from current social science research that we reviewed as part of our study, that many American youth are *starved* for positive interaction with adults. In my view, "starvation" is not too strong a term to describe this phenomenon.

In the focus groups that we conducted as part of the Carnegie study, one of the strongest, clearest themes was the *hunger* that young people described for *positive, supportive relationships with caring adults*. Many of the youth we interviewed expressed a desire to interact with adults whom they can trust, who respect them, and who can teach them to "do the right thing." We should not underestimate this desire for guidance. All of the youth we interviewed noted that communications skills were very important; they wanted to be with adults who could talk with you, listen to you, respect you, and understand your point of view.

There is also no question, from our own research and that of our colleagues, that America's youth have *too much time on their hands*. This theme, in fact, found its way right into the title of the Carnegie report. Fully forty percent of young people's waking hours are discretionary—that is, not already committed to activities like school, household chores and homework. Many of America's youth spend virtually all of this discretionary time without companionship or supervision from responsible adults. They spend the time alone, with peers, or—in some cases—with adults who may exert negative influences on them or exploit them.

One reason American youth have so much discretionary time is the comparatively short school day (six to seven hours, not all of which are spent in academic pursuits) and short school year (180 days). By comparison Japanese adolescents attend school for nine hours a day, 240 days per year. So what do young people do with all this free time? Those of you who are librarians, in schools or in public libraries, would probably like to believe that they are *reading books*. However, the research doesn't bear this out. In fact, according to University of Michigan researchers, young adolescents spend about 1.3 percent of their waking hours reading and 3.5 percent studying. By contrast, they spend 20.7 percent of their waking hours doing *guess what*??? You're right—watching television. And it's probably not public TV. Even if the programs they are watching are full of sex and violence (and, of course, there's a good chance that they are), these programs are likely not contributing very much to young adolescents' cognitive or social development. Reflect for a moment on the many developmental tasks of adolescence; there's hard work to be done and many milestones to achieve. It's pretty clear that watching twenty or more hours of television per week probably represents a lost opportunity.

So, young adolescents need libraries and the many kinds of resources they can offer: books and videos, computers and CD-ROMs, homework help, access to information, opportunities to learn how to access information; safe places, serious places, fun places, nurturing places; people, including adults with knowledge, skills and commitment; peers; other age kids, including opportunities to tutor young children or be tutored by others. Libraries can meet the major developmental needs of young adolescents—for competence, belonging, identity and self-worth. They can contribute to all five domains of human development—cognitive, moral, social, psychological, even physical. They can offer a range of roles, from patron to helper to employee.

OK, you say, but *why do libraries need young adolescents*? They are sometimes noisy, sometimes messy, sometimes scary—especially when they start getting taller than we are and as opinionated as we are. But libraries need young adolescents for several reasons: demographically, they represent one out of every twelve of our citizens; and, if my homework is correct, they represent an even much larger proportion of current library users. Without their active participation, libraries wouldn't be doing their jobs, and the public would surely notice. But beyond simple issues of demographics and accountability, libraries need the strengths that young adolescents bring: their knowledge, their curiosity, their candor, their energy. Talking with and listening to young adolescents can make your services more relevant. And young adolescents, adequately supported and supervised, can contribute to many of the library's services as paid or volunteer assistants.

Why Libraries Need Community-Based Organizations

In today's world, no organization—whether it's a public library, school library, or community-based youth-serving organizations can afford to operate in isolation. It's just not good practice. No single entity can meet the complex needs of today's youth. School and public libraries need one another to supplement and complement one another's work; and libraries and youth agencies need one another if either is to meet its youth development goals. For example, libraries can (and do) work with youth-serving organizations to enrich their programming, to help them reach underserved groups of youth, to share in the work of advocating on behalf of youth, and to testify on their behalf at times of budget-cutting. Similarly, youth agencies need libraries to enrich their programming, to help them document the needs of youth in the local community, as sites for paid employment and community service projects, and as advocacy partners. In the Carnegie study, we outlined the current trends and challenges facing public libraries in their work to promote positive youth development. And we highlighted the work of one innovative library program–the Bay Area Youth at Risk Program in the San Francisco Bay Area.

In my current work at DeWitt Wallace-Reader's Digest Fund, I am involved as a funder of several programs that involve school and public libraries. One effort, the Connecting Libraries and Schools Program (CLASD), fosters collaboration between the New York Public Library and New York City Public Schools and also between the branch libraries and youth serving organizations, such as the Children's Aid Society and the YMCA. Another major program supported by the Fund is Library Power, designed to revitalize school libraries in communities around the country. The Fund has worked closely with the American Library Association in designing and implementing this initiative, which is currently operating in 13 cities.

I tell you this not to invite proposals but to let you know that at least two major national foundations—my former employer, Carnegie, and my current employer, the DeWitt Wallace-Reader's Digest Fund, recognize the importance of libraries in contributing to the well-being of America's youth. I am heartened to see that the federal government shares this view by funding this conference, and I applaud the Rutgers School of Communication, Information and Library Studies for convening this conference. This is a too-rare gathering of people who need one another and who are needed by our nation's youth. I am pleased to have been able to make some introductory remarks and I wish you much success in the deliberations and dialogues that will be part of the conference over the next two days. [October 1994]

Read My Genre: A Reader's Advisory Workshop
Judy Sasges

It might happen at a library conference where technology vendors greatly outnumber the book publishers. Or after attending another workshop on information access. It could happen while interviewing MLS candidates who have no idea who the current fiction writers are because they read "only the classics." It could even happen at the public service desk when a patron asks for a good book to read—and you can't think of a single title. Sooner or later, it happens: the realization hits that those of us who work in libraries hardly ever talk about novels, or reading for pleasure, anymore.

At the Santa Clara County (CA) Library, Deputy County Librarian Carol Jaech and I talked around this topic for months. We knew that staff, for whatever reason, was not reading as much fiction as in the past. We also knew several individuals who read voraciously in at least one genre. People wanted to keep up with titles and genres but could not find the time. In 1989, we decided to take a proactive role and plan a workshop that focused on fiction. Thus, the almost annual reader's advisory series got its start.

The goals for the first workshop, called *How to Be a Novel Guide*, were simple and remain consistent:

1. The focus is fiction: old favorites, new titles, genres, personal recommendations—whatever the presenter chooses.
2. Participants want to attend and actually read some of the titles mentioned. Attendance is encouraged but not mandated.
3. The fun and pleasure of reading are emphasized by both the presenters and the audience.
4. Bibliographies and handouts are included.

The Basics

The first workshop was targeted to those who work at the adult information desk. Early in the planning process, we decided to encourage the participation of other local libraries so Carol Jaech called personal contacts, explained the workshop and its goals, and asked for volunteers. Four libraries, other than Santa Clara County, "volunteered" staff. Each person then selected his/her topic. The genres represented were romance and family sagas; mysteries; poetry; war stories; "kinder, gentler novels"; science fiction and fantasy; and adult novels for young adults.

With the speakers confirmed, we structured the workshop. Two sessions were scheduled to accommodate various shifts: different days, one morning and one afternoon, each about 3 1/2 hours. Presenters were given 20-30 minute slots with a half hour break so that people could mingle and look at the books, reader's advisory tools, bibliographies, and featured titles on the display tables. Food was served. A trading post featured bibliographies from many library systems. All participants received a packet of bibliographies prepared by the presenters.

Apart from requesting that a bibliography be included (which the sponsoring library typed, reproduced and collated), instructions to the presenters about their genre talks were minimal. Comparisons between authors and titles were encouraged, (for example, if you like King, try Koontz), but not required. Each speaker developed a presentation that was both enlightening and fun.

The first year, 109 people from seven library systems attended the *How to Be a Novel Guide* workshop. Evaluations were very positive, including, "It's so good to see a literature based program," to "You should take this show on the road!"

Building on the Basics

In 1992, after three successful reader's advisory workshops, we began planning number four. Many evaluations from previous years indicated a need for information about young adult titles, especially suggestions for the high school age. The focus for 1992 became young adult titles that also appeal to adults and, I, as Young Adult Services Coordinator, was in charge of the year's effort.

The workshops are traditionally (if four years constitute a tradition) offered in June so planning actually begins in January. By November, I was worried about finding 1992's "volunteers." Although speakers from other library systems were successfully recruited previously, it was becoming more difficult to find volunteers and young adult genres made the pool even smaller. I decided to approach my library's young adult librarians about the project since they are generally recognized as good sports.

Rereading the ever-useful evaluations, discussing recent YA reader's advisory questions, and analyzing school assignments helped define topics and genres of interest to young adults. The selected genres were: readable historical fiction; romances for the older young adult; fantasy; biographies (not fiction but definitely a heavily requested genre); multiculturalism; and humor. Whereas in previous workshops, presenters already had basic knowledge in their selected genres, the YA presenters would, for the most part, be becoming familiar with the genres as they prepared for the June program. Having recently completed my term on YALSA's Best Books for Young Adults committee, I lured three YA librarians into volunteering with promises of preselected books in their genres. That covered romance, biography, and multiculturalism. Historical fiction was chosen by the librarian in the next office who, besides being an avid historical fiction fan, tired of hearing me wail about how no one would touch the subject. For fantasy, I called an old friend in another system who knows the genre and was too kind-hearted to refuse me. I volunteered to do humor because I was working on YALSA's Humor Genre committee and (mistakenly) assumed I could read the same titles for both projects.

With presenters and genres chosen by January 1992, a timeline was the next step. It included cut-off dates for choosing the title of each presentation and submitting bibliographies, as well as a date for a timed run-through of each segment of the workshop. Presenters could either ask me to proof bibliographies or submit camera-ready copy. Most chose the proofing route although that meant a shorter deadline. As in past years, Santa Clara County Library designed, typed, and reproduced the bibliographies.

The serious work began in earnest. Selecting, reading, and annotating titles became a way of life, but more stressful for the presenters was creating a unique approach to the genres. In most cases, presenters say a few words about their interest in the genre, how they define it, and then move into brief mini-booktalks, mentioning the type of patron who might enjoy the books. Occasionally, a presenter reads a short passage but because time is so limited, this is not recommended.

For the humor genre talk, I mentioned that humor is so subjective that the patron should be offered more than one choice. I spoke about some of the novels that made me laugh and why. After highlighting titles on the bibliography, I distributed a list of funny books suggested by high school aged males, pointing out the lack of crossover between their list and mine. (Their all time favorite is Thomas Rockwell's *How to Eat Fried Worms*.) I planned to finish by reading the description of the school librarian in J. Clarke's *The Heroic Life of Al Capsella* but ran out of time. Twenty minutes in front of your peers may sound like an eternity but it flashes by when the audience is receptive.

Davi Evans provided a creative approach to historical fiction. Grouping titles loosely by time periods with a date card on top of each stack, she asked the audience, "How about a date?" The books she highlighted reflected the audience's response. Then, because Davi always gives a kiss on the first date, volunteers received a Hershey's Kiss.

These are only two examples of the different approaches to the genre talks; each speaker is individualized and brings something unusual to the presentation.

The reader's advisory workshops are rewarding. They bring people together from different libraries. They allow presenters a chance to show off their knowledge and creativity. They inform and entertain. They inspire people to read.

One thing they are not, however, is perfect. Aside from the minor difficulty of recruiting speakers, three components need some modification. First, there are a few subjects almost no one wants to tackle. Techno-thrillers, for example. Maybe some genres only have closet fans. Another problem is the participants' reluctance to bring additional materials for the trading post. No one does. The audience is also encouraged to mention favorite titles in the "quick picks" time slot. No one does that either. However, these are small glitches in an otherwise successful workshop.

Francoise Sagan once commented, "The one thing I regret is that I will never have the time to read all the books I want to read." That certainly holds true for today's readers—and librarians, as well. The reader's advisory workshops highlight books which may otherwise be missed and offer staff a better chance of putting just the right novel in a patron's outstretched hand.

Basic Hints

Here are a few hints that will improve the chances for the workshop's success and make life a little easier for those involved.
1. Choose a date (or dates) that doesn't compete with other workshops or holidays. If there is a master calendar somewhere, make sure the workshop is listed.
2. Plan two sessions—preferably a morning and an afternoon, on different days but within a week or so of each other. Different locations are also a good idea if the staff has long commutes.
3. Three hours is about the maximum length for this kind of program. Six presenters given twenty minutes each with a half hour break and time for questions/evaluations at the end is the right pace.
4. Be sure the facilitator starts promptly, keeps speakers on track, and ends the workshop on time.
5. Use a microphone for large groups.
6. Do not be shy about asking people to help. Most potential volunteers are flattered to be approached and will at least consider speaking.
7. Structure the workshop so that presenters can be creative and have fun with the genres. Remember that speakers are sharing their personalities as well as their reading tastes.
8. Presenters usually have more titles to discuss than time. Since people like to take notes, the presenters should either clearly announce the author/title of each novel or arrange the bibliographies in the order of presentation. Evaluations indicate that it is better to talk about fewer books in depth rather than try to cover everything in the bibliography.
9. Energy is always high at the workshop, the people are *right there*, so grab them and sign them up for next year. The new recruits will then

have a year to plan their twenty minutes of fame. At the 1992 session, I recruited volunteers for two of the most requested genres: westerns and techno-thrillers. And, no one has ever canceled after making the commitment to speak. No one has missed deadlines, either.
10. Allow enough time to gather drafts of bibliographies to proof, type, and reproduce. With clerical priority and using quick print services, the shortest deadline is one and one half months before the program.
11. On the 1992 evaluation, an added space allowed participants to suggest names of genre readers. It worked—apparently, people like to volunteer others but not necessarily themselves.
12. Read the evaluations and use them as a planning tool.

Planning a Reader's Advisory Workshop: Almost Step by Step

Before the workshop:
1. Recruit speakers about six months in advance. Be sure the genres are varied and general enough to interest public service desk staff. Suggest that speakers bring books for discussion.
2. Choose, book, and confirm dates and locations ASAP.
3. Send out information flyers to library directors, supervisors, and staff announcing the dates and genres. Mention that registration forms will follow.
4. Set deadlines with presenters for receiving bibliographies. Allow time for proofing, typing, designing cover art, and reproducing.
5. Send registration flyers one month in advance. Assign someone to receive registrations, collect fees (if needed), update list of registrants, and make name tags.
6. Prepare an agenda and an evaluation.
7. Collate agendas, evaluations, and bibliographies into packets.
8. Collect basic reader's advisory tools for the display table. Possible inclusions: *Genreflecting, Best Books for Senior High Readers*, copies of *Library Journal*'s Word of Mouth column, etc.
9. Organize the food and drink. Delegate responsibility for this!
10. Test all audio equipment that will be used.
11. Arrange for someone to register people at the workshop, collect evaluations, and troubleshoot.

12. The day before, call each site and make sure that the chairs will be set up, the coffee pot will be visible, and that podiums and display tables will be nearby.

The Day of the Workshop:

1. Arrive early to reassure yourself that the room is set up. Take a key to the building if necessary.
2. Start the coffee and organize the food.
3. Retest the audio equipment.
4. Post directional signs.
5. Place a table by the door for participants to check in, pick up packets, get name tags, etc.

Supplies Needed

Mundane as the following list sounds, a successful program inventory consists of: (1) The list of registrants; (2) folders with bibliographies; (3) change and receipt book (if needed); (4) pens; (5) tape; (6) printed and blank name tags; and (6) items for setting up the display tables and trading post area.

Be sure the facilitator starts and ends on time and keeps the presentations on track.

Relax and enjoy the speakers.

After the Workshop:

1. Write thank-yous to the speakers.
2. Write letters of commendation to the speakers' supervisors.
3. Analyze information: attendance, money, evaluations, problems, etc.
4. Follow up on suggestions for next year's speakers.
5. Work on post-workshop publicity such as articles for *VOYA* and recaps for library newsletters.

[June 1993]

For Young Adults Only—
From Teen Volunteers to Young Adult Library Advisory Boards: North Regional/Broward Community College Library

Leila J. Sprince

Introducing a Prototype Training Manual

One of the most interesting parts of editing ALA's new publication, *Excellence in Library Services to Young Adults: The Nation's Top Programs*, was getting to know a lot of great librarians doing great things with kids. While many people and programs in that publication could easily compete for anybody's favorite, I was particularly struck by the YA Library Advisory Board program established by Lee Sprince in Broward County's West Regional Library. The multicultural LAB was so popular that the kids themselves limited annual membership to thirty to keep things manageable. The LAB did all the programming for their peers in the library so successfully that they were asked to create programs for other age groups. Even more impressive, when Lee was promoted, her LAB kids from the West Regional came to help her set up a new LAB at her new site. The whole program is a model of how to offer youth development opportunities in a library setting.

When I talked with Lee by phone, we chatted about a book promotion video the kids had made which shows a scene of a vampire (played by a LAB member) coming out of his coffin at night. Lee said that she was worried that nobody would be able to see the scene on film because the vampire was played by an African American kid wearing black, arising from a black coffin in the shade of a large palm tree, but she then said, "I didn't say anything, though, because they have to figure these things out for themselves." I knew then why her program was so successful, and when she volunteered to share the LAB manual with *VOYA* subscribers for possible publication, I grabbed at it.

The text that follows is the codification of how a great librarian and youth worker does library-based youth participation good. Using it to replicate her YALAB success in other library settings would be the next best thing to cloning Lee, something Jane Quinn would no doubt very much like to see happen—and so would we.—Mary K. Chelton

Statement of Purpose: It's a Matter of Pride

We at North Regional/Broward Community College Library feel that a planned, multi-dimensional program for Young Adults within the Youth Services Department, is indeed, a matter of pride. This feeling of pride should be shared by staff and teens, as the programs should be of mutual benefit and interest.

The initial creation of a Teen Volunteer program should provide opportunities for young people to practice such qualities as efficiency, patience, promptness, and self-confidence, as well as to develop a sense of responsibility. Teens will not only form friendships and have fun, but they will become aware of the library as a viable resource in their lives.

From this group of interested teens will come a more dedicated teen group, known as a Young Adult Library Advisory Board. This group will learn even more skills, such as library technology, and will have the opportunity to work directly with the patrons, under the direction of the Youth Services staff. This group will also be involved in planning and implementing Youth Services sponsored programs.

The mutual benefits are almost endless! The teens will learn job skills, while having fun and developing a sense of community involvement. At the same time, they will be a wonderful human resource for the library, by relieving staff of certain time-consuming tasks, which can be performed well by teens. As a very real bonus, the teens will also become a source of goodwill and good public relations within the Youth Services Department, and throughout the entire library.

At a time when our teens face a world of violence and of alienation from society, we, at the library, must recognize their needs, and make clear our commitment to them.

Teen Recruitment: Go for It!

Nothing succeeds like personal contact. One visit is worth a hundred flyers, and once that first impression is created, printed materials can be used effectively as reminders, and reinforcement of the initial information.

Try to locate a map of your area schools, either from your library, or from your local school board. Call the school principal and the media specialist, and schedule a visit at the school. Try to see as many students as you can. I visit every middle and high school that will give me time, and young people to see.

How you introduce yourself to the teens is a matter of personal choice. I am a storyteller, so I always have a strange, and quirky little story to tell, preferably one with a tricky ending. After I have gotten their attention with the story, I tell them what YA literature is, and I booktalk a few real grabbers as examples. My personal favorites are *Killing Mr. Griffin* by Lois Duncan, *The Face on the Milk Carton* by Caroline B. Cooney, and *The Other Side of Dark* by Joan Lowery Nixon.

Now they are ready for your message. Make sure that you know what you want to say to the teens. You do not want to create a false impression, or to make unrealistic claims or promises.

Tell them about the Teen Volunteer Program, stressing the opportunities it provides for job experience, service hour credits, and certainly, for interest and fun. I also tell them that teens who are interested will have the further opportunity of joining a new group, called a Young Adult Library Advisory Board. This organization will have even more responsibility in the library. Teens who belong to the YALAB may participate in many activities. Among them may be: training new teen volunteers, peer tutoring, creating programs for themselves and other teens, helping with programs for younger children, helping the public to use new library technology, and having some input into YA titles ordered by the Youth Services Department.

I try to leave the teens with the impression that there was something for everyone to do in YALAB, and that no one would be involved in an unwanted activity.

Finally, I told them how much I needed their help with both the Teen Volunteer program, and with the formation of the YALAB. I invited them to visit the library, and to meet the Youth Services staff.

I always save some time for a question and answer period. Your goodbye should be as warm as possible, and should include your hope to see them again.

Teen Volunteer Guidelines

Hi! Welcome to NR/BCC Library. We are very happy that you have decided to become a teen volunteer. We hope that you will serve here with pride and pleasure, and we will do our best to make the volunteer experience a rewarding one for you. Your work at the library makes it possible for us to provide even better service to our community, and we appreciate the commitment you and your family have made to devote both time and energy for this purpose. Remember that when you wear a Teen Volunteer badge, you represent both Broward County, and NR/BCC Library, so be as courteous and professional as you can.

We hope you will think the following guidelines are fair and reasonable. If you have any suggestions, please let us know, and we will discuss them with you.

Responsibilities

1. Keep to your schedule and be on time.
2. Please call in and let us know if you are unable to come in.
3. Sign in every time you come to work, and remember to wear your volunteer badge.
4. Your volunteer session always begins with a shelving and a shelf reading assignment.
5. Check in the volunteer box for further duties.
6. Never leave the Youth Services area without informing the librarian.
7. Sign out when your volunteer session is over.
8. Remember to fill in your time sheet neatly, correctly, and legibly.

Schedules

The NR/BCC Library open hours are listed in "Bookings." If you would like to work on a day other than originally scheduled, please call in first. We will let you know if there is work for you to do.

Breaks

You will probably be working a two hour shift. During this time, you may take one 15 minute break. While wearing your badge, you are welcome to use the staff lounge. There are drink and snack machines in the lounge, if you wish to buy some refreshments. If you bring food with you, you will be able to use staff refrigerators and microwave ovens. For teens who work more than two hours, break times will be adjusted.

Teen Volunteer Assignments

1. Shelve books and read assigned shelves.
2. Set up and clean program room before and after programs.
3. Reinforce and string name tags.
4. Prepare crafts for programs.
5. Photocopy.
6. Label new books as directed by Youth Services staff.
7. Use department stamps to stamp books, etc. as directed by librarian.
8. Tidy Children's Room on request, and exchange full clean-up cart for an empty one when necessary.
9. Direct patrons in need of assistance to staff members.
10. Assist all patrons in use of Wise Guide.
11. Attend teen volunteer meetings as required.
12. Perform other duties as required.

Advantages of the Teen Volunteer Program

1. If you follow the rules and do your job properly, you will be gaining

valuable job experience. You will have the chance to demonstrate good attendance, dependability, creativity, accuracy, and interpersonal skills during your work with us.
2. You may be eligible to receive a letter of recommendation for job references, and school or community awards.
3. Volunteer hours may enable you to receive a Silver Cord upon graduation from high school.
4. You may fulfill service hour requirements for schools, organizations, or awards such as Honor Society.
5. Your work is a valuable contribution to your community, and helps people of all ages.

Teen Volunteer Training

All teen volunteers receive training at a Teen Volunteer Orientation, which is specially planned to teach you all you will need to know about your job at the library. This orientation will be given four times per year. It will be held in the Youth Services Department, on a Saturday morning, from 9-11 a.m. Remember that attendance is required, and that you cannot work as a volunteer without participating in this valuable learning opportunity. At the orientation meeting, you will tour the library, and schedules will be arranged. We try to accommodate individual needs when assigning schedules, while also considering the needs of the Youth Services Department.

Future Plans

In the near future, dedicated teens will be invited to join a NR/BCC Young Adult Library Advisory Board. This leadership group will plan recreational, informational, service, and book-related programs for local teens, and will have duties of increased responsibility in the library. Teens who are invited to join this group will be considered charter members.

Important!

Please note that for purposes of Broward County insurance, all teen volunteers must be at least 12 years of age. No exceptions can be made. Once again, welcome to NR/BCC, and good luck!

A Step By Step Procedure

1. Eight weeks in advance, advertise a Teen Volunteer Orientation meeting. Try to arrange your meeting on a Saturday. Publicize your meeting with signs in the library.
2. Call your area middle and high schools and arrange school visits. Plan an interesting program, such as storytelling, and talk about your library, and your plans for teen activity. Stress benefits of teen programs to teens and to the library. Be friendly, and let them know that their interest and help will be welcome at your library.
3. Prepare a Volunteer Orientation Guidelines sheet, and include the following:
   a) a list of responsibilities and jobs which teens can fulfill in your library.
   b) simple rules and regulations for teen volunteers.
   c) advantages of being a teen volunteer, such as job experience.
4. Create, or ask your Volunteer Coordinator's Office for, Volunteer applications, time sheets, and badges. Have these available for your first orientation meeting.
5. Prepare a chart to facilitate scheduling of teens.
6. At the orientation meeting, welcome the teens and be as warm and friendly as possible.
7. Go over the Teen Guidelines with the teens, and ask if there are any questions.
8. Teach the teens how to fill out a time sheet clearly and correctly, stressing the importance of these sheets as a permanent record of their job experience hours with the library system.
9. Train teens to shelve picture books. Emphasize the importance of this job to the patrons, and to the Youth Services Department.
10. Demonstrate the use of copy machines, and any other simple

technology that teens will be using to help the department.
11. Repeat this orientation meeting as needed, but no less than every three months.
12. Once you have a group of teen volunteers, introduce the idea of a Young Adult Library Advisory Board. Explain your vision of the board, and ask for charter members.
13. Hold an organizational meeting to discuss YALAB aims and goals, and follow that meeting up, within a month, with a brainstorming meeting to discuss program ideas.
14. Elect committee chairpersons, the most important of which, at this point, is the Communication Chairperson. All of your YALAB members must be involved in all plans, and feel part of this very new organization.
15. Draw up job descriptions for each chairperson so that their duties and responsibilities will be well defined.
16. As a staff advisor, work with your teens in choosing interesting, challenging but practical programs. Do not set the new Board up for failure by choosing activities or programs that cannot possibly succeed.
17. As staff sponsor, it is your responsibility to create and send all initial, follow-up, and thank-you letters.
18. Evaluate all programs and activities upon their completion. Everyone should take part in this process. Make sure that the teens understand that not everything will be wonderful. We learn from our mistakes.

Young Adult Library Advisory Board Introductory Meeting (Date)

Long Range Goals

1. To establish, throughout our library system, recognition of Young Adults as a great human resource.
2. To create a series of programs and services that will serve area teens, as well as other patron groups.

3. To be a prototype for system-wide YALAB groups.

Short Range Aims

1. To plan and implement programs for area teens, ages 12-18.
2. To train new teen volunteers in the library.
3. To assist with YA paperback collection.
4. To maintain a list of "Best Teen Picks" in the YA area.

Sample Brainstorming Session YALAB: Program Ideas

1. CPR Training for teens
2. Babysitting Workshop
3. Run a game, such as *Jeopardy!*
4. Back to School Fashion Show
5. Rock Party with a local DJ***

Committees were set up to run the Rock Party, once letters produced a local radio station ready to send us music and a DJ. These committees were as follows: tickets, posters, decorating, hosts, and cleanup.

Duties of hosts included welcoming guests, taking tickets, encouraging dancing, introducing all staff and performers, preparing a large poster for the DJ with autographs and thanks from all the teens.

Following this successful program, the staff sponsor wrote a letter of thanks to the promotions manager of the radio station. The next week, YALAB met to evaluate this program, and to begin plans for another.

Some Final Thoughts

1. Motivation is very important in forming a YALAB. If you are excited about the idea, if you recognize that Young Adult is a viable term, both as a literary genre, and as a special patron group, you are on your way.
2. YALAB does require time, dedication, enthusiasm, some money for programs, and some space for activities.
3. Remember that it can take years to form a really cohesive group, as well as time and publicity to spread the word.
4. You must have the understanding and support of your Branch

Librarian, and the entire library staff. Only a warm and welcoming staff will keep the library doors open to your Young Adult patrons.
5. Remember that when YALAB begins to be successful, many more teens will join in. After all, nothing succeeds like success, so good luck, and have fun with "your kids"!!

[October 1994]

Cooperative Dialogue: Using an Instrument to Empower
Kay E. Vandergrift

There is a long history for cooperation between school and public libraries in this country. Unfortunately, the actualities of such cooperation often fall far short of the aspirations. Sometimes differing institutional goals, personality conflicts, or turf wars impede cooperation, but most often it is the everyday demands of librarians' own immediate responsibilities that prevent them from doing what they genuinely want to do to improve service to young adults. Until cooperation becomes a priority for professionals in both institutions, the ongoing process of developing cooperative ventures that benefit both remains a distant goal. The instrument that follows may be used as an evaluative tool, but it is more useful in the process of implementation. Used to initiate a dialogue among youth services providers in school and public libraries, it can help focus attention on current practices, key concerns and potential benefits from working together. At best, it will encourage professionals to go beyond these suggestions to explore alternative means of cooperation to better serve our shared clientele.

The instrument (see pp. 247–251) begins with the simplest and most basic concern—communication. It is amazing—and disturbing—to discover how many youth librarians do not even know the other key people in their community who provide parallel services to young people. (No. 1) The very existence of a ready-reference sheet with names and phone numbers of appropriate contact persons in the other institution may itself encourage that contact. Although young adults do many school assignments in the public library, there is often little or no communication about these assignments. If there is little communication between the school and public library about assignments, there is even less about more general curricular changes (No. 4) that have implications for collection development, programs, and services. The public library is a logical source of information for parents about new content or methods introduced in the school curriculum. Displays, exhibits, bibliographies, or programs in the public library, especially when planned cooperatively with school personnel, can help parents understand and cope with changes in their children's schooling. They can also help young adults themselves who often feel that such changes are made without giving them adequate information about new expectations for their work.

What, for instance, does it mean to restructure our schools? Can the whole language movement so popular in elementary schools make a difference in secondary education?[1] How could a literature-based curriculum work in the midst of the "canon wars" in high school English classes?[2] What are the canon wars anyway? How can we expand the content of the curriculum to make it more inclusive and more multicultural while, at the same time, subject specialists are developing national standards and the tests to measure them in each of the disciplines? These are just a few of the questions parents, students, and others are asking about education today, and they ought to be able to get answers at the public library as well as the school. Since each school system answers these questions differently, the public library needs more than just the latest reports of national studies, suggestions for reform, and education exposés. Youth services specialists in the public library need to be informed about what is happening in *their* schools and collect the specific materials to support those educational endeavors. They also need to be able to inform parents and the community about local schooling. This requires continuing communication between school and public library personnel. (No. 2)

In recent years many schools and public libraries have cooperated in ALA's efforts to put a library card in the hands of every young person. (No. 14) What is not clear, however, is if this cooperation extends beyond library registration. Do school and public library personnel continue to work together to ensure that appropriate programs and services are available for young adults and that they are informed about and encouraged to participate in them? (No. 16) Summer reading programs are a case in point. (No. 15) Do youth services librarians involve teachers and school library media specialists in planning these programs; and do school personnel actively work to enroll students? Is there cooperative research to indicate whether such programs make a difference in attitudes, reading behaviors, or school achievement? Even more critical is the need to cooperate in efforts to find out why so many young adults do not use either school or public libraries and figure out what to do to remedy that.

Technology is a major player in both school and public libraries today and is a prime site for cooperation and compatibility. (No. 18) Although youth services personnel may not be the primary decision makers in respect to automation and other technological developments in their schools or libraries, they need to make their voices heard and often can be very influential in winning community support. Most community members are far more likely to support new technologies or electronic systems that benefit both school and public libraries since both are funded by their tax dollars. Even when one library has already brought up a particular system, dialogue among those in both institutions might ensure that newer systems are compatible with existing ones. Cooperation can enhance a community's information environment and provide the best possible access for all the young people who reside there. Establishment of local area networks is a mutually beneficial endeavor. Cooperation in the selection of hardware and software can result not only in financial savings but also in increased access to all community resources. Community licensing, particularly of more elaborate and expensive CD-ROMs, is a more efficient and cost-effective means of making such materials available to users. (No. 19) Such networks could encourage shared storage and access to bibliographies, newsnotes, email messages, and crisis information for young people within a community.

Even some well established, if sometimes problematic, practices can be revitalized through the use of electronic media. Many local or regional groups attempt to bring school and public librarians together for the evaluation of new materials. (No. 10) The major problem is often one of scheduling. Afterschool hours are the busiest for youth service providers in the public library, but it is difficult for teachers and library media specialists to attend meetings during the school day. Posting reviews as email messages obviously eliminates the benefits of face-to-face communication, but it might encourage greater participation and a greater range of personal responses. Multiple responses might be far more useful in the process of evaluation and selection than a single reviewer's comments. Young people could also be encouraged to participate in this exchange in ways that would be beneficial both to them and to the adults who select materials for them.

The instrument presented here is intended to initiate dialogue. It is hoped that the interaction that occurs in relation to these topics will encourage participants to continue their discussions of other issues of concern to young adults. How might we present a unified front in planning, proposal writing, or other aspects of our work that will encourage greater community support for both school and public libraries and encourage young adults as lifelong learners? Such dialogue and cooperation between institutions might also encourage reflection upon and action in response to current social problems which impact on young adults. For example, there is now a great deal of evidence that gender bias exists in most schools, but, to date, there has been little investigation of similar biases in public libraries.[3] How might the two institutions cooperate to identify biased behaviors both by young adults themselves and by the adults who work with them? More important, how might they work together to eliminate such behaviors?

A related problem is that of sexual harassment.[4] While gender bias is often subtle, sexual harassment is usually overt, but it is also frequently excused as the "natural" behavior of young men. Thus, it may be dismissed with comments such as "boys will be boys" or "they're just clowning around." Youth services providers from school and public libraries might work together to purchase resources to help them expose and understand this problem and then establish policies and procedures to deal with it. Joint action in response to such concerns not only deals more effectively with the issues, it also is an indication to both young people and the community that we are concerned and committed to action.

One area in which we are sorely in need of dialogue is that of selection of "sensitive" materials. We seem to be in an age when political correctness is often pitted against a kind of confrontational politics of intellectual freedom. We need open and honest debate between those who sincerely believe they are serving young adults by upholding current standards of political correctness and those who are equally sincere in their absolutist positions on intellectual freedom. As one who waivers between these two positions, I know how important it is to engage in the kind of dialogue that forces me to sharpen my thinking and face my own prejudices. I like to think that I hold two values as absolute; one is a respect for young adults and their abilities to deal with challenging ideas; the other is the belief that we have no right to spend tax dollars on materials that offend or hurt others or perpetuate stereotypes. I also know that these two absolutes are frequently in conflict. It is in sustained and informed dialogue with others, adults and young adults, who share my concerns and commitment that I find ways to reconcile my sometimes conflicting beliefs. In doing so, I also find better ways to serve young adults.

These are just a few examples of ways this instrument may be used to encourage cooperation among school and public librarians. The issues raised in the tool itself are basically non-confrontational ones. If a real dialogue is initiated, however, youth services professionals may go on to work together on many other issues and projects that will empower both them and the young people with whom they work.

SELF-EVALUATION INVENTORY:

School-Public Library Cooperation

School Library Media Specialists
1. Do you know the names and phone numbers of the director and youth services personnel in your local public library?
2. Have you made every effort to inform the public library about the school curriculum and assignments and to inform students and teachers about programs and activities of the public library?
   - Requested information from the public library?
   - Requested information from classroom teachers to be shared with the public librarian?
   - Devised simple but informative questionnaires to keep yourself and public library personnel abreast of topics and assignments?
   - Arranged specific times and procedures for sharing such information with public librarians?
   - Requested time to meet with youth services specialists *in the*

public library?
- Asked to be included on the distribution list of newsletters and other public library publications?
- Attended Friends of the Library meetings to inform yourself about the public library and offer your support?
- Requested reference copies of textbooks to be placed in the public library for assistance with homework assignments?
- Sent lists of new materials prepared for teachers or students to the public library?

3. Have you made every effort to work with public library personnel to assist students?
   - Worked together in goal setting and data collection, recognizing similarities and differences in mission?
   - Offered to help set up curriculum-related collections in the public library?
   - Participated in a joint evaluation of the use of such collections?
   - Informed classroom teachers about student informational needs that *can or cannot* be met at the public library?
   - Explored the possibility of resource sharing to meet student needs, including the possibility of school library media center loans to the public library, especially during school vacations?
   - Invited public library personnel to the school library media center to observe and discuss resources and services?
   - Worked with the public library to establish a Homework Helper program?
   - Established an efficient document delivery system between schools and the public library?

4. Have you informed the public library about potential changes in the school curriculum and about current topics of discussion such as the Whole Language movement or cultural literacy and the core curriculum?

5. Have you contacted special area teachers (art, music, physical education, etc.) to inform them of school and public library resources that might assist them in their work with students?

6. Have you invited youth specialists from the public library to participate in planning sessions in the school?

7. Have you requested an opportunity to join public library youth

Focus on Adults

services specialists in speaking to their library administrators or the library board about the library and information needs of young people?
8. Have you offered to advertise public library programs and services to parents, teachers and students?
9. Have you offered to share new materials with public library personnel—either in the public library or the school library media center?
10. Have you asked public library youth specialists to participate in cooperative reviewing of materials and then made every effort to schedule meetings at their convenience?
11. Do you invite public librarians to do booktalks in the school on topics of special interest to teachers and students?
12. Do you keep public library personnel informed about changes in media center policies and procedures, especially about technological changes such as an Online Public Access Catalog (OPAC)?
13. Have you asked public librarians about your students' abilities to use the library and cooperatively planned bibliographic instruction to meet student needs?
14. Do you work with the public library to enroll students in summer reading programs?
16. Have you planned and participated in cooperative programming with your public library youth services specialists?
17. Do you share professional development opportunities—or at least share transportation to professional meetings?
18. Are you purchasing hardware, particularly computers, that are compatible with those in the public library?
19. Are you at least working toward establishing an electronic network among the schools and the public library (especially email and a union catalog)?

Public Library Youth Services Librarians

1. Do you know the names and phone numbers of all the school library media specialists and school principals in your community?
2. Have you made every effort to inform yourself and your colleagues about the school curriculum and student assignments?

- Requested information from the school library media specialist?
- Requested information from classroom teachers?
- Devised simple but informative questionnaires to keep abreast of topics and assignments?
- Arranged specific times and procedures for the collection of the above instruments?
- Requested time to meet with the school library media specialists and teachers in the school building?
- Asked to be included on the distribution list of curriculum bulletins, newsletters, etc.?
- Attended school board and open informational meetings for parents and community about curriculum changes, etc.?
- Requested reference copies of textbooks for the public library?
- Sent lists of new materials to school library media specialists?

3. Have you made every effort to inform school personnel about how the public library can assist them and their students?
   - Worked together in goal setting and data collection, recognizing similarities and differences in mission?
   - Offered to set up curriculum-related collections in the public library?
   - Provided feedback to school personnel on the use of such collections?
   - Informed school personnel about student informational needs that can and cannot be met at the public library?
   - Offered loans of materials to the school library media center or to classrooms?
   - Invited school personnel to the public library to observe and discuss resources and services?
   - Worked with the schools to establish a Homework Helper program?
   - Established an efficient document delivery system between schools and the public library?

4. Have you helped to inform parents about the school curriculum, especially about educational change and current topics of discussion such as the Whole Language movement or cultural literacy and the core curriculum?

5. Have you contacted special area teachers (art, music, physical education, etc.) to inform them of library resources that might assist

them in their work with students?
6. Have you invited school library media specialists to participate in planning sessions of youth services personnel in the public library?
7. Have you requested invitations to speak at teachers meetings and back-to-school nights or at least prepared materials to be distributed at such meetings?
8. Have you offered to display school-related materials and student work in the public library and then given appropriate publicity to such displays?
9. Have you offered to share new materials with school personnel—either in the public library or the school library media center?
10. Have you asked library media specialists and classroom teachers to participate in cooperative reviewing of materials—and then made every effort to schedule meetings at their convenience?
11. Do you offer to do booktalks in the school on topics of special interest to teachers and students?
12. Do you keep school personnel informed about changes in library policies and procedures, especially about technological changes such as an Online Public Access Catalog (OPAC)?
13. Do you offer bibliographic instruction for students in the public library?
14. Do you work with the schools to register students for public library cards?
15. Do you work with the schools to enroll students in summer reading programs?
16. Have you planned and participated in cooperative programming with school library media specialists?
17. Do you share professional development opportunities—or at least share transportation to professional meetings?
18. Are you purchasing hardware, particularly computers, that are compatible with those in the schools?
19. Are you at least working toward establishing an electronic network between the schools and the public library (especially email and a union catalog)?

[June 1994]

Notes

1. Ralph Peterson. *Life in a Crowded Place: Making a Learning Community*. Portsmith, NH: Heinemann, 1992; Kenneth S. Goodman. *What's Whole in Whole Language*. Portsmith, NH: Heinemann, 1986; and Linda L. Lamme and Linda Ledbetter. "Libraries: The Heart of Whole Language," *Language Arts* 67 (November 1990): 735-41.

2. P. Lauter. *Canons and Contexts*. New York: Oxford University Press, 1991; Kay E. Vandergrift. "Literacies of Inclusion: Feminism, Multiculturalism and Youth," in *Journal of Professional Studies* 3:1 (Fall-Winter) 1995: 39-47.

3. See, for example: *The AAUW Report: How Schools Shortchange Girls*: Washington, DC: Wellesley College Center for Research on Women/American Association of University Women, 1992; Lois Weis and Michelle Fine, eds. *Beyond Silenced Voices: Class, Race, and Gender in United States Schools*. Albany, NY: State University of New York, 1993; and Barrie Thorne, *Gender Play: Girls and Boys in School*. New Brunswick, NJ: Rutgers University Press, 1993.

4. See, for example: *The AAUW Report: Hostile Hallways: The AAUW Survey of Sexual Harassment in America's Schools*. Researched by Harris-Scholastic Research, a division of Louis Harris and Associates in partnership with Scholastic, Inc. Study No. 923012. June 1993. Washington, DC: American Association of University Women, 1993; Robert J. Shoop and Debra L. Edwards. *How To Stop Sexual Harassment in Our Schools: What Parents and Teachers Need To Know To Spot It and Stop It*. Needham, MA: Allyn and Bacon, 1993. In addition, there are videos such as: *Sexual Harassment: What Is It and Why Should I Care?* Quality Work Environments, Inc. PO Box 1945 Manhattan, KS 66502.

The Junior High School Comes to the Public Library

Elizabeth Vollrath and Diane Kippenhan

"You did what?" and "How brave of you!" was what we heard when we announced the joint venture between our school library and public library. Beginning September 5th and November 9th, 1995, eight classes of P.J. Jacobs Junior High School students were bused to the Portage County Public Library daily to provide library service to them while a new school library media center was being built.

When Bob Strack, coordinator for Library Media and Technology of the Stevens Point school district approached the public library director, Bob Stack, in July to request this special service, we saw an opportunity too good to pass up. Media Specialist Diane Kippenhan prepared the school to do without the school media center and without her for most of the day. She purchased multiple copies of periodicals and placed them in study halls. She asked teachers to postpone library units until the LMC (Library Media Center) was opened. She placed carts of books in classrooms on request and then boxed and stored most of the collection. She also checked out materials from the public library and delivered them to teachers. She had limited time to deliver, troubleshoot, and schedule AV equipment for teachers, however, as she spent most of her school day at the public library.

She arrived at the public library at 8 a.m. to greet the first busload of students and returned to school after the last group left at 2:45 p.m. She was given a study room at the public library for an office. It was located in the Reading Area of the library near the Reference Area and the nonfiction collection where the students would work. Basic communication with teachers was through school mailboxes and a portable telephone supplied by the school system.

Youth Services Librarian Elizabeth Vollrath met with public library staff to work out the details and to keep staff informed of management plans, especially since the public library would be opening early to allow the students to enter. (Normal hours begin at 9:30 a.m.) She held a staff in-service session on how to anticipate the special needs of younger teens. The circulation department revised its schedule so that staff would be available to check out materials earlier than normal. Elizabeth and the Reference staff arrived early to be at the Reference Desk for the first group.

Other details were worked out ahead of time. The library director and school administration decided that AV materials would not be checked out, as the school would be responsible for damages and losses. The students would be responsible for their own overdue items. Elizabeth gave Diane an overview of the Reference Department with emphasis on some of the books most useful to teens in the public library.

The P.J. LMC Aide rode with the students on the bus. Seventh, eighth and ninth graders were bused from study halls twenty students at a time each period during an eight period day. Students with teacher passes were allowed to sign up first. Students carried a large (10" x 11") numbered cardboard pass corresponding to the number next to their name on the pass sheet. They showed the pass to the aide to get on the bus and gave it back to the aide when they returned to school. Students were required to have the pass with them at all times while at the public library.

This worked out well, too, for the library since we regularly had other school tours, and it was easy to know which students belonged to which group. The students were limited to the second floor of the library for easier supervision, although they could leave the floor to look for materials on other floors. Public library staff decided that students should have their library card with them in order to check out materials, as it takes time to call up records. Sometimes students were disappointed when they discovered they couldn't check something out that day, but we did put the item on reserve for them so they were able to check it out the next time they came in with their card, usually in a day or two.

Students were at the library for approximately twenty minutes. They were required to be busy and quiet. If they were not, they were given one warning. A tone was sounded twelve minutes before the next period began, so students and school staff had time to get on the bus, take roll, and return. (The junior high is about a mile from the library.)

The students were told that using the public library was a special privilege and they should be on their best behavior. Other library patrons would judge P.J. and teenagers in general by the behavior they chose to display.

A few library staff wondered initially if some adults would be put off by so many junior high students in the same reading areas. However, when Elizabeth noticed adults looking around when they heard Diane with her tuning fork, she told them what it was for, and to a person, they said it was a wonderful idea. Other library users seemed supportive. We announced the project in the *Stevens Point Journal* and their photographer took pictures of students at the library. We also hung a banner in the library's entry welcoming the P.J. Jacobs Junior High students.

The first week Elizabeth spent training the classes how to use the on-line catalog and microfilm machines. The first month most students eagerly searched microfilmed newspapers for their birth announcements. After the novelty wore off, they settled down to work on school assignments or read magazines.

Many young people told us that it was "cool" to come to the library. They were glad to learn how to do research and use the on-line catalog effectively. They were especially happy to find out the public library is not a stuffy place where they had to keep totally quiet. They liked being able to work in groups and talk quietly. Some were amazed to discover the library had things that teens wanted, like their favorite musical groups, computers for typing papers or playing games, study rooms, and teen oriented magazines. They became comfortable in the library, and because of their experience, they will probably be back.

Word of mouth of the good experience students had visiting the library encouraged other students to sign up. Even during the last two weeks we saw new faces.

The visit allowed students and staff to get to know each other better. The Library Media Specialist explored and used the public library holdings. P.J. students received library cards, many for the first time, and checked out library books and magazines. Diane and Elizabeth were able to recommend books to each other. We are already planning more joint projects.

During the two months 5,648 rides were given to 442 junior high students. We are proud of these kids. Not only did they represent their school during their visits to the Portage County Public Library, but they proved that teens are considerate, thoughtful, interesting, and interested. [October 1996]

About the Contributors

Contributor identification is as of the time the article was written unless we have direct information that it is no longer applicable.

ALAN BERN is a Children's Librarian at the Oakland, CA, Public Library.

BARBARA BLOSVEREN is the Head of the Young Adult Department in the Stratford (CT) Library Association and is also one of the most active advocates for youth participation in libraries.

MARGARET BROWN is the Young Adult Supervisor for the Arlington, VA, County Public Library.

MARILYN BROWN is the Head of Children's Services at the Herrick Public Library in Holland, MI.

PAM CARLSON is a library specialist with the Orange County, CA, Public Library and a *VOYA* reviewer.

MARY K. CHELTON is Assistant Professor at the School of Library and Information Management, Emporia, KS, State University.

LYNN COCKETT was the Young Adult Librarian at the Nutley, NJ, Public Library when she wrote the included article. She is currently finishing work on a Ph.D. at Rutgers University.

MARY ALICE DEVENY is the Youth Section Manager of the Selby Public Library in Sarasota, FL.

KAY FINNEY works as a Reference and Young Adult Librarian at the South Branch Library in Berkeley, California. This program has been selected as one of the top fifty young adult programs included in the American Library Association publication entitled *Excellence in Library Services to Young Adults: The Nation's Top Programs* (ALA, 1994).

NANCY GARDEN is a long established author whose attacked book, *Annie on My Mind* remains the only young adult novel told from the viewpoint of adolescent lesbians.

NANCY GORMAN is the Young Adult Librarian at the Longwood Public Library in Middle Island, NY.

KATHRYN L. HAVRIS is the Reference Librarian at the Mesa, AZ, Public Library.

BETH KARPAS is the Young Adult Librarian at the Amelia Branch Library of the Clermont County, OH, Public Library.

DIANE KIPPENHAN is the Media Specialist at the P.J. Jacobs Junior High School, Portage, WI.

LUCRETIA LIPPER is the Young Adult Librarian at the East Brunswick, NJ, Public Library.

CATHI DUNN MACRAE was the Young Adult Services Librarian at the Boulder, CO, Public Library at the time she wrote the included articles. She is currently editor of *Voice of Youth Advocates*.

MARY MAGGIO is the Youth Services Librarian at the Mastics-Moriches-Shirley Community Library in Nassau County, NY.

KIM MCCOMBS was the South Branch Library Student Worker in Berkeley, California.

ANNE MERKLE is Reference and Young Adult Librarian at the Herrick Public Library in Holland, MI.

ARTHUR S. MEYERS was the Director of the Hammond, IN, Public Library and is currently Director of the Middletown, CT, Public Library.

NANCY MOORE is the Media Specialist at the Base Line Middle School in Boulder, CO.

PAT MULLER is the Youth and Young Adult Coodinator for The Library Network in Southgate, Michigan.

MARY BETH OLIVETO, Children's Librarian at the Farmington, MI, Community Library is now Mary Beth Tacy.

FRANCES PLESSER is the Young Adult Librarian at the East Meadow, NY, Public Library.

Notes on Contributors

JANE QUINN is Program Director for the DeWitt Wallace-Reader's Digest Fund and a firm believer in library services for youth.

LINDSAY RUTH is the Young Adult/Reference Librarian at the Geneva, NY, Public Library.

JUDY SASGES is Library Manager at the Lynnwood, WA, Public Library.

CAROL SHAMA is the School Media Specialist at the Geneva, NY, Middle School.

MARTHA SIMPSON is the Children's Librarian in the Stratford (CT) Library Association.

JOAN STAINFORTH is retired from the Orange County, CA, Public Library.

ROGER SUTTON, currently Editor of *Horn Book*, was Executive Editor of *The Bulletin of the Center for Children's Books* when he delivered this important speech at the November 1991 meeting of the Michigan Library Association. In offering the speech to *VOYA*, Sutton suggested we might not want it because so many of the examples are from children's books. The specific examples of titles pale before the significance of the issues and principles of selection Sutton examines!

JANICE T. UNGAR was the Young Adult Library at the Farmington, MI, Branch Library.

KAY E. VANDERGRIFT is a full Professor, School of Communication, Information and Library Studies, Rutgers University. The selection included here uses an instrument from her *Power Teaching: A Primary Role of the school Library Media Specialist* (American Library Association, 1994).

SHARON VINCENT is the Young Adult Librarian at the Farmington, MI, Community Library.

ELIZABETH VOLLRATH is the Youth Services Specialist at the Portage County, WI, Public Library.

BARBARA OSBORNE WILLIAMS is Manager of the Youth Services Division, Central Library, Queens Borough. NY, Public Library.